The Collected Plays

VOLUME ONE

GENERAL AUDAX

HONEST URUBAMBA

LIVING ROOM WITH 6 OPPRESSIONS

A SPLITTING HEADACHE

THE VIRGIN AND THE UNICORN

ISLAND

VOLUME TWO

THE MONK WHO WOULDN'T

THE SENSIBLE MAN OF JERUSALEM

PROFESSOR SNAFFLE'S POLYPON

ADAM ADAMSON

THE FATAL FRENCH DENTIST

OF ANGELS AND ESKIMOS

BOOKS BY OSCAR MANDEL

A DEFINITION OF TRAGEDY, *New York University Press, 1961*

THE THEATRE OF DON JUAN, *University of Nebraska Press, 1963*

CHI PO AND THE SORCERER, *Charles E. Tuttle, 1964*

THE GOBBLE-UP STORIES, *Bruce Humphries, 1967*

THE FATAL FRENCH DENTIST, *Samuel French, 1967*

SEVEN COMEDIES BY MARIVAUX, *Cornell University Press, 1968*

FIVE COMEDIES OF MEDIEVAL FRANCE, *Dutton, 1970*

THE COLLECTED PLAYS, *Unicorn Press, 1970*

Oscar Mandel
Collected Plays
Unicorn Press

VOLUME ONE

General Audax; Honest Urubamba;

Living Room With 6 Oppressions;

A Splitting Headache; The Virgin and the Unicorn; Island

Typography by Alan Brilliant
Type-set in 11 Palatino Linotype by Achilles Friedrich
Printed by Halliday Lithograph Corporation

Library of Congress Catalogue Number 70-134738
Standard Book number 0-87775-000-9

Indede, into the worlde now must we to and fro,
And where or how to rest I can nott say at all.

Contents

FOREWORD 11

GENERAL AUDAX 13

HONEST URUBAMBA 63

LIVING ROOM WITH 6 OPPRESSIONS 95

A SPLITTING HEADACHE 113

THE VIRGIN AND THE UNICORN 145

ISLAND 179

Foreword

General Audax was first published in Henry F. Salerno's *First Stage: A Quarterly of New Drama*. *Living Room With 6 Oppressions* appeared in the successor to this magazine, *Drama and Theatre*. An early version of *Honest Urubamba* was printed in *The Literary Review*, edited by Clarence R. Decker and Charles Angoff. Early versions of *Island* and *The Virgin and the Unicorn* appeared respectively in *The Massachusetts Review* and *The Minnesota Review*.

Island has been performed in various places, among them Amherst, Smith College, Los Angeles City College, the California Institute of Technology, and the studios of station KPFK in Los Angeles. The Pacifica Network stations have repeatedly broadcast a production directed by John Houlton in which Harold Innocent, Barry Atwater, Harold Gould and David Ossman took the leading roles. *The Virgin and the Unicorn* was staged by Ted Roter at the Santa Monica Playhouse.

General Audax is based on Cervantes' *La Numancia*, supplemented by Appian's histories. *Island* derives from the *Philoctetes* of Sophocles. *The Virgin and the Unicorn* comes out of medieval legend. It will be apparent, however, that I have used my sources to take directions entirely my own. For the three "modern" plays in this volume — *Honest Urubamba*, *Living Room With 6 Oppressions*, and *A Splitting Headache* — I am not aware of any specific indebtedness. Besides, I have blithely fabled the facts I needed in any of these plays — turned Lemnos into a luxuriant island, made the War of the Gran Chaco contemporaneous with the United Nations, and invented a conflict between "Istria" and "Friuli," to name only these. On the other hand, I wish to thank my colleague Robert W. Oliver for providing me with the economic realities for *A Splitting Headache;* as I thank my wife who first brought *La Numancia* to my attention, and Henry Salerno who has opened the pages of his magazine to my work year after year.

I owe a debt of gratitude, too, to the California Institute of Technology and the Andrew W. Mellon Fund for assistance in the preparation of this book for the press.

O.M.

GENERAL AUDAX

A Play in Seven Scenes Concerning the Roman Invasions of Spain

Ser, nada más. Y basta.
Jorge Guillén

CHARACTERS

Numantians

RETOGENES, *Governor of Numantia*

CARAVINO, *Vice-Governor*

AUDAX, *General of the Numantian Army*

CONNOBA, *his son*

AVARUS *and other members of the Peace Party*

MARANDRO, *a merchant*

JULIA, *sister-in-law of Audax*

LIRA, *a friend of the family*

MARCIUS, *a citizen*

THREE GRAVEDIGGERS

OFFICERS, SOLDIERS, CITIZENS

Romans

PUBLIUS CORNELIUS SCIPIO AEMILIANUS, *Consul and General of the Army*

MAXIMUS, *his brother*

BUTEO, *his nephew*

POLYBIUS, *historian and officer attached to Scipio*

MINUCIUS, *in command of Scipio's private guard*

MUMMIUS, *a slave on an Italian estate*

OFFICERS, LICTORS, SOLDIERS

SCENE ONE

(A villa in the Italian countryside. Night time and moonlight. A portico, a garden, a fountain, a few trees, shrubbery and flowers. Marandro, an old man, is sitting quietly at a table under the portico, lit by a single candle. He is examining a ledger and other documents, occasionally picking at a grape from a bowl which has been placed on another low table within reach. A deeply peaceful scene. A slave, Mummius, enters quietly from within the house. He sets another bowl of fruit on the low table.)

MUMMIUS. Excuse me, sir.

MARANDRO. Mummius?

MUMMIUS. Yes, sir.

MARANDRO. It's so dark where you stand, I can only see your voice.

MUMMIUS. Shall I set another light on the table, sir?

MARANDRO. No no.

MUMMIUS. My master has asked me to bring you more refreshments and to inquire whether you have any other wishes.

MARANDRO. I don't wish anything else. I've t-t-told you, you can all go to sleep. I know the way to my room. But why hasn't old Audax come yet?

MUMMIUS. He's our only night watchman, sir, and also he's a bit slow on his legs.

MARANDRO. But he's sure to come?

MUMMIUS. Absolutely sure, sir. You'll hear the jingling of the keys and him I'll bet humming one of his Spanish ditties.

MARANDRO. Spanish ditties. . . . Who'd believe it? . . . And you're sure it's General Audax?

MUMMIUS. Oh yes, sir. We're very good friends, so of course I know. He's told us many stories about his glorious days in Numantia, how he led the war against Rome, and how he made Scipio himself tremble.

MARANDRO. Hmm.

MUMMIUS. Sometimes we don't believe a word of it. A decayed night watchman in Italy that was a Spanish general sitting at table with governors and ladies — prove it, we say, and he goes all red in the face.

MARANDRO. It fits.

MUMMIUS. Excuse me for asking, sir, but is that where you're from, Numantia?

MARANDRO. Yes, that's where I was when the Romans t-t-took it. And I wasn't eating grapes that day, let me t-t-t-tell you.

MUMMIUS. So it's really true, sir?

MARANDRO. What's really true?

MUMMIUS. His having been the commander and all?

MARANDRO. I don't know, my boy. All I know is that Audax was the name of our commander in chief.

MUMMIUS. Excuse me for asking.

MARANDRO. Well, that's all, Mummius. Go to bed, and tell your master I'll be t-t-talking to him after I t-t-tour the estate in the morning.

MUMMIUS. Very good, sir. Good night, sir. (He leaves)

(Marandro sits back again, dreaming. Then he looks at the ledger. His finger marks the place)

MARANDRO. "Audax. Place of origin: Numantia, Spain. Age: approximately fifty-five." And that was seven years ago. (He sighs) "Purchased in fair health from the tribune Pomponius at Capua" and so on. It figures. . . . Ah — there he must be.

(We hear the keys and the humming, as promised, and then Audax appears, old but hale, lit by the lantern he is carrying. He vanishes for a moment, and we hear him securing a door. Then he is seen again)

MARANDRO. General Audax.

AUDAX. Mummius? Never mind the general. I won that jug, and you'll pay up, young puppy.

(Marandro rises and shows himself. Audax is surprised)

AUDAX. Beg your pardon, sir. I didn't know there were guests at the house. Wait — was it you? — did you call me General Audax?

MARANDRO. I did. You don't know me, but I know you. Or do you recognize me? Numantia, eighteen years ago.

AUDAX (with extreme astonishment). Numantia! (He lifts the lantern up to look at Marandro, whom he inspects close and long) Were you in the troops? Yes, one of my officers . . .

MARANDRO. No. I was a merchant. Of course, I only knew you from a distance.

AUDAX. A merchant. And you survived.

MARANDRO. Like you.

AUDAX. Like me?

MARANDRO. Well, not exactly. But I survived.

AUDAX. How did you know I was here?

MARANDRO. I didn't know. I happened to see your name in the ledger of slaves. And I d-d-decided to wait for you and see for myself. Hey! To think I'm t-t-talking to our c-c-commander!

AUDAX. A commander who locks up stables.

MARANDRO. Sit down, old man, sit down beside me. On a chair, by God.

AUDAX (hesitant). On a chair?

MARANDRO. That's right. Everybody's asleep in the house. And I don't f-f-fuss about etiquette. I'm a b-b-businessman.

AUDAX. All right. But I can't stay long. I'm the night watchman here.

MARANDRO. I know.

AUDAX. What's your name again?

MARANDRO. Marandro.

AUDAX. Marandro. No, I don't think I knew you. How did you manage to save your skin, Marandro?

MARANDRO. Well — to tell you the truth — on the day we f-f-found out about you — you know —

AUDAX. Speak up, merchant: on the day I defected, say it and don't quibble.

MARANDRO. Well, on the day you went over, I said to myself, I said "Marandro, you're not going to die either." So I moved myself to an abandoned shack in a lot, and when people began to k-k-kill themselves like it was the end of the world, and the Romans c-c-came in, I k-k-kept quiet and waited.

AUDAX. And here you are, eighteen years later, a guest on the noble if crumbling estate of Quintus Pompeius Aulus. Look at that silk! My congratulations.

MARANDRO. Come on, old fellow, don't b-b-blame me for my luck. When you're lucky, it means that the gods love you.

AUDAX. Guzzle your luck in peace! I'll kiss the rim of your goblet, I will.

MARANDRO. That's more like it.

AUDAX. You've come here on business? Wait a minute. You're not buying the estate, are you?

MARANDRO. I might be doing just that.

AUDAX *(whistling)*. And I'll be your man! *(Confidentially)* Listen, old merchant, don't bid too high on the property. The soil is fair enough, but you can barely see it under the pile of debts.

MARANDRO. The debts are to me.

AUDAX. Triple gods! To you! Marandro, if you buy — what will you do with me?

MARANDRO. Don't worry. You can have your f-f-f-freedom.

AUDAX. Let me kiss your hand. But — instead of freedom — look, why lose a good man like me? The master allows me to live in an old cabin at the edge of the wheat field. Give it to me outright, Marandro, and I'll serve you well. Give it to me in writing — cut my night duty a bit — and also — damn it, I might as well come out with it — don't scatter my family.

MARANDRO. Your family!?

AUDAX. Try to understand, Marandro. I'm an old man. The past is past, oh God, the dead are dead. . . . A man needs a warm place.

MARANDRO. Sure.

AUDAX. So there's a woman under my roof; who do I harm? and two children — not mine — but I don't care. Let me keep them together.

MARANDRO. Don't worry, they're all yours.

AUDAX. May the gods keep prospering you, sir.

MARANDRO. And you too, Audax.

AUDAX. Sure; me too.

MARANDRO. Why not? To each his turn. The way I see it, you've paid heavily enough for your — (*he stops short*)

AUDAX. Treason, Marandro, treason.

MARANDRO. Who said treason?

AUDAX. Nobody.

MARANDRO. I'm a p-p-plain businessman. You didn't rob me, did you? So I don't judge.

AUDAX (*bursts out*). But I do. I judge. Audax has sat for eighteen years over Audax: who led an army; who twice defeated the Roman legions; who dared to say No in the end; who accepted the name of coward; who became a slave, and suffered, and regretted nothing. Judge all you like, my friend. There is a courage for which trumpets do not blow.

(*Darkness now covers the scene. Silence. Then, very faintly, in the far distance of many years before, a sound of trumpets as in elegy. The sound gradually increases, and turns into a shattering fanfare as the next scene opens*)

SCENE TWO

(*Sound of trumpets. Heralds off-stage shout "Scipio Africanus!" Preceded by lictors and flanked by officers, Scipio enters and quickly ascends a wooden tribune*)

SCIPIO. Soldiers, I salute you! Some of you know me. Some of you stood at my side under the walls of Carthage. And some of you broke into Carthage behind me and lived to remember the day. I greet you in the name of Rome, and call you friends. But to the others among you I am only the next general sent down from Rome to roll with you in the Spanish dust. That is why I have come to greet you in particular. Lift up your heads and look at me: Scipio himself is here to take command. Soldiers, in the name of Rome, I salute you!

    Men, how long, how bitterly long have you been serving before Numantia? Ten years, many of you! Ten years of fighting or dawdling. Defeats. Stagnation. And incompetence: why should

I deny it; sometimes incompetence among your leaders. Though I've just arrived, believe me I know, and what I don't know, I smell. I've been here before. I was fighting in Spain when some of you were in diapers. And now, as I look at a few of you slouching instead of standing smart, I keep those ten years in mind. Also when I see a few dozen whores, and fortune-tellers, and lunatic priests, and when I see card-games, drinking and dicing — some of you are grinning, I notice — well, I keep those ten years in mind too. *(He suddenly slams the railing with his fist)* But the games are finished. Off with the cooks, the flute-players, the priests and the actors! From now on, you'll work the fat off your bellies! You'll stand square in the ranks! Every man here, beginning with myself, every officer that's got two legs with two feet and ten toes, every twitching body will be assigned his job until the job is done. What job? Numantia taken. Taken and occupied. Occupied and colonized. By Roman farmers. You. Your families. Numantia a safe civilized Roman city, and the country a safe civilized Roman country. But for this I need hard bodies and clear minds. Myself, I've come to this camp naked: no servants, no pillows, no ivory tables and no Persian candy; not so much as a bed. I'll be sleeping on a cot and so will you. Away with the wagons of clothes, the jolly stuffed beds, the beads and trinkets! Instead of pins for your girls you'll play with picks, axes, mattocks and spades. Away with the harlots and the gypsies! Away with glassware and dishes! To each man — officer and private alike, me and you — a pewter cup, a dish and a spoon: period. At nine the camp is asleep. Guards caught napping: off with the left hand. Scipio will snoop and Scipio will poke anywhere anytime. He's not proud. At five, up. Half of you training. The other half digging and building. *(He raises his arm as though to silence the soldiers)* Digging and building I said. A trench clean around Numantia except where the river is. Next: a palisade around Numantia. And last: behind the palisade, a stone wall around Numantia: thick, tough and high. Parapets. Towers. Stairs. Architecture! Numantia will starve inside a hoop! Not a drop of Roman or allied blood will be lost! Provided we keep a Roman discipline. Alert twenty-four hours a day. Steady work. Patience. One solid front. Your reward will come when Numantia is in our hands. Yours, I should say: its money, its shops, its cellars: yours. And triple pay in the month of victory! A week of dancing and the rest of it! Let Hell pay the bill! Numantia is yours. And there· will be no favorites then, as you will see none now. Where Scipio commands, the great get no favors and the humble suffer no wrongs. You'll not be riding chariots to and from work; but neither will I. You'll have no Portuguese slaves to wash your bodies; but neither will Scipio. And you'll be spading the dry soil from light to dark; but so will your general: spade in hand you'll see me beside you and puffing with the best of you. Romans and allies! My grandfather fought and died in Spain. My father campaigned in Spain. Myself I served in Spain eighteen years ago as prefect to Licinius Lucullus now dead. I have been elsewhere since, you know where. The man who comes from Carthage does not tolerate defeat! In a year Numantia will be ours. Today we outnumber them three to one. Tomorrow more are coming! Four thousand fresh men — my nephew in charge — another Scipio! Volunteers from every part of our dominions — sent to me Scipio by kings and princes who remember Carthage. Romans and allies, hold onto Discipline, Work and Patience. Under these three hammers Numantia will sink into the floor of the world: and God be with us. (*He abruptly descends as the trumpets sound once more. Off-stage cries of "Dismiss!"*)

SCENE THREE

(*Numantia. Meeting of the Military Council. Retogenes, Caravino, and Audax around a table. Behind them, a few officers, including Connoba. Maps on the table. Off-stage, the tolling of the death-bell, gradually receding. Caravino has been speaking. His finger is jabbing a map.*)

CARAVINO. Here. Is it or isn't it a fact that he has sent half of his seventh legion away to Termantia?

AUDAX. He has. And it is also a fact that half of it remains.

CARAVINO. I have made that calculation too. What of it? Are they supermen? They're men like our own, just as tired, just as hot under the sun.

RETOGENES. So then.

CARAVINO. So then. My plan is simple enough. We send a squad out on the first moonless night, that is to say a week from today. The men swim across at this point here. They scale the cliff. They surprise the enemy on his flank. Meantime we open the Minervan Gate wide — something the enemy never expects —

AUDAX. Because he thinks better of us, perhaps.

CARAVINO. Something the enemy never expects, and we launch a frontal assault smack against him with our fourth, fifth and eighth.

RETOGENES. The casualties would be high.

CARAVINO. They will be high. But twenty-five percent will come back.

RETOGENES. Can we afford it?

CARAVINO. Can we afford anything else? We've got to shake up Pallantia; prove to them we're alive and capable of putting meat into an alliance; what they need to convince them is a show like this one.

AUDAX. A show like this one will bleed us dry.

CARAVINO. I expected nothing else from you, General Audax.

RETOGENES. Gentlemen . . .

AUDAX. It's not blustering over a map will get you through the Roman lines. Retogenes, we are being asked to engineer an idle massacre of our own best men. I want no part of it. Let this be understood.

RETOGENES. You mean there's no chance for the plan to succeed?

AUDAX. Of course there's a chance. But the chance must be weighed against mischance. You take one in two, one in five, but not one in ten, in twenty! To count on surprising Scipio — that, for example, is lunacy.

CARAVINO. Scipio again!

AUDAX. Yes, Scipio again. This is no amateur you're fighting, my friend. Whether or not he expects us to march out at the great gate to tweak his nose, the point I am making is that one does not surprise Scipio Africanus. One may defeat him in pitched battle, one might buy him off, but one does not plan a campaign which depends on surprising him.

CARAVINO. The invulnerable Scipio! There we have him again. Take it from me, I know where Scipio succeeds. Not in starving our bodies. Good, he has starved our bodies too — you needn't prove it to me, I hear the death-bell and I can smell bodies too; but that's not it. Scipio is starving our wills. Our wills are sick. One against a hundred we used to crack the Roman lines. Now we let them huddle us into the city, we sit down and starve, we grumble and we die, we send peace delegations, we allow a Peace Party in our midst: we don't *move*. One good blow! That's what I demand. Not only to smash through the Roman lines, but to get our own blood circulating again.

AUDAX. Circulating? You mean flooding the land. Gentlemen, you are both respected administrators, but you are not soldiers. This is not the rostrum, you are not making speeches to our good citizens. The squad you want to send up the cliff will be picked off and killed. Fine. It's their business to die: signed, General Audax. But what next? Scipio knows better than to be taken in by a feint. Our men throw their bodies against the wall he's built, or into his trenches. Scipio butchers us with his left hand, and laughs at us besides. Now I understand Caravino's intentions: they are good, but they are political. Not good enough to justify a military catastrophe. I'm ordering no frontal attack.

CARAVINO. Here you have it, this is the very flabbiness I spoke about. I allowed the general to have his say.

AUDAX. We'll not be saving Numantia with insults.

CARAVINO. If only Scipio were defending this city instead of attacking it! ... This hopelessness, this unwillingness to make sacrifices: there's the true enemy. General Audax, I'll say freely that I reject your policy of inaction.

AUDAX. And I reject your policy of reckless action. It makes me mad — ten years of fighting, lives and more lives — the waste — the ruin — the fanatics — and now all I hear is more more more — "no sacrifice is too great," and I see you ready to depopulate the city for the sake of a "policy of action." If you want victory, Caravino, leave us a few people alive to know we've won.

CARAVINO. Are you suggesting that the war is lost, General Audax?

AUDAX. Not lost and yet lost, and if not lost, lost anyway.

RETOGENES. *That* is a conundrum you must kindly explain to our lesser minds, general.

AUDAX. I mean, Retogenes, that we might yet win in the legal sense, especially if we are able to suck in Pallantia, Malia, and Lutia. But we cannot win back those ten years. Those are ten defeated years. The dead are dead, the waste is wasted.

RETOGENES. Perhaps you have taken certain personal losses too much to heart.

AUDAX. Your own have been as great as mine, Retogenes; that's not to the purpose.

RETOGENES. Well, you're an elusive sort. You think well, Audax, no man better in this city, but undoubtedly you think too much. However, let's come to some kind of agreement. What do you propose, Audax? Specifically now.

AUDAX. My proposition is far from heroic — or new, for that matter. Scipio still likes money. We've bribed him before. Let's bribe him again. Or accommodate him with a loan, in civil language.

CARAVINO. To make him lift the siege? What?

AUDAX. No such foolishness. But we might be allowed to buy a little food again. Last time he sold us his own — stolen from his men, thank you. That's risky for him; so let's propose that he allow a single one of our men to needle in. Let him allow the man to reach Pallantia, ostensibly to buy food in secret. The supplies can trickle in at night by way of the river, provided the Romans look the other way again. And then, while our man is in Pallantia, why shouldn't he reopen the subject of alliances?

CARAVINO. Extravagance. Until we prove to Pallantia that we've got muscles — enough to give *them* a few knocks when the day comes — they won't show their noses to the Romans.

AUDAX. Possibly. And yet our argument, namely that the cities are only waiting to be plucked off one by one, is hard to refute. We must propose a coordinated attack, rear and front. If the move is carefully prepared, then we can open the gate at last and try Caravino's plan. But not without safeguards.

CARAVINO. Safeguards! Safeguards! That's all I hear in the council nowadays. The chimney-sweeps have more courage than some of us.

AUDAX. Then make the chimney-sweeps your generals.

CARAVINO. There are those who think too much of safety, sir.

AUDAX. And others who have reasons of their own perhaps for not caring any more. Let the world collapse with them!

CARAVINO. The meaning of this?

AUDAX. Gladly!

RETOGENES. Gentlemen —

CARAVINO. I'm proud to be on Scipio's blacklist, General Audax, and on that honor roll second only to Retogenes, and shame on you, and something more, who knows, for not standing in it.

AUDAX. Call me traitor, say traitor to my face, miserable politician.

RETOGENES. Enough! Silence! Both of you. Now look why Scipio picked one to die and another to escape alive. Here is the fruit. Numantia will tear itself to pieces while Scipio snickers. Caravino, you have gone too far. I must ask you —

CARAVINO. Yes yes — I apologize.

RETOGENES. And you —

AUDAX. Sweep it under. Peace.

RETOGENES. Let's consider your plan, general. I don't see any reason for not trying it out. If it fails, there's still time for other ideas. We'll risk one man — and try to blind Scipio with golden coins over his eyes. Caravino?

CARAVINO. Very well. Try it. I agree.

RETOGENES. Remains the choice of a man to undertake the little cold swim in the river at night, the dart through the Roman patrols, the scratchy climb along the face of the cliff, and the long run to Pallantia; and actually, I can't think of anyone more suitable than our prefect of the second cohort. What do you think, gentlemen? (He is addressing the officers)

OFFICER. An excellent choice.

CARAVINO. First-rate.

RETOGENES. General? I can't better express my confidence —

AUDAX. My son is ready. I can speak for him; but let him speak for himself.

CONNOBA. Name the time and give me precise instructions. I'll do the rest.

RETOGENES. Good. We'll reach Scipio through the usual muddy channels, and find out whether he'll dance if we fiddle. Anything else, my friends? If not, I bid you good night. Let me shake your hand, Connoba; and yours, General Audax. Remember, all of you: unity is our strength. (*He leaves*)

CARAVINO (*as he is leaving with the other men*). In short, we need a Scipio of our own. Buying artichokes in Pallantia, ha-ha . . . (*They are gone*)

(*Audax and Connoba are left alone*)

AUDAX. God be with you, my boy, God be with you. They took my breath away. How was I to guess?

CONNOBA. I think we can count on Scipio.

AUDAX. I daresay. But I never meant you. Mongrels. Did you see Caravino grin and pretend to hide it?

CONNOBA. Father —

AUDAX. Yes?

CONNOBA. Don't worry about me.

AUDAX. I won't.

CONNOBA. But you. You'd better be careful.

AUDAX (*suddenly furious*). If I were a man! A man! Not a patriotic ox of a coward, I'd pick you up and put you down before Scipio, me and you, and tell him "Enough, enough! My wife died in the second epidemic, my first son is killed, I've lost the war already, save this one at least!" The clowning has gone too far. I've forgotten why thirty thousand people died last year. To save Numantia from the Romans? Is it possible? Have I decided that it's better to die thirty thousand times than to become the clerk of a Roman? Have we gone insane?

(*He becomes aware of his son's gaze*)

CONNOBA (*cold*). Better I hadn't heard you.

AUDAX. You're right.

CONNOBA. You only lost your temper for a moment.

AUDAX. That was it.

CONNOBA. Be careful.

AUDAX. I will.

CONNOBA. Well, I'm overdue at the barracks. Equipment to check, orders to give, and all the rest before I go.

AUDAX. Maro will replace you for the few days.

CONNOBA. He'll do.

AUDAX. I'll see you again tonight.

CONNOBA. If you wish. I'm off now.

AUDAX. Connoba . . . One reason is what you know. I swore to your mother I would pester you into safety . . .

CONNOBA. I'm not a child any more. I have duties. Excuse me —

AUDAX. Go.

(*Connoba leaves. Audax sits down and looks at the maps, his forehead in his hand*)
AUDAX. Twenty years old . . . Not even . . .

Scene Four

(*Scipio's tent. Two bunks, a table, a chest: the minimum. Scipio sleeps at one end, Maximus at the other; both almost fully dressed. Buteo enters and shakes Scipio*)

BUTEO. Uncle.
(*Scipio sits up*)
SCIPIO. What is it? Oh, it's you. What's the matter?
BUTEO. They've caught a man.
(*Maximus wakes up*)
MAXIMUS. What is it? Buteo?
BUTEO. Yes. Sorry to wake you up, but there's been a commotion.
SCIPIO. Start again. What commotion? And why bother *me* with it?
BUTEO (*lower voice*). Fulvius Flaccus made this one.
(*Scipio and Maximus get up with oaths*)
MAXIMUS. Shall I go see?
SCIPIO. Wait. Let Buteo tell us. All right, nephew. Hand me my belt. Now, in three words.
BUTEO. Fulvius went on a patrol before dawn with a few of his boys, and I followed discreetly at a distance.
MAXIMUS. Good.
BUTEO. He noticed somebody lifting himself out of the river on our side of the wall.
SCIPIO. Whereabouts?
BUTEO. Near Tower Six.
MAXIMUS. God split him.
BUTEO. He cries out "What's this? What's this? Isn't the river supposed to be triple-watched? Stop that man!" And three of his men dive quietly into the brushwork down the hill. I could see the shape clearly now. I saw them pounce. The man fights back, but they pinion him in a second. That's when I shot away to tell you.
SCIPIO. Go meet them, Buteo. Quickly. Tell them Scipio's been informed — don't say how — and say I want to see the prisoner alone. At once, in fact. And bring the prisoner to me yourself.
(*Buteo leaves the tent*)
SCIPIO. A catastrophe. Fulvius Flaccus caught him. How did he know?

Or was it an accident? And is the man talking? A catastrophe, I tell you. Expect the worst.

MAXIMUS. But are you sure it's the man?

SCIPIO. By Tower Six, idiot! Tonight was the night, Tower Six was the spot. Who else was it? The ghost of Achilles? And where else would that scabby Fulvius be except where there's trouble against me?

MAXIMUS. One of these days that snooper is going to find his neck broken.

SCIPIO. And where the devil is Buteo? Is he giving Fulvius time to make another investigation?

MAXIMUS. Let me take a look. (He looks outside) They're coming. Brother, listen to me. Maybe it's somebody else. Maybe!

SCIPIO. Shut up.

MAXIMUS. All right, it isn't. What are you going to do?

SCIPIO. We took the money and yet he was captured. He'll be shouting this every step of the way.

MAXIMUS. Think, brother.

SCIPIO. I'm going to be erased by a snivelling dandy whose only speech in the Senate has been "Gentlemen, I propose we decorate the vestibule with a painting of Justice and Virtue." This prig is trampling on me!

MAXIMUS. Think what you'll do about the prisoner, brother.

SCIPIO. I'll do what I have to do.

MAXIMUS. Quiet.

(Enter Buteo and Connoba. Connoba's hands are tied)

CONNOBA. Which one of you is Scipio?

SCIPIO. One minute. (Aside to Buteo) Where's Fulvius?

BUTEO. Back in his tent.

CONNOBA. I want to see Scipio at once! Bring him to me!

MAXIMUS. Quiet! You'll see him plenty soon.

SCIPIO (same). Did he question him?

BUTEO. Don't know.

SCIPIO. Suspicious?

BUTEO. Of course.

SCIPIO. Go now. Don't let anybody come near till I call you. (Buteo leaves) I am Scipio.

CONNOBA. I thought so. Why am I here? Answer me.

SCIPIO. Are you the son of General Audax?

CONNOBA (draws himself up). Prefect of the second cohort of Numantia.

SCIPIO. Your name?

CONNOBA. Connoba. And more you'll not hear from me. Scipio, listen to me.

MAXIMUS. You listen to me, young fellow; you remember who you're addressing.

CONNOBA. I'm remembering it, my Roman friend; I'll be remembering it as long as I live. Scipio, you've put our money in your pockets. Deny it.

SCIPIO. I don't deny it.

CONNOBA. Why do these Roman hyenas live? Their generals pick-pockets. For this miserable money you were letting me reach Pallantia — God curse you! — to beg a few loaves of bread for our children. Didn't you swear? Deny it!

SCIPIO. I don't deny it, Connoba. And I stood by it.

CONNOBA. You stood by it? Can a man sink lower? What am I doing here with a rope around my wrists?

MAXIMUS. We stood by the agreement, Connoba. Tell it to your father and to the Council. Publius Scipio's own guard was at Tower Six, with private orders.

CONNOBA. Three of them knocked me to the ground. What's this drivel?

MAXIMUS. Those were other men. Another patrol. We didn't know — what can we say?

SCIPIO. We didn't know.

MAXIMUS. The third legion had a patrol out last night — night duty — and we hadn't been personally informed. That's the whole story and God's truth.

CONNOBA. You take me for an imbecile. All right. I'm satisfied. Are you going to cut the rope?

SCIPIO. Gladly. But remember you've been seen. Tell me first — exactly and word by word — what you told the men who caught you — what you cried out, or deliberately spoke, or dropped before you could think.

CONNOBA. Nothing. There wasn't much time for gossip, and I'm no fool. I said and repeated one thing strong and loud: "Take me to Scipio."

SCIPIO. Ah, very good.

CONNOBA. Look, Scipio, I'll swallow your story. Done. Now will you keep your pledge? We paid for it with heavy gold. My mouth is shut; you can trust me; and nobody denies your word's always been good.

SCIPIO. Don't worry, we'll find a way for you to escape. Be patient a day or two. I'll post one of my own men over your cell and you can manage the rest.

CONNOBA. Agreed. But let me warn you. You try foul play on me and I won't die I promise without every man in this camp hearing the facts.

MAXIMUS. Insolent brat!

SCIPIO. I understand. You have my word, Connoba. Be patient a day or two.

CONNOBA. I'll wait.

SCIPIO (to Maximus). Please call Buteo and a couple of his men. (Maximus *leaves)*

SCIPIO. Sit down, sit down. You've had a rough excursion. And a drench besides. But we'll give you dry clothes. Sit down. *(Connoba sits heavily)* Why don't your people give up, Connoba? You've been brave; none braver; but —

CONNOBA *(quietly)*. But nothing. The word is never. We've kept your faces in the dust for seventy years. We've demolished fifty of your legions. We killed your grandfather here in Spain, Scipio, and he with forty thousand men, and proud, like some others we've seen in their glory.

SCIPIO. Your people are sending a peace delegation to me tomorrow.

CONNOBA. Let them watch out for themselves. We know the difference between peace and surrender.

SCIPIO. Words, wind.

CONNOBA. Besides, summer is coming. Your first, Scipio. You won't be so gay under our sun.

(Maximus and Buteo enter)

SCIPIO. Here comes your escort. Go quietly. Keep your mouth shut. Sleep in peace, and wait for a signal from me. And we'll feed you, my boy. *(To Buteo)* Take our prisoner away, Buteo, and see to it that he is given dry clothes, a good meal and decent bedding.

BUTEO. Yes, sir.

CONNOBA. I've taken your word, Scipio. I'll eat the food because I need strength.

(He is led out)

SCIPIO *(to Buteo, aside)*. Come back a minute.

BUTEO. In a second. I'll tell my men to hold him.

(He goes out and returns at once)

SCIPIO. Put him in Barrack S. Make him comfortable and see that *nobody* talks to him. And send me Polybius and Minucius.

BUTEO. I will. *(He leaves)*

(A long silence)

SCIPIO. The sun is up.

MAXIMUS. Looks like another warm day. Summer is coming.

(Another silence)

MAXIMUS. For God's sake, brother, tell me what next.

SCIPIO. Yes; what next. I'd better be the only one who knows. *(He falls silent again and then explodes)* Strutting about the camp with his "mantle of office"! Rome sets a spy on me! On me! I took Carthage for them! They're sitting in their villas lapping champagne while I kill myself in this desert. And they send me a spy; a prig who never saw a spear before except in a museum; a duckling!

MAXIMUS. I don't recognize you, brother. What's the use of crying? Tell

me instead what you propose to do. Are you going to let him escape?
Personally, I think you should.

SCIPIO. "Take me to Scipio."

MAXIMUS. What's that?

SCIPIO. "Take me to Scipio" is what the Numantian boy was shouting all
the way at Fulvius Flaccus.

MAXIMUS. Oh. That's right. Still, it could —

SCIPIO. Of course. It could, it could. But it doesn't. And why, says Fulvius,
wasn't the river guarded? And how comes it, he'll ask tomorrow,
that the prisoner escaped? What an odd concourse of events! And
"Take me to Scipio!" No, Fulvius is giving me no choice. I must
prove there was no bargain.

MAXIMUS. How do you prove that?

(Buteo appears)

BUTEO. Minucius and Polybius are outside. What's the matter, uncle?

SCIPIO. Nothing. Send Polybius first. And then Minucius.

(Buteo leaves. Polybius enters the tent)

POLYBIUS. Good morning, Publius and Maximus Scipio. You have orders
for me this morning?

SCIPIO. Not exactly. But do sit down.

POLYBIUS. Thank you.

SCIPIO. Fulvius Flaccus caught a Numantian officer this morning.

POLYBIUS. Yes.

SCIPIO. He was trying to reach Pallantia.

POLYBIUS. If Pallantia goes in with them —

SCIPIO. If Pallantia goes in with them, the politicians in Rome may sweat
a little and learn to appreciate their general.

MAXIMUS. The monkeys.

SCIPIO. But that's another story. The man who was caught turns out to
be a son of General Audax.

POLYBIUS. Yes.

SCIPIO. Ah, you know.

POLYBIUS. I do.

SCIPIO. Now I suppose they wouldn't have sent a man of his rank without
some expectations in Pallantia.

POLYBIUS. I agree. And yet it might also be an act of desperation.

MAXIMUS. We've had them in a vise for eight months and thirteen days,
you know. Fourteen counting today.

POLYBIUS. No doubt about it. They are down to licking hides, eating straw,
and even boiling limbs of the dead. They chuck people into mass
graves. And according to reports, they also talk with extremely
noble words about Saguntum.

MAXIMUS. Saguntum?

POLYBIUS. Another Spanish town. Your brother knows. Hannibal besieged it. He too put a ditch and a wall around it, like Publius Scipio.

SCIPIO (*laughing*). Well, Polybius, I'm not a "great originator of strategic maneuvers" and so forth! But it takes something, doesn't it, to choose what to imitate?

POLYBIUS. My respected general, Hannibal crushed Saguntum, but you crushed Hannibal. That speaks for itself.

MAXIMUS. Tell me what happened at Saguntum.

POLYBIUS. When the deathly hour drew near, the men burned their own city, melted down all valuables, destroyed every sitting and standing object in town, murdered the prisoners, dispatched their own women and children, and then neatly disemboweled themselves.

MAXIMUS. And that's what the Numantians are talking about?

POLYBIUS. So I hear. I'll hear more tomorrow, of course.

SCIPIO. That's why I sent for you. I'd like this siege to come to an end, Polybius. They're starving, to be sure, but we're not sipping honey either. And I've got them in a vise, but how long can I pinch them in it? Let them hold out another year, and I'll have twenty towns at my throat, and ten more years of campaigning. Well then, when you meet their delegation tomorrow, I want you to make a pretty effort.

POLYBIUS. I've been making a pretty effort for six months, Scipio! What else can I do? Do you have new ideas? Concessions?

SCIPIO. Yes, concessions.

MAXIMUS. What's on your mind, brother? You've told me nothing about this! Why concessions?

SCIPIO. I'll guarantee the safety of every man, woman and child in Numantia, except those on the list. And I'll find new land for them.

POLYBIUS. But that's nothing new. You're talking to Polybius, my dear general, not to your enemies. Come, what *new* proposals have you got?

SCIPIO. Well, reduce the tribute, God blast it!

MAXIMUS. What?

POLYBIUS. You surprise me.

SCIPIO (*red-faced*). You all think I'm a robber, a squeezer, a purse-snatcher! They kick my name about in Rome as though I were a pawnbroker. They send accountants to sniff into my "practices"! And you too, Polybius —

POLYBIUS. I didn't say a thing!

SCIPIO. But you smiled. Well, I say reduce the tribute. Take ten per cent off and let's have peace, by all the thunder in heaven! Rome won't let me do more for them. Talk to them.

POLYBIUS. I'll try, Scipio. You know my feelings. Is that all?

SCIPIO. Yes, that's all.

(Polybius is leaving)

SCIPIO. Offer it at the end. If you must.

POLYBIUS. Of course. Good day, gentlemen.

MAXIMUS. I'll breakfast with you.

(Polybius leaves)

MAXIMUS. Ten per cent, Publius! Are you mad?

SCIPIO. We'll force the Senate to take half the loss.

MAXIMUS. Oh.

SCIPIO. I can't do anything in my own straight way. Rubble across my
path. But my conscience is clear.

MAXIMUS. They don't know your value; that's what I maintain. What have
they got against you? Only that you're too popular.

(Enter Buteo)

BUTEO. Minucius is still waiting, uncle.

SCIPIO. Send him in.

(Buteo leaves)

SCIPIO. Maximus —

MAXIMUS. You'd better do the rest alone.

SCIPIO. Right.

*(Maximus, glad to leave, makes his way out. Minucius salutes him as he
enters, then stands in front of Scipio, who is now sitting at the table)*

SCIPIO. Trouble at dawn, Minucius.

MINUCIUS. I know, sir. We saw it all.

SCIPIO. Oh.

MINUCIUS. I couldn't see nothing we could do about it, sir. We had no
orders. Sure, we could have jumped them. But I said to myself it
wasn't what you'd be wanting us to do, out in the open.

SCIPIO. Right. Tell me what happened exactly.

MINUCIUS. Not much to tell, sir. Me and the other five was on duty at
Tower Six. I took my turn about two in the morning, on account of
the man you said was supposed to show up about three. About four
o'clock sure enough I hear a quiet kind of splash in the river, and
the man comes swimming up to the bank. He looks around, and I'm
looking at him from the tower — of course he don't see me — and
then him and me see the others at the same simultaneous time. A
squad of our own men. He tries to get away —

SCIPIO. Fine. I know the rest.

MINUCIUS. I hope we did right, sir.

SCIPIO. You did. You're not to blame for a thing. But now we've got the
prisoner on our hands, and there may be a nasty job for you.

MINUCIUS. Anything, sir. You know me.

SCIPIO. Yes. That's why I called you. *(He opens the chest, takes out a locked box, opens it with a key, and retrieves a bag, which he fills with pieces of gold and gives Minucius)* This is for you even if I don't give you the sign.

MINUCIUS. Thank you, sir.

SCIPIO. Listen carefully. We're expecting a delegation from Numantia tomorrow. There will be talks. The talks will be fruitful or useless. If they are fruitful, that's the end. No orders for you. Keep the money — you're my man and what I give I don't take away. Now: if the talks go wrong, I'll drop you a word: I'll say the talks went wrong. Exactly these words. And that's your sign. You follow me?

MINUCIUS. Yes, sir. My sign is, the talks went wrong. Otherwise no orders.

SCIPIO. Good. Now, if you hear those words, you'll assign two of your youngest boys to watch over the prisoner. You'll pour some sleeping powder in his wine. Before dawn you'll dismiss the guards. You in person and alone will carry him out a short way on the road to Pallantia. Kill him quietly: through the back. Kill him easy; don't let him wake up.

MINUCIUS. Where is the prisoner now, sir?

SCIPIO. I've thought of that. He's in Barrack S; convenient. When you've finished, you report back to me that the prisoner was killed while escaping.

MINUCIUS. Very good, sir.

SCIPIO. But only if I tell you clearly, the talks went wrong. I'll say nothing else.

MINUCIUS. I understand, sir. I don't do more than enough.

SCIPIO. That's all then.

(Minucius salutes and leaves)

SCIPIO. Maximus!

MAXIMUS *(outside)*. Yes. I'm coming. *(Enters)* Well?

SCIPIO. I've taken steps. Fulvius has nothing.

SCENE FIVE

(A public square in Numantia, bordered by houses, and backed by a parapet overlooking the country beyond and below. There is a monument whose broad base will serve as a platform for the speakers. The death-bell is heard for a little while. Audax, his back to the audience, gazes out over the ramparts. To one side, by one of the houses, a ragged man sits weakly, head down, on a doorstep. There is a long silence. A second and third

man enter and aimlessly join the sitting man. They are pale, ragged, long-haired)

SECOND. Still watching his dead soldier lad.

FIRST. Who?

SECOND. The general. Look.

FIRST. I don't know.

SECOND. I said the general is watching his dead soldier lad.

FIRST. You said, you said.

SECOND. Did your boy find anything?

FIRST. A dead dog. With flies.

SECOND. You can die eating it, in my opinion.

FIRST. Why?

SECOND. What do you mean — why?

FIRST. Why should I die eating it? The flies don't die..

(The third man laughs)

SECOND. Flies don't die so easily.

FIRST. That's what I said.

SECOND. Flies are a good sign, in fact.

THIRD. Why are flies a good sign?

SECOND. They mean summer. I hear the Romans will have to give up when the hot weather comes.

THIRD. Who said?

SECOND. I heard it. Now I think of it, it's what Retogenes said on Sunday.

FIRST. What did he say?

SECOND. "We must persevere, stand firm, tighten our belts, bury our dead, and fight on." I always like the way he puts things.

FIRST. Then why did he send a bunch of traitors out to talk to Scipio? What a joke.

SECOND. We've got to explore, I suppose.

FIRST. I wish I could stand up.

SECOND. What would you do?

FIRST. But I get spots before my eyes and I faint.

SECOND. It's a bad sign.

THIRD. Not necessarily.

FIRST *(for the first time he raises his head)*. Some people are eating dinners.

SECOND. What's that?

FIRST. I said some people are eating dinners.

SECOND. What do you mean? Who is eating dinners?

THIRD. Such a fool.

FIRST. When I saw the bunch of traitors come back from talking to Scipio, I said to myself when I saw them, "They have dined with Scipio."

SECOND. I don't know about that. They didn't look very happy to me.

FIRST. If I had dinner with Scipio I'd watch out to look unhappy too.

THIRD. Rot and nonsense.

FIRST. Good old Peace Party — the gang. They look fat. You can look unhappy when you've had a meal but you can't look skinny.

SECOND. I didn't notice.

FIRST. You got weak eyes. There was grease on their lips. I noticed. Don't tell me they join the Peace Party for nothing. Scipio gives them bread and butter and then they talk about peace while we're chewing hunks of timber, and my woman is dead sure enough and only one of the boys is left to me.

SECOND. I don't know. Nobody knows. But I know the hot days are coming soon.

(Enter Marandro)

SECOND. What's the news, Marandro?

MARANDRO. They've arrested the p-p-p-peace delegation.

FIRST. Good. But I don't believe it.

SECOND. The ones that went to Scipio?

MARANDRO. The same. Arrested. I saw it.

THIRD. But why? Why?

MARANDRO. How do I know? But they're all c-c-coming this way. A mob. Speeches. Retogenes and everybody.

THIRD. Retogenes likes to give us shows.

FIRST. Traitors all of them.

SECOND. They're coming this way?

MARANDRO. On the way to jail. They're t-t-tied together already. Avarus in front. Everybody roped.

SECOND. Another trial, I guess.

THIRD. And more executions. It never fails. It hasn't failed yet.

FIRST. All traitors, A to Z.

THIRD. You're a damn fool.

FIRST *(a flicker of strength)*. Who? Me?

THIRD. That's right. You.

FIRST *(down again)*. They'll arrest you too.

THIRD. Let them.

MARANDRO. What are you talking about?

SECOND. What's the good of quarreling? We must remain united.

THIRD. United dead in a ditch. Or out there with a sword through the gut but no father or mother alive to look at us and pray peace over the bones.

MARANDRO *(seeing Audax)*. Still there!

SECOND. What do you suppose a man feels that has sent his own son off to die?

MARANDRO. I wouldn't p-p-p-put it that way.

THIRD. I thought surely this time they'd be coming back with terms.

SECOND. The delegation?

THIRD. Yes. Why should anybody arrest them?

FIRST. Because they came back with a bellyful of Roman dinner they did.

THIRD. I'll swear they did come back with terms! And that's why — that's why these politicians will murder them!

SECOND. Terms — I'll say! Give up the city! Move your baggage out! Pay tribute! Settle in the sand two hundred bitter miles away! Not me! Leave my house to the first hooligan that comes and demands it of me? A Roman dog sleeping in my bed? I tell you the hot days are coming and they'll rot down to their bones.

THIRD. The hot days are coming and you'll be stinking in the grave with the rest of us and the Roman dog will sleep in your bed all the same.

SECOND. You're a maniac! I tell you the hot days are on our side, and in another month we'll be seeing a Pallantian army on the hills. Wait and see.

THIRD. Thank you, say my bones. Five more years of the same. Glory be.

FIRST. They'll arrest you.

MARANDRO. No no, they won't. Don't t-t-t-talk so much, my friend.

THIRD (laughing). It's better than listening to my belly making speeches. Damn, now my eyes are rolling too. (He leans against the wall and sits down. The first man moves a little way)

SECOND (helping him). Talking uses you up.

MARANDRO. We'll f-f-fight together to the b-b-b-bitter end.

(Enter Lira and Julia)

MARANDRO (to Lira). G-g-g-good afternoon, madam.

LIRA. Good day, Marandro.

MARANDRO (to the men). A f-f-fine woman. I used to supply the f-f-family with wine. She went to school with Audax's wife.

SECOND. Isn't the other his sister-in-law?

MARANDRO. I don't know.

FIRST. She'll die anyway.

JULIA. Audax. (Audax turns around) What's the use? Don't look . . .

AUDAX. It's so far away, I can almost pretend, no, it isn't Connoba. But all the same, it's somebody, isn't it? (He holds each woman by the hand) Lira, I'm glad to see you.

LIRA. We wondered if we could help. At your house, perhaps.

AUDAX. Yes — at my house — thank you. Fortunately, I'm on duty day and night. My house . . . . Julia, your husband?

JULIA. It will be over soon. One of us today, the other tomorrow.

AUDAX. I'll bring some food again after dark.

(Meanwhile, a number of citizens have appeared. Now an officer enters and approaches General Audax)

OFFICER. Excuse me, general.

AUDAX. Yes — what is it?

OFFICER. The governor requests that you join him. He is actually coming this way and the prisoners after him, but he would like to be met and attended.

AUDAX. I'll go meet him. Let him know. *(The officer leaves)* Retogenes is delivering the prisoners to jail in person. But I don't know why he is coming on before them.

LIRA. Roman prisoners? What do you mean?

AUDAX. Oh. You haven't heard. Our own peace delegation is going to jail.

LIRA. I don't understand.

AUDAX. You're lucky. Well, I have to leave you. I advise you not to stay.

LIRA. Isn't there anything we can do for you?

AUDAX. Yes, of course. Tell the housekeeper I'll come home in two or three days, and not to worry about me.

LIRA. We'll do everything.

JULIA. Audax, please, for your own sake — don't look any more.

(Audax presses her hand and leaves)

LIRA. God knows what the men are up to again.

JULIA. Murder, what else?

LIRA. But why? Because they couldn't agree? I don't understand.

JULIA. Who knows?

LIRA. Maybe we shouldn't stay.

JULIA. It hurts, but I want to see it.

(Now they are swallowed up by the crowd of tired, ragged and skeletal citizens. A few soldiers are among them. Most of the people sit quietly on the ground. Some listless conversation. A late citizen asks whether this is the place where "he" will speak. Then the fourth citizen suddenly accosts the fifth)

FOURTH. Why you staring at me?

FIFTH. Staring at you?

FOURTH. Yeah. Staring at me.

FIFTH. I've been staring at you?

FOURTH. That's what I said. You've been staring at me.

FIFTH. So I've been staring at you. But not because you're a picture of Apollo.

FOURTH. What do you mean? Is there something funny about me?
    (To the sixth citizen) You too? Anything funny about me?

SIXTH. No. Nothing funny about you. I ain't laughing. Nothing except what everybody knows.

SEVENTH. All right. That's enough.

FOURTH. What everybody knows? What does everybody know, you bastard? I'll kill you.

SIXTH. You call me bastard?

FOURTH. That's what I call you. And anybody else that stares at me.

SEVENTH. Come on, that's enough.

FOURTH. Because there's nobody in this town got a human right to stare at me. That's right. I was a soldier in the service twelve years.

FIFTH. Sure. Raiding the stalls in the market.

FOURTH. You stinking bastard!

FIFTH. That's enough. *(They fight)* You ain't fit to be seen among decent people.

FOURTH. I'll show you who's fit.

(Others try to interfere, but the fourth citizen has the upper hand)

EIGHTH. For shame! Retogenes himself is coming to speak to us.

FIFTH. Let go! Let go!

FOURTH. Twelve years in the service while you was putting on weight and now you think you got the right to stare at me. Bastard, bastard, bastard!

SEVERAL. Let him go! You're choking him! God damn you! There's an assembly of the people here!

(But the fifth citizen has finally disengaged himself. He strikes a violent blow. The fourth citizen falls backward)

FIFTH. Cannibal!

(Suddenly everybody falls silent. The fourth citizen slowly picks himself up. He is weeping. He drags himself away)

FIFTH. He provoked me. Leave me alone.

EIGHTH. Forget it.

SEVENTH. Yes. Forget it.

SIXTH. He provoked you.

NINTH. Anyway, I think Retogenes is bringing good news.

TENTH. Me too.

ELEVENTH. I think we can manage another go at the wall. Masses of us. Torches. Ladders. And when that's done we'll talk peace.

TWELFTH. They'll have to carry you into battle on a stretcher.

ELEVENTH. Maybe you'd like to join the peace delegation. There's rope enough for everybody's neck.

TWELFTH. You don't scare me. I've got my thoughts.

EIGHTH. Don't start another quarrel, if you please.

(Various remarks and grumbles. The group subsides. During the episode, Marcius has come in with a friend)

MARCIUS. Is he here?

FRIEND. I'm looking. Yes, he is. Don't look now. But in a moment turn casually to the left and glance at the Tax Collector's house. The man standing up is Marandro.

MARCIUS. The one in black? With the finger in his ear?

FRIEND. That's the man.

MARCIUS. All right. Stay here. (*He walks casually*) Are you Marandro?

MARANDRO. Marandro, import and export; in the good days, alas.

MARCIUS. May I have a word with you — on the side?

MARANDRO. At your service. (*They walk aside*)

A WOMAN IN THE CROWD. Food! Give us food instead of fighting like dogs!

A MAN. Stupid woman.

MARCIUS. I'm told you've got food stored away.

MARANDRO (*frightened*). Who t-t-told you this trash? Food? In Numantia?

MARCIUS. Calm down. We're safe in the crowd.

MARANDRO. Who are you?

MARCIUS. I'm somebody whose children are hungry. I'm nobody else. And I'll pay you whatever you want for whatever you've got. Caro told me about you.

MARANDRO. What did he tell you?

MARCIUS. That you sit like a dragon on a heap of victuals.

MARANDRO. It's not true. Like a what? Do I look like I have f-f-food? Why did Caro tell you this trash? You're from the p-p-p-police, that's clear enough.

MARCIUS. If I were from the police I'd be searching your cellar. Come on, Marandro, talk business or else the police *will* hear from me. (*Grim*) Besides, I'll kill a man for a piece of bread. What have you got and how much do you want?

MARANDRO. I haven't got anything. But I might get in touch with somebody. Maybe!

MARCIUS. What has your somebody got, and how much does your somebody want?

MARANDRO. A p-p-pound of flour for sixty silver denarii.

MARCIUS (*quietly*). Your somebody is lower than a dead stinking mongrel. What does he hope to do with silver? Bribe an eagle to fly him out of Numantia?

MARANDRO. That's his business. Good-bye.

MARCIUS. Wait. I'll pay. Sixty in silver. For two pounds of flour.

MARANDRO. A p-p-pound and a half.

MARCIUS. It's children, Marandro; not myself, children. What kind of a beast are you?

MARANDRO. All right. Two pounds. Let it be.

MARCIUS. Where and when?

(*Marandro takes him aside. His answer is drowned in shouts from the crowd. A few distinct calls can be heard*)

VOICE. Here they are!

VOICE. Retogenes!

VOICE. Caravino!

VOICE. Audax!

VOICE. Speech! Hurrah! Hang Scipio!

VOICE. Where are the prisoners?

VOICE. Action!

VOICE. They'll sell us to Rome for a pound of meat!

(Audax and escort enter)

AUDAX. Peace! Silence! Order! No riots here!

VOICE. Bravo for the general!

AUDAX. The prisoners — *(uproar)* — silence! The prisoners are being taken
to jail. No violence will be tolerated.

VOICE. Are you going to feed them in jail?

VOICE. Make them starve! *(Shouts of approval)*

AUDAX. Peace everybody! Let the court try them! *(The crowd is on its
feet. Soldiers try to enforce some order)*

VOICE. The Romans don't hold trials. Why should we?

VOICE. Did they try your son? *(Voices silence him)*

VOICE. Forget the prisoners! Give us bread!

(Shouts of approval, "Food, food," etc.)

AUDAX. Make way for the governor!

*(Enter Retogenes, Caravino, soldiers, escort. Retogenes is waving a scroll.
He leaps up to the base of the statue. Caravino is at his side.)*

RETOGENES. Citizens and neighbors! Let me speak with you! *(The crowd
shouts approval)* As you know, we have arrested the peace delegation —

VOICE. Good work!

RETOGENES. And Avarus at their head —

VOICE. Off with it!

VOICE. Is it because they didn't make peace, or did make peace, or would,
or wouldn't?

VOICE. He's a lawyer! *(Laughter. They parody and silence him)*

RETOGENES. Patience! I'm here to report to you — the people! Listen to me!
The prisoners are going to jail. But I have come ahead in order to
give you an account; an account of the actions of your government.
And I hold in my hand a document I beg to read to you. A document
from Scipio himself! A document from the enemy to men in our
midst — to Numantians — traitors — here in my hand — a letter from
Scipio's agent — found this morning in the possession of Avarus.
Yes, Avarus! The intelligent and patriotic leader of the opposition!
You will see him presently, neighbors and friends, loaded with
chains.

VOICE. What happened, sir? We were hoping for peace at last.

VOICE. That's right. The bins are empty. How long can we hold out?

VOICE. Your knees wobbling?

VOICE. Shut up. Let him talk.

VOICE. Cowards all!

VOICE. Babies!

VOICE. I'm for peace!

RETOGENES. Friends friends friends. Let me say my word for God's sake! Who sent Avarus to negotiate with Scipio? Who but ourselves? There are whispers that we are opposed to peace. Opposed to peace! Are we maniacs or butchers? Is my son not dead in this war? No, let us have peace, let us have peace by all means, let us negotiate fairly, bravely, honorably — I said honorably, neighbors, like free men, because free men is what we are! Who will oppose this? Is there anyone here who would oppose honorable peace? Let him speak up! Thank God, the time hasn't come when any honest man is afraid to speak his mind in this land. Let only the traitors beware. No, my friends, we are not opposed to negotiations. We have negotiated before, and will do so again and again — but from a position of strength and honor, the brave to the brave! Not crawling like beaten dogs. What shall we do — my friends, what shall we do, I ask you! Tell me! I am your servant! You call me your governor, but you — the people of Numantia, you are the governors. I ask you what shall we do? This letter asks us to capitulate. Simply to capitulate! And this infamy is acceptable to our Peace Party. They are invited by their Roman friends to spread defeatist propaganda in our midst. How shall we reply to them? Have we lost our manhood, that we should go begging when the tide of war is turning in our favor?

VOICES. Well said! Read the letter! Take a breath! Read the letter! That's right, read the letter!

RETOGENES. The time for speeches is over. Here is the letter. Read it, Caravino.

CARAVINO. The letter is from Polybius, secretary to Publius Cornelius Scipio Aemilianus, called the African, and it is addressed to Avarus, President of the Numantian Peace Commission and Chairman of the Peace Party of Numantia. It begins "My good friend."

RETOGENES. "My good friend."

CARAVINO. I am reading now. "It is with deep personal regret that I view, once more, the failure of our negotiations to bring about an honorable settlement of the tedious conflict between our two nations. Yet we Romans are determined — and I myself am determined — to continue these negotiations indefinitely, in the hope of averting a final catastrophe. That you yourself, Avarus, and your Party, share in our eagerness for peace prompts me to entrust you with this letter, in which I express certain personal views, certain private feelings perhaps, which might not transpire during our official meetings.

Take these words of mine, Avarus, and if possible spread words of peace among the citizens of Numantia; let the good cause of peace flourish quietly; let an atmosphere —"

RETOGENES. And so forth and so on! Skip the ceremony, Caravino, and come to the meat.

CARAVINO. "And to this effect, illustrious Avarus, I send you the following. And first, I will have you know that slavery is not so much what is imposed by the conqueror, as what is induced by the defeated. Yes, I will boldly say that the defeated *ask* for slavery. For the conqueror's cruelty is aroused by cruel resistance against him. The defeated who have not resisted live on, prosper, and often become subtle conquerors of those who conquered them. The defeated who did resist are oppressed or exterminated. For set this down as a fearful axiom: the height of a nation's resistance determines the depth of its fall; while, on the contrary, a tyrant without enemies is a tyrant no longer." *(Looking up)* Who understands this gibberish? "Slavery, I repeat, is rather induced by the conquered than imposed by the victors. And so well did your countrymen in Saguntum know it that, when their walls crumbled after a long and bitter siege, they killed themselves one and all rather than await the fury of the Romans they had foolishly opposed so many years."

RETOGENES. Foolishly opposed! My children, he mocks our brothers and sisters of Saguntum, whose ashes the wind still blows over our Spain. *(Moans are heard)* Hush! I'll not be guilty of making tears fall. Let Polybius and Scipio jeer at our Spanish martyrs. Read on, Caravino.

CARAVINO. "Look instead, I ask you, at that other city of Spain, wealthy, growing, charming Emporium —"

A VOICE. Collaborators! *(Boos)*

CARAVINO. "Emporium made no resistance; Emporium, if you will, capitulated, collaborated, surrendered, temporized, compromised — oh, call it what you will, do words frighten us, noble Avarus? I am not frightened by words. Very well, Emporium surrendered. Surrendered ingloriously, as your leaders say — "

A VOICE. Pissing with fear! *(Laughter)*

CARAVINO. "And now Emporium is the jewel of Spain. Port of entry, city of parks and boulevards, mansions and shops, active citizens, sound laws, and by special privilege exempt from taxation and military service!"

A VOICE. Bastards by special privilege.

RETOGENES. Patience, my friends, you have heard nothing yet.

CARAVINO. "But, you will answer me, Emporium is no longer free! Oh Avarus, who ever possessed this freedom except the few powerful men of this earth, and the most intelligent of the intelligent? The people? Give them a little money; entertain them with races and dances; protect them from envy and ambition, the two scourges of mankind; humor their habits; and then they will think they are free. Freedom, my friend, is a word, a puff of smoke."

RETOGENES. Attention! Scipio says freedom is a puff of smoke! Do you know why? I'll give you the answer in an old country saying of ours: "Don't praise the sun in front of the owl."

A VOICE. "And don't try to sell wings to a mole." (*Laughter*)

RETOGENES. It's not in Numantia that Scipio is going to find the slaves he found in Africa. But wait. You've heard nothing yet. You won't be laughing when you hear about Scipio's special friends in Numantia. On with Avarus' letter, Caravino.

CARAVINO. "Now, of course, if we Romans meant to kill you, your people would be right to fight us to the end. Well may a man risk his life to save his life. That is a sensible sort of bargain. But shall he die to save his house? his money? his city? his place in society? his reputation? Let your leaders say what they will, but we Romans, though we may be harsh, we are not murderers."

RETOGENES. Not murderers! He says not murderers! Shall we look over those ramparts for the evidence? But go on, Caravino, go on. Listen to the Roman abusing your own elected government.

CARAVINO. "And this, noble Avarus, brings me to a great point. Tell the people to distrust their leaders — indeed, to distrust all leaders. What are leaders? Political men: men who believe, and who cause people to believe, that political life is the alpha and omega of existence. Naturally! It is their profession! A physician believes all men need treatment; a poet believes that poets build cities; and a cobbler, no doubt, believes that men cannot live without shoes: don't they all talk to him about shoes? Now, these political men, these leaders, persuade the people that no horror can exceed the horror of being ruled by foreign political men. The foreigners will oppress you, beware! I reply: They will oppress you only if you draw your knives when they come near. Tell the people of Numantia, my good Avarus, that only the leaders suffer when a nation quietly surrenders. But the grocer and carpenter continue to sell lettuce and to build tables. Do not frighten your conquerors, for only the frightened are cruel. Surrender to us, Numantians, while there is time, and we will give you governors as good as your own. Do not provoke our cruelty. Disarm us by disarming."

RETOGENES (*his face in his hands*). Disarm! Surrender! Listen to it! Listen to it! Surrender when the summer is about to decimate them, when we are even now stirring up half of Spain for another great upheaval against Rome; disarm, when another year, two years at most of sacrifices will make the dogs lick our feet. And yet there are men here, among us, in Numantia, who listen to this voice out of hell and who tell us to disarm!

AUDAX *(to Retogenes)*. Haven't they heard enough?

A VOICE. Go on reading!

CARAVINO. "And I pronounce the word 'surrender' freely, Avarus, but to you only; do not use dangerous words with the common people, who are dull in spirit and heavy of understanding." That's you, gentlemen!

RETOGENES. Dull in spirit and heavy of understanding, ladies and gentlemen. Into the mud with your faces! Your turn!

A VOICE. Does he really say that, governor?

RETOGENES. What? Do you think we're making it all up? By thunder you do! Show him, Caravino. No — give it to me. You there — come on up — take a look!

VOICE. Me?

SEVERAL. Go ahead. Take a look.

RETOGENES. Come here — don't be afraid. Have a good look. *(He shows him the letter)* Read it! Read it aloud!

THE MAN. Where? I —

RETOGENES. Here, my good fellow.

THE MAN. "Wise men fear things —"

RETOGENES. Where are you? No no no, begin here! Follow my finger.

THE MAN *(to those behind him)*. Stop shoving, damn you! "Do not use —"

VOICES. Louder, louder. We can't hear!

THE MAN. All right! It says: "Do not use dangerous words with the common people, who are dull in spirit and heavy of understanding." That's what it says. And it's a Roman hand sure enough!

(Uproar)

RETOGENES. Citizens — good people — patience — patience above all! Let Caravino continue!

CARAVINO. I continue. "Wise men fear things. But children and common people fear words. Their leaders frighten them with witchcraft phrases: 'ignominious surrender' and 'humiliating defeat' and 'abject compromise' and 'cowardly retreat.' No wonder; it is they, the leaders, who will lose job and life when the conqueror marches in. No wonder they inspire in the people that bloody patriotism, that blind and odious national fervor, that unnatural heroism, that stupidity which they call 'self-sacrificing devotion' —"

RETOGENES. Don't cry out! Ask the gods for patience!

CARAVINO. "For that 'self-sacrificing devotion' is chiefly what is going to keep them in office. Without it, the cobblers and carpenters would open the gates to the conquerors, wrangle and deal with them, worship the new gods, marry their daughters off to the new men, and carry on in peace and satisfaction. Oh Numantians, you have no enemies!"

RETOGENES. We have no enemies! Scipio has been joking with us all year.

A VOICE. Let him give us a dinner for a joke!

RETOGENES. Wait! Don't get angry with Scipio! He has more friendly words for us, and it would be bad manners not to listen. Continue, Caravino.

CARAVINO. "But finally, my friend, tell the people that should the worst be true, should the conqueror enslave them, beat them, rob them, rape them, mutilate them, still, all this is better than not to be at all. For this is still life, and life when it is most bitter is still sweet, but death is neither bitter nor sweet, and who would choose this neither, this nothing? Our terms, I cannot conceal the fact, are harsh. It is too late for complete forgiveness. Your leaders will pay, and your people will suffer. You have fought us too long. Only our friends will be treated with especial regard."

RETOGENES. Patience, patience!

CARAVINO. "Only our friends will be treated with especial regard; those few brave and lonely men who have dared to stand up against the folly of their compatriots, and who prefer a tax, a tribute, a restriction of privilege here and there, even a complete loss of rights, even exile from their ancestral home, prefer all this, I say, to endless massacre and utter extinction. Not that such horrors are destined for your people, unless by longer resistance you finally arouse the ferocity you fear. Avarus, a man who has himself witnessed and recorded twelve wars, and whose soul is weary with slaughter, sends you this, in hope of human peace. Your brother Polybius embraces you."

RETOGENES. Your brother Polybius embraces you. Read it again!

CARAVINO. "Your brother Polybius embraces you."

RETOGENES. Embraces you. Your Roman brother.

(Uneasy stirrings in the crowd)

RETOGENES (with sudden fury). So be it! Freedom is a puff of smoke! Your leaders are bandits! You the people are idiots! Exile is not so bad! So be it! Let's embrace Avarus too! Let's all of us get especial consideration like Avarus! Down with Numantia! Numantia has stood a thousand years, but down with it, down over the graves of your fathers and grandfathers, down over the graves of your sons who have died for it, down over the son of General Audax who lies out there on a plank murdered under our eyes, down with it, and out with us into the desert, begging proud Scipio for an acre of alien inhospitable land, while he repopulates Numantia with Romans and Asians. Surrender! Why not? Vote for it here and now! Who votes for surrender in this Assembly? Who votes for opening the gates to Scipio, for yielding him the keys to our houses, for washing his feet as he enters, tired of trampling over our dead? Who votes for enlisting in his armies to fight our old allies on his side? Who votes for delivering our wives and daughters to his bed, and to the beds of his bearded Asians? Who votes for groveling before him, yes and thanking him for throttling our freedom? Who votes for handing over our children as slaves to wash his latrines for him?

VOICES. No, no, never. (Moans)

RETOGENES. Not I, citizens of Numantia! Don't ask this of me! I, Retogenes, will not be alive to disgrace my name when that day comes. Elect another governor. Elect Avarus! Here's the letter again. Your brother Polybius embraces you. Avarus will surrender you to the Roman butchers in person! But as for me, citizens of Numantia, here, before you all, here is what I do with that letter (he shouts) which burns my hands! (He tears, and punctuates with) Freedom! Freedom! Freedom!

(He scatters the pieces)

A VOICE. Freedom!

CROWD. Freedom!

CARAVINO. Down with the traitors!

VOICES. Hang 'em! Burn 'em alive! Crucify them!

VOICE. We're not crawling for nobody!

VOICE. There's blood in us yet!

VOICE. Long live Retogenes!

CROWD. Long live Retogenes!

VOICE. Long live Audax!

CROWD. Long live Audax!

VOICE. Long live Caravino!

CROWD. Long live Caravino!

RETOGENES. Which shall it be? Surrender or victory?

CROWD. Victory! Victory!

RETOGENES. Then send it to the heavens. Fight to the death!

CLAMOR. Fight to the death! (Tumult)

CARAVINO. Retogenes! The soldiers are coming with the prisoners!

RETOGENES. Let them come! Off to jail! Special consideration!

(Uproar of the people)

AUDAX (to Caravino and Retogenes). What are you doing? They'll be massacred! Take them another way!

CARAVINO. Don't be a child, general.

AUDAX. Retogenes! Keep those men away!

VOICES. The prisoners!

AUDAX (to his men). Make a circle around them! (They hesitate) A circle around them, do you hear? Keep the crowd away! (Shouting) No violence! Hands off! Back! Back!

CARAVINO. General —

OFFICER. Make room for the prisoners!

(A group of four silent and cowed prisoners is brought in. The mob surges against them, but is rather tentatively held back by Audax's men. Several men throw stones and one of the prisoners stumbles to the ground. A woman screams and tries to reach him)

WOMAN. Let me through! Let me through! They stoned my husband!

SOLDIER. Step back.

AUDAX. Arrest that man! Here — that one — there — grab him.

(A soldier grabs the stone-thrower)

THE MAN. Somebody help me!

AUDAX. Get back, all of you! Away with him!

WOMAN. Let me help my husband!

VOICES. Let her get through for God's sake! Clap her in jail with the rest of 'em! Special consideration! Hang 'em all! Give her a chance! Shame! Etc.

AUDAX. Let her help the man! The next one who throws a stone is killed on the spot!

VOICE. Don't be too rough on us, general! (Laughter, noise)

RETOGENES (to Caravino). Wait.

(The woman kneels by her husband. He is getting on his feet again)

WOMAN (shaking her fist). Rabble! Rabble! Retogenes, tell them! Tell them you're on Scipio's blacklist! (Her husband tries to stop her) You want the people to bleed with you! You're going to kill my husband — let me talk! Let me talk! — you're going to kill my husband so —

CARAVINO. General! There's one trying to escape!

RETOGENES. Hold him! People! (Uproar)

AUDAX. Where? Nobody's escaping!

VOICE. They're trying to escape!

VOICES. Hold them! Hang them!

AUDAX. No violence! Nobody's escaping! Step back all of you!

RETOGENES. All right! Let the prisoners march quietly.

WOMAN. Take me along.

RETOGENES. Yes, take her along, the witch, take her along. Open a way for them.

AUDAX. Make a circle. Keep out — you! Away! (To an officer) Your responsibility. On your life.

OFFICER. Make way. March. March.

(The mob grumbles but allows the prisoners, the woman, and the escort to pass and leave)

CARAVINO. People of Numantia, rest assured, the prisoners will be tried fairly, and they will not escape. Meantime, gird yourselves — the struggle continues. Our allies are arming. We are strong. The summer is falling on the Roman army. That letter, citizens, that very letter shows how weak the Romans are, and how desperately they want peace. Let us be guided by patience, loyalty and resolution. And now disperse, go home, be of good cheer, one people united and free.

VOICE. And hungry!

(Laughter and groans. The crowd slowly breaks up. A few people are left, among them Marandro, Julia, and Lira. Retogenes is gone, but Caravino lingers)

CARAVINO *(privately to Audax)*. You were a trifle uncooperative —

AUDAX. Don't make me raise my voice, Caravino. I saw your agents in the crowd. And murder is not my duty.

CARAVINO. Murder? General, if I were you I'd think of murder elsewhere. *(He gestures toward the ramparts)*

AUDAX. What I think of is my business.

CARAVINO. I happen to disagree. We are all extremely interested in your thoughts.

AUDAX. I'm grateful. So grateful that I'll give you a sample of my thoughts. How did you happen to catch that useful letter?

CARAVINO. No mystery about that. We've never prevented the Romans and the Peace Party from exchanging secret messages. Quite the contrary. So I can assure you that *we* didn't write the letter.

AUDAX. You were just lucky enough to intercept a good one.

CARAVINO. Not even that. Avarus gave it to us.

AUDAX. *Gave* it to you! *(He looks at Caravino)* Yes — he would! Out of simple innocence he would!

CARAVINO. Or prudence.

AUDAX. That trusting simpleton! Yes, I believe you.

CARAVINO. Thank you. And confess that you rather enjoyed that letter, general.

AUDAX. Confess?

CARAVINO. I mean, there were a few principles in it, I don't know —

AUDAX *(his hand touches his sword a moment)*. I may be harder to truss up than some others you've caught.

CARAVINO. The people saw you in action. We'll be talking again.

AUDAX. No doubt.

(Caravino goes. Audax notices the two women)

AUDAX. Were you two watching this pathetic circus? You shouldn't have

stayed. If you approved of it, you're fools; if you didn't, you're
suspects.

JULIA. Audax —

AUDAX. Yes?

JULIA. Be careful . . .

AUDAX. Ha! Just what Connoba said to me.

LIRA. We mean well, and we're concerned for you. I've known you all
so long —

AUDAX. I am thankful, Lira, don't misunderstand.

JULIA. Audax, I don't know what right I have — I want to ask you a
question — not an easy one —

AUDAX. Ask me anything Cornelia might have asked.

JULIA (low). Why haven't you resigned? I'm terribly afraid . . .

AUDAX (low). Because the next day I'd be arrested, and the day after
hanged; along with Avarus and the rest.

(Julia looks into his face, and then lowers her head)

JULIA. They do horrible things — but how can anyone keep decent and
sane — with all this? And when all's said and done —

AUDAX. It's us. I understand.

JULIA. This is our home. I was married here. You too. You and Cornelia . . .

LIRA. And how else can they act? You can't win a war with prayers. I'm
sorry for these people. I don't think Retogenes is always right. But
people who get secret letters —

JULIA. We mustn't stay any longer.

AUDAX. Thank you, both of you.

LIRA. We'll look after everything.

(As the two women move away, the death-bell is heard off-stage)

JULIA. Come the other way . . .

(Julia and Lira leave. A tumbril now rattles on stage. It is drawn by two
men between the traces, and is loaded full of bodies. The gravedigger
walks behind ringing the death-bell. At one of the windows a woman
appears. She speaks in a forlorn blank voice)

WOMAN. Here.

GRAVEDIGGER. Age and sex? (No answer) Age and sex, up there?

WOMAN. A little boy. Eleven years and two months old.

GRAVEDIGGER. Bring him down.

WOMAN. I can't.

GRAVEDIGGER. Why can't you?

WOMAN. I can't.

GRAVEDIGGER. All right. Keep him.

AUDAX. Wait. (To the woman) We'll fetch him down, and decently. Open
the door for us. (He sees Marandro) You there, citizen. Come with
me.

MARANDRO. Me, general?

AUDAX. Yes. Come along. Don't dawdle.

(Marandro reluctantly follows him into the house. A few moments later they reappear carrying the dead boy on a makeshift litter. Marandro is nauseated and tries to avert his face)

AUDAX. Lift up. He'll fall. *(Impatiently)* Up!

(He manages to place the boy carefully in the wagon)

GRAVEDIGGER. There's usually something for us.

(Marandro has stepped aside. Audax looks at the window, which is empty, then gives the gravedigger some money)

GRAVEDIGGER. Thank you, general.

(The cart moves off to the shaking of the bell)

MARANDRO. Some people get used to it. I can't.

(He and the one or two remaining citizens move off. The bell is heard to the end of the scene. Audax is alone. He remains in deep reflection, looking again toward the plain where Connoba lies. Julia returns by herself)

JULIA. I didn't want to leave you with her words, as though I meant them.

AUDAX. I know you better, Julia. Sister . . .

JULIA. Yes?

AUDAX. I was going to tell you tonight. I am leaving soon.

JULIA *(frightened)*. What do you mean?

AUDAX. What *can* I mean? Leaving.

JULIA. Leaving for where? *(Whispering, as he gestures toward the plain)* Going over to Scipio? You can't — your own child — Audax — you can't —

AUDAX. I'll bury him myself. I'll be an example to Numantia.

JULIA *(incredulous)*. Your own child —

AUDAX. I had chosen him — in my mind — you understand — I had chosen him to survive. Now the last one is myself.

JULIA. They murdered him!

AUDAX. The war murdered him.

JULIA. And say we win the war?

AUDAX. I've lost my taste for victory. The old soldier is giving up.

JULIA. Your city.

AUDAX. I am my city.

JULIA. Audax, let me sit down . . . I'm trembling. Are you in serious danger?

AUDAX. That's not it.

JULIA. You're not going to lead the Romans against us?

AUDAX. No, Julia.

JULIA. Is there something I don't know? Has it all been wrong?

AUDAX. Nothing you don't know. And as for what's right and what's wrong, I'm done with that. Were we right to oppose the Romans? Yes we were. We were right, they were wrong. Rapacity sent them into Spain. They want slaves, gold, soldiers, markets. We were right, they were wrong. We have been right for two generations, they have been wrong for two generations. The young men died for the right, then the old people began to die for the right, then the women, then the children; and the houses fell down for the right, always for the right, mind you. I don't deny it. But now I'm sick of being right, I want this people of mine to give in to the wrong and to live. The wrong isn't all that wrong, and the right isn't all that right.

JULIA. You destroyed Aemilius and Brutus in the field before Scipio became consul. You could destroy Scipio himself.

AUDAX. In three years? five years? ten years?

JULIA. In three years.

AUDAX. In three years of fighting and siege, might a child die? Yes, a child might die. It isn't worth it.

JULIA. Your city.

AUDAX. I am my city. Julia . . .

JULIA. Yes?

AUDAX. You'll be left alone soon. Marcellus is dying.

JULIA. Yes.

AUDAX. You have no children.

JULIA. I have no children.

AUDAX. Fortunate woman. The unborn don't die. If the worst should happen —

JULIA. Yes?

AUDAX. There will be a great self-destruction here. It has been secretly discussed in the Council. Take my words seriously, Julia.

JULIA. I do, God help us, I do.

AUDAX. Don't cry.

JULIA. I won't.

AUDAX. Retogenes and Caravino want to teach Scipio a lesson no one will let him forget. They can do this even if we lose the war, by wiping out the city.

JULIA. Why?

AUDAX. Scipio has his troubles in Rome. They suspect him of wanting to be king. He needs money and a brilliant success. Besides, you heard the woman. Retogenes and Caravino are on the blacklist.

JULIA. Is it true?

AUDAX. It is. And it makes them a little more reckless. Julia, listen to me. Scipio may be beaten yet in the open field; but if he is not, and the day comes, play dead in your cellar, take whatever food you can find, don't stir, lock the door, answer to no one, and wait until the Romans

are in possession. If they let me live I will find you again; if not . . .
(Julia is crying) Julia . . .

JULIA. Is that your advice to me? Welcome to the first soldier that knocks
down the door? Allow them to sell me? Become a charwoman in
a Roman kitchen? Or worse? I'd rather die, it's ten times easier, I'll
go with Marcellus, I'll kill myself when he is dead . . .

AUDAX. Julia —

JULIA. And you're running away, oh my God, my God . . .

AUDAX. Julia — how can I say it? — there's always time to make an end
of it, don't you see? If you can bear it no longer — God knows it's
easy, nothing else in this dirty world is easier. Don't die as a pre-
caution, Julia, it's too absurd — promise — swear — raise your hand
to me and swear!

JULIA. I can't. I'll be alone now. I can't bear it. My God, where are you,
where are you, God, why do we suffer so much? *(She is sobbing)*

Scene Six

*(The ruins of Numantia. Three elderly citizens — two men and a woman
— crouching in the rubble, tied up and guarded by a Roman soldier. Enter
Polybius. He walks slowly, as though looking for something. He stares at
the prisoners a while. In the distance, the shouting of a crowd. Enter
Buteo.)*

BUTEO. Oh, Polybius.

POLYBIUS. Buteo. Anything? Anyone?

BUTEO. Plenty of broken shoulders, scratched faces and bleeding hands.

POLYBIUS. What do you mean?

BUTEO. I mean our men digging into the rubble. We're taking losses
without meeting an enemy.

POLYBIUS. Haven't you found anything alive?

BUTEO. Children. They seem to have spared the children here and there.

POLYBIUS. No one else?

BUTEO. Don't ask. *(Pointing to the prisoners)* More of those. More raggle-
taggle odds and ends that couldn't afford the knife to stick into their
gut; and more children, starved and too astonished to be scared.

POLYBIUS. God have mercy on the innocent. Will I ever forget that first
child? You and your legionaries at one end of the street, swords,
spears, helmets, breastplates, and that child at the other end,
wondering whether all this was for her.

BUTEO. I'm grateful for one thing.

POLYBIUS. What's that?

BUTEO. The men aren't hungry for females. Otherwise, pah! Scipio was right, as usual. Our whores were bugled out of the front door with great ceremony, and whistled back through the cellar with greater discretion. I know why you're smiling.

POLYBIUS. How your military purity was offended when you first met our harlots! And how your manly integrity was affronted when you saw Scipio winking! We couldn't calm you down!

BUTEO. Have you seen my uncle?

POLYBIUS. Oh yes.

BUTEO. How is he?

POLYBIUS. Wild. Keep searching, Buteo. He *demands* prisoners.

BUTEO. Well, mine's only one sector. Maybe the others will dig up some flesh for him. Has anyone found Retogenes yet? There's my great hope — No!

POLYBIUS. Killed in state and lying in the middle of the Council Chamber all by himself. He fooled us. Not like Hannibal, who went down with his ship, and came up again into ours.

BUTEO. Retogenes killed himself.

POLYBIUS. Makes us look rather shabby. As in fact we are. When Scipio saw him —

(Another shout in the distance)

BUTEO. What's that? What are they shouting about? Good news maybe.

(Another shout)

POLYBIUS. Can't you make it out?

BUTEO. No!

POLYBIUS. They're crowning Scipio and giving him a new name.

BUTEO. What name?

POLYBIUS. He is now Scipio Numantinus, in honor of this victory.

BUTEO. Not bad. Whose idea was it?

POLYBIUS. Mine.

BUTEO. I shouldn't have asked!

POLYBIUS. I thought it might distract your uncle. Perhaps give him something to tell the Senate. I whispered the hint to Maximus, who passed it on to the tribunes and down the ladder. All quite spontaneous.

BUTEO. Never mind. He deserves it. I tell you he does.

POLYBIUS. I don't deny it.

(Enter a soldier)

SOLDIER. Beg your pardon, sir.

BUTEO. Yes?

SOLDIER. General Audax is asking permission to look for some of his people in the city.

BUTEO. Why not? Keep two men with him.

SOLDIER. Right, sir. *(He leaves)*

POLYBIUS. I hope he finds somebody.

BUTEO. Isn't his wife dead?

POLYBIUS. Yes. She died in one of the epidemics. Look!

(Enter Scipio hurriedly, followed by Maximus and several officers. He wears a crown of laurel which he angrily throws aside)

SCIPIO. Prisoners! Give me prisoners, not crowns! Look at this! this! this! Shambles! Think of the promises I made to my men! *(Looks at his officers)* And you! What are you staring at? Don't follow Numantinus about! Go to Fulvius Flaccus! Or get me some prisoners! Scatter and find me some prisoners! Scratch the rubble!

BUTEO. Uncle —

SCIPIO. And keep the children away from me! *(To the soldier who is standing guard over the old prisoners)* You — what are you doing with these people?

SOLDIER. This is a kind of temporary receiving point, sir. I'm supposed to collect a dozen prisoners before I carry them away.

SCIPIO. Cut their ropes.

SOLDIER. Yes, sir.

SCIPIO. Roping up old people! Have I come to this? Shame... There, let me do it myself. Old fellow, don't be scared. What's your name?

OLD WOMAN. He's hard of hearing, my lord.

SCIPIO. Why are they kneeling here? Give them something to eat, for pity's sake, and let them sit or stand.

POLYBIUS *(to Buteo)*. He's crying.

BUTEO. Uncle —

OLD MAN. Thank you, your excellence.

SCIPIO. He thanks me. And the city is broken, the temples down, the citadel burned, the people dead. Worse than Carthage. Oh Polybius, let me rest my arm on your shoulders. Why did they kill themselves? Am I an ogre? Is this courage? Wasn't there a man among them man enough to throw the sword away? Insanity! Name it in your chronicle, Polybius; insanity! And write this with your pen: Scipio entered Numantia victorious again, and wept.

MAXIMUS *(aside to Scipio)*. Brother, control yourself. You're making things worse for us. Proclaim it all went according to plan.

SCIPIO. Run away from me, Maximus. I'm done for. Give Fulvius a box of sweets.

MAXIMUS. What do you take me for?

SCIPIO. Where's Audax?

BUTEO. I allowed him to do a bit of searching on his own.

MAXIMUS. Under guard?

BUTEO. Sure.

MAXIMUS. Don't forget you've got Audax, brother. An authentic prize.

The only survivor! It'll look dramatic in Rome.

SCIPIO. Dramatic! and I'll be the buffoon in the drama. *(Angry)* I had Rome knee deep in my prisoners! Polybius!

POLYBIUS. Yes, sir.

SCIPIO *(taking him to one side)*. I want you to keep looking for the gold, do you hear? I'll give you five hundred men to dig up foundations, debris, empty lots, anything. And we'll question every prisoner we get, babies, lunatics, cripples.

POLYBIUS. I'll keep at it, Scipio, but —

SCIPIO *(cold fury)*. Don't but me. Find the gold.

POLYBIUS. I'll do all I can.

(Enter a soldier)

SOLDIER. Beg to report, sir.

SCIPIO. All right. What is it?

SOLDIER. Five more prisoners in the south sector.

SCIPIO. What kind?

SOLDIER. A couple of them are old, but the others seem to be in pretty fair condition, sir.

SCIPIO. Bring them to me. I'll question them myself. *(The soldier leaves. To Polybius again, pointing to the prisoners)* What information did you get out of these?

POLYBIUS. I haven't —

SCIPIO. Why not? Why not? *(He grabs the old man)* You! Try to remember — did you hear any rumors about the gold in the temple or treasury?

OLD MAN *(frightened)*. They burned the furniture.

SCIPIO. The gold!

OLD WOMAN. We don't know, sir. He's a little deaf, and we made sandals, out by the gardens . . .

BUTEO. Uncle —

SCIPIO. Pah! *(He lets the old man go)* Where's Audax? Oh yes. Leave me alone! Stare at each other. *(He pokes in the debris)* Watch me returning to Rome now. Ahh.

MAXIMUS. What's the matter?

SCIPIO. Nothing. A splinter. It's a foretaste, an omen, a reminder . . .
    (He sits down heavily and loses himself)

BUTEO *(to Polybius)*. What does he want you to do?

POLYBIUS. He wants me to find the gold.

MAXIMUS. The gold's melted down, gone, he knows it, damnation!

POLYBIUS. I know. But we'll keep digging.

SCIPIO *(looking at them suddenly)*. Died for what? For the glory. But what's the use of glory you can't glory in? Idiots.

MAXIMUS *(to Polybius)*. Go to him. All this talk about dying. It gives the wrong people ideas.

BUTEO. He owes it to the army to look cheerful.

(A soldier has entered. He talks to Maximus)

SOLDIER. A report from the western sector, General. May I hand it to Publius Cornelius Scipio?

MAXIMUS. Let me see it first. *(He reads it quickly. Polybius and Buteo look at him. He shakes his head)* Better not just now. I'll keep it. Go on back. *(Exit soldier)*

SCIPIO *(his back turned to them)*. Yes, better keep it from Scipio. *(He rejoins the group)* All right, let's move along. I want to see every corner of the city. Buteo: the officers are to maintain absolute order, no grumbling, no petitions, no meetings. Let the prisoners be fed so they can be sold. Hands off the woman and all officers to report under the citadel's ruins at sunset.

BUTEO. I'll see to everything.

SCIPIO. Where's Fulvius Flaccus?

BUTEO. Writing a dispatch.

MAXIMUS. Naturally.

SCIPIO. All right. You can go.

BUTEO *(to a couple of officers)*. Follow me, please.

(They leave)

SCIPIO *(to Maximus)*. What was that report?

MAXIMUS. From the western sector.

SCIPIO. Well?

MAXIMUS. Nothing.

POLYBIUS. Here's Audax . . .

(Enter Audax, carrying Julia's body. Two soldiers are with him. He places the body gently on the ground)

OLD WOMAN *(whispers to the old man)*. Look! Look! It's General Audax!

POLYBIUS. I'm sorry.

AUDAX. I washed her face at the fountain. So be it. I'm too dazed to think about it.

SCIPIO. Who is this?

AUDAX. My wife's sister.

SCIPIO. Let her be buried, and enough.

AUDAX *(to Polybius; he is kneeling by the body)*. Have you found anyone?

POLYBIUS. Here and there . . .

AUDAX. Marquinius, the high priest?

POLYBIUS. Dead.

AUDAX. Retogenes, Caravino? *(Polybius shakes his head)* Dead? Caravino dead? By his own hand?

POLYBIUS *(his hand on Audax's shoulder)*. Let's cover her. *(He removes his cloak)*

AUDAX (*grasping Julia's face*). Unbearable!

POLYBIUS. Let me . . . (*He covers the body*)

(*Audax rises, and notices the prisoners*)

AUDAX. A few remain, thank God. My people, my people.

(*As he moves closer to the prisoners, the second old man suddenly stands up*)

SECOND OLD MAN. Turncoat! Renegade!

OLD WOMAN (*terrified*). Hush, for pity's sake!

MAXIMUS. What's that!

SECOND OLD MAN. Renegade! I spit in your face! Your woman had more guts than you, you slimy coward!

FIRST OLD MAN. I didn't say anything!

SCIPIO. Take them away.

SOLDIER. All right, you. Get moving.

SECOND OLD MAN. Let the world know it! He knifed us in the back! He'll do the same for you, Romans! Renegade! May you rot like a leper!

OLD WOMAN. Hush up — oh God —

FIRST OLD MAN. I didn't say anything!

SOLDIER. Go on, damn you, shove off, on your feet, all of you!

SECOND OLD MAN. You're a mongrel without race —

POLYBIUS. Away!

SOLDIER. Move!

SECOND OLD MAN. I don't care. Renegade!

(*The prisoners are gone*)

SCIPIO. God love the common people. There's more truth in that scum than in most of us. Audax, turn around. I might as well have done with you now. I fed you because I thought you could save Numantia for me. You didn't. As for what you are, you heard your compatriots.

AUDAX (*low*). Give me a dagger, Scipio.

SCIPIO. After the pains you took to save your precious hide? Too late.

AUDAX. Kill me! (*The guards hold him*)

POLYBIUS (*aside to Scipio*). Why not use him in the city, Scipio? Look at him; so much misery is pitiful.

SCIPIO (*loud*). I could taunt him to where he would bite his own flesh. Didn't I kill his son? Eh? Didn't I murder his son? And didn't he come to me begging for my favor all the same?

POLYBIUS. Scipio, be generous.

SCIPIO. You're right, my friend. Audax is a lamb, but that's no reason for Scipio to be a wolf. Tell Fulvius Flaccus, while he's about his dispatches, to write to the Senate as follows. "Disposition to be taken with regard to the former Numantian general Audax." Audax, stand erect for your sentence!

MAXIMUS. Stand tall, Audax.

SCIPIO. "The former general, having deserted from the Numantian army, will be conveyed to the Spanish coast under heavy guard, and thence shipped to Greece, the land of slaves, and sold into slavery. For Scipio Africanus Numantinus will not permit a renegade to defile our sacred homeland, lest his presence carry a curse and corrupt the Roman people." Let Fulvius be instructed to write this to the Senate. Did you hear me, Polybius?

POLYBIUS *(low)*. I did.

SCIPIO *(to the guards)*. Now take him away and don't show him to me again.

AUDAX. Before they made you consul, Scipio, I destroyed Aemilius and Brutus.

SCIPIO. Listen to the tattered bankrupt — "I used to drink out of silver goblets." Take him away. I'm sick enough as it is.

GUARD. Come along, Audax.

AUDAX *(struggling)*. I'm an officer! I have a right to my sword!

GUARD. That's enough.

AUDAX. Give me a sword! Hands off! Respect! *(As the guards lead him away)* Kill the mongrel! Kill me! Connoba! *(He is gone)*

SCIPIO. My stomach heaves.

MAXIMUS. What next, brother?

SCIPIO. Next? To my own hole. Come here, Polybius. If I don't keep you busy you'll be running to Audax to hold his hand. Gold, Polybius, I need gold for the Senate, fasten your mind on *that*.

MAXIMUS. What about the troops?

SCIPIO *(wearily)*. The troops. Make more promises. Organize thanksgiving services to the gods.

MAXIMUS. Why not athletic games, too? But try to look satisfied, Publius, that's what matters the most. Come on, give us a hearty word.

SCIPIO *(picking up the laurel crown he had thrown away)*. There's my crown, brother. Keep it for your grandchildren.

(They move on)

SCENE SEVEN

(The setting of Scene One again)

AUDAX. My life nauseated me. I thought the ghost of my son would rise — with such hate in its face —

MARANDRO. Yes, I had forgotten, he murdered your son.

AUDAX. The war murdered my son.

MARANDRO. Either way — you've paid for it all, old soldier.

AUDAX. The old soldier is an old pitcher leaking out through twenty cracks. But still pouring, mind you.

MARANDRO. You've had your day, remember that too. Riding high.

AUDAX. It gives me a ticklish strange feeling to meet somebody who remembers. My life went into another language, and now I'm hearing the old tongue again. . . . When I remind the young rascals hereabout who I was, "Run for your lives," they cry, "the old man's off on his Spanish horse again!" All in fun, maybe, but Tuccia gives them a scolding anyway.

MARANDRO. Tuccia? Oh yes, Tuccia.

AUDAX. She's no queen or princess, but I've learned not to be fastidious. She's as cozy as an old pillow, a good cook besides, and the children, well, they're worth living for, after all.

MARANDRO. If the townspeople could have g-g-g-guessed you'd be here with your Tuccia, and children in your lap, they'd have howled twice as much as they did.

AUDAX. I wanted to give an example.

MARANDRO. That's a good one! There was a black p-p-p-panic, I tell you, when they missed you.

AUDAX (flaring up). It didn't keep you from fighting another eight months, getting Pallantia and Malia demolished, and killing and dying like drunkards. I watched it. I was in Scipio's camp, don't forget, I talked to envoys, I pleaded, but what for? The national honor was involved, "Numantians will never be slaves," and you don't plead with national honor. And on the last day —

MARANDRO. Don't talk about it.

AUDAX. I entered Numantia with Scipio. Like a madman. Bellowing for life, looking for — looking for those I knew. Even Scipio broke down and wept.

MARANDRO. Well, Scipio is dead, you're telling stories —

AUDAX. Spain is a Roman province.

MARANDRO. And all is back to normal.

AUDAX. Except for half a million dead.

MARANDRO. That's life for you.

AUDAX. Who knows? Maybe I saw you that day in Numantia.

MARANDRO. Maybe. Thank God, a few of us survived. You know, to c-c-c-carry on the name of Numantia.

AUDAX. Don't talk rot, Marandro. Oh! I beg your pardon.

MARANDRO. Never mind. Sit down, sit down . . .

AUDAX. I forgot . . .

MARANDRO. That's all right . . . How things do turn around, though . . .

AUDAX. You don't know the tenth part of it, Marandro. You don't know the sorry days I've seen . . . I saw Scipio lying in a bloody heap in

Rome. And was I glad? Not even. A slave doesn't care. I've learned to dig in the fields and I've built bridges for armies and I've carried stones for monuments to governors and heroes, usually dead ones, and I've been struck in the mouth and I've bowed to idiots and I've had three ribs smashed and I've been sold and sold again and now I'm a broken old man.

MARANDRO. With Tuccia in a cabin.

AUDAX. Yes. To be sure. And the air in my nostrils. Take a breath, Marandro. *(He breathes deep)* Do you taste it? Do you smell the moon? Every five seconds of your life there's that bacchanal of air, if you'll only bother to notice. I learned the alphabet when I fell to the bottom. A for air; B for bread; C for cover. Which reminds me; I ought to get up and finish my first round. *(He doesn't move. Long silence)* Once I had a master ninety-seven years old. I don't remember where. I think in Smyrna. I fed him, dressed him, combed his three hairs, wiped the drool off his lips, sat him on his chamber pot, and scratched his back. That was the only pleasure left to him — so I scratched. But those were the good days. Look — *(He shows Marandro his ankle)* wait — here too. *(He shows his neck)* See the dent? Go on, touch it!

MARANDRO. I don't have to. I see —

AUDAX. The ankle is from working in a chain gang in the fields. And in silence, or else, clak! Chained up at night, too. But the neck wasn't so pleasant. That was in Brundisium, in a bakery. They put a wooden saucer round your neck — I suppose you've never seen one?

MARANDRO. No — I —

AUDAX. They clap it around your windpipe — about this wide around — you can just see over the edge to work the dough, but you can't lift any of it to your mouth.

MARANDRO. Why remember those awful times?

AUDAX. You're right. When I was sold at the market in Delos, they put me in a cage, naked and oiled, and I did tricks. Lifted stones to show my muscles.

MARANDRO. Why remember? A quiet night like this.

AUDAX. You're right, you're right. The advantage of being rich and free is that you can order any stories you like. You live. Look at you! I just survive.

MARANDRO. Fiddlesticks! There's nobody keeps *my* nest warm. And how about right here? It doesn't look like a t-t-terrible bad life.

AUDAX. I suppose not.

MARANDRO. If I come back, I'll let you stay home nights.

AUDAX. That will be a good thing too, though to tell you the truth —

MARANDRO. What?

AUDAX. One Spaniard to another?

MARANDRO. Of course.

AUDAX. I don't really stay up all night. About midnight something comes over me and I creep back under the covers with Tuccia.

MARANDRO *(laughing)*. Old horse-thief!

AUDAX *(laughing too)*. No harm done, you know. And if a tramp makes off with a few hens now and then, why the hens are as happy with him as with the master. But it doesn't happen much. Mummius is in the house. Mummius is the lad with the serious face who takes care of you here.

MARANDRO. Yes, I know.

AUDAX. We're friends. He sleeps light, and he tells me to go home and warm my feet.

MARANDRO. So there it is.

AUDAX. So there it is. Oh well, I'd better be going. The horses don't sleep easy until I've gone by the stable.

MARANDRO. Yes, time for bed. *(They rise)* Good night, old soldier. It was a good talk. With luck, we'll meet again.

AUDAX. I'll be a faithful servant to you, sir. If only for the sake of Numantia.

MARANDRO. I'm sure of it. *(He presses some coins on Audax)* Good night, Audax.

AUDAX. Oh no, sir, I won't —

MARANDRO. For the children. Not a word. I'm off.

AUDAX. For the children. Thank you.

MARANDRO. Not a word.

AUDAX. Thank you.

(Marandro is gone. Only his voice is heard)

MARANDRO. Oh, Audax.

AUDAX. Sir.

MARANDRO. There's some fruit on the table. T-t-take everything home.

AUDAX. I will, sir. *(Alone, he looks at the coins)* Shoes this winter, little devils! *(He takes one coin away and hides it)* You never know . . . What a night! *(He draws near the table)* Three peaches! Should I? *(He drops two peaches into a scrip and contemplates the third)* Beautiful . . . I'll take a mouthful, and Tuccia will eat the rest. It isn't every day. *(He bites into the peach)* It rivers into my mouth, it licks me. Hmm. Too luscious for a soldier. *(The peach goes into the bag. He picks up his lantern and starts away)* Marandro. Strange sudden meeting. Two sodden elderly rascals. *(He kneels at the fountain, wipes his mouth and drinks. He plays with the water)* And the moon trickles in it. Liquid eyes. Rightly considered, so is the world sodden. Juice of a peach. Water of the fountain. Tears in the eye. Sap in a tree. Milk in breast and udder. Flowing time. A stone sweating. An insect's gum. Male seed and woman's secreted answer. Venus . . . Trickle for me, affectionate water . . . Eighteen years . . . *(Silence)* Almighty pitiless gods, grant that all men and all women may live as long as their bodies are able, for it is once only and then never again. Grant us joy in duration. To be is to be enough.

(A window opens sharply in the second story)

MUMMIUS *(from the window)*. Is that you, old Spaniard?

AUDAX. Who is it? Mummius?

MUMMIUS. Yes. Are you talking to yourself now?

AUDAX. I — I was making up a story for the children. But I'm off on my round.

MUMMIUS. Are you locking the greenhouse?

AUDAX. I am.

MUMMIUS. And going by the tool shed?

AUDAX. I am.

MUMMIUS. Very good. I'll see you tomorrow. *(He closes the window. Audax picks up his lantern. He is on his way)*

AUDAX. I am. Speak it with humble commendation. I am. *(He vanishes)*

THE END

HONEST URUBAMBA

CHARACTERS*

A CROWD, including a little boy
A NEWSHAWK *(Blodgett)*
ANOTHER NEWSHAWK *(Pimpkin)*
A FAT MAN
A SMALL MAN
THE VIRGINS OF LA PAZ
A BOY IN A VISION
SOLDIERS
A GENERAL
MAJOR CUCUCHABAZ
TWO FARMER LADS
A FOREIGNER
FORTUNATO CONCEPCIÓN URUBAMBA
URUBAMBA'S AIDES
THE WOUNDED SOLDIER
SEVERAL DELEGATES TO THE UNITED NATIONS
THE PRESIDENT OF THE ASSEMBLY
HIS AIDE
ONESTO MORALES
A REPORTER
DANIEL SALAMANCA, *President of Bolivia*
SAN MARTÍN, *Minister of the Exterior*
PRADO, *Minister of the Interior*
AYALA, *Minister of Transportation*
CARRIÓN, *Minister of Defense*
ORTIZ, *Minister of Commerce*
GÓMEZ, *Minister of Information*
AIDES
A NURSE
THE MESSENGER
A CHERUB
THE CIA MAN
MRS. URUBAMBA
PEPE, *her little son*
AUNT URUBAMBA
GENERAL COCHÓN
A BEGGAR, *formerly* CHOCOLATE MAN
A WAR VETERAN

* Most of the actors and actresses can take two, three or four roles in the play.

SCENE ONE

(The stage is bare except for a few platforms, a Bolivian flag, and a conspicuous loudspeaker. Another loudspeaker is located in the theatre itself. The curtain rises on a cacophony of rumba music and military marches. Jolly atmosphere of frenzy throughout this scene. A siren ululates above and under the music as a joyous colorful crowd dances and waggles across the stage. Bells peal. Soldiers march in and out. Automobile horns give the V toot. The music is on or off in this scene as convenient. Additional dialogue can be improvised)

A LITTLE BOY. Bolivian flags! Ten cents each, worth at least twenty-five! Bolivian flags! Made in Bolivia! Bolivian cotton!

CROWD. Here! Give me one! I'll take two! Etc.

BOY. One at a time! Wait for your change! No bills, please, no paper money, no personal checks! Ten cents each! List price is twenty-five cents! Here you are, here you are . . .

MAN. On a day like this, young man, a flag is worth fifty cents! *(He brandishes a coin)* Fifty loyal native cents!

(Hurrahs from the crowd)

BOY. Thank you, sir. *(He has sold out his flags)* Long live Bolivia! Down with Paraguay!

(Crowd cheers)

BOY. More flags coming soon! *(He leaves)*

RADIO. Citizens of Bolivia!

CROWD. The radio! Quiet! Shhhh.

RADIO. Here is the voice of our Minister of Defense, Dr. Constantino Carrión.

VOICE OF CARRIÓN. Citizens! Descendants of Simon Bolívar! — These are historic hours! Hours that challenge the greatness of a nation! The government of Paraguay threatens to unleash its brutal hordes against our sacred territory, our national inheritance, our Chaco! Bolivia longs for peace, but when Bolivian land is invaded, Bolivia stands up and fights!

CROWD. Bolivia fights!

VOICE OF CARRIÓN. While this administration will take every honorable measure in its constant striving for peace, you, the people of Bolivia, have the solemn pledge of your freely elected government that we shall not rest until the last Paraguayan hireling is driven out of the Chaco, the land of our inheritance. Bolivians! This is a time for heroic sacrifice and patriotic rededication. Our dead shall not be dying in vain!

(Wild cheers)

RADIO. You have heard the voice of the Minister of Defense, Dr. Constantino Carrión, in an informative broadcast on the true facts of the border crisis.

(*Music resumes. Two newshawks appear on either side of the stage*)

NEWSHAWK 1. War imminent! Read it in the Observer!

NEWSHAWK 2. Showdown at the United Nations tomorrow! Read it in the Sun of the Andes!

NEWSHAWK 1. Bolivian delegate to the United Nations, Dr. Fortunato Concepción Urubamba, flies to New York this afternoon, carrying emergency instructions from President Salamanca!

NEWSHAWK 2. Second Division called to arms! Paraguay refuses to evacuate Fort Vanguardia! Bolivian embassy boarded up in Asunción!

NEWSHAWK 1. President Salamanca discloses Argentine oil interests are urging Paraguay behind the scenes to provoke an armed conflict!

NEWSHAWK 2. Paraguayan atrocities! Read the second installment of "I was defiled in Paraguay," told by a Bolivian maiden! More sensational disclosures! Breath-taking dirty photographs in full color!

(*Crowd buys papers. Roar of planes*)

CROWD. The air force! Bomb the navels off their bellies! Good boys! Over the Chaco and away!

WOMAN. Lookeee — the pilot is waving!

MAN. Off he goes! Bomb the pants off of them!

MAN. Bolivian bombs are sacred bombs!

(*Cheers. A large fat man dashes across the stage, pursued by a small man swinging an axe*)

SMALL MAN. Filthy Paraguayan! (*Uproar*) No — leave him to me!

(*Both off*)

RADIO. The entire world has witnessed this example of Paraguayan cowardice. (*More music*)

NEWSHAWK 1. The federation of Bolivian Miners affirms its solidarity! (*Cheers*)

NEWSHAWK 2. The Football League of Bolivia rallies to the fair cause! (*Cheers*)

NEWSHAWK 1. The Women's Volunteer Organization reveals it has stocked 50,000 bottles of iodine for our brave soldiers at the front! (*Cheers*)

(*The fat man, pursued by the small man, rushes across the stage in the other direction*)

FAT MAN (*bawling*). My grandmother was born in Nicaragua!

SMALL MAN. Foreigner!

(*Both off*)

CHOCOLATE MAN. Chocolates. Bolivian chocolates. Instant energy for the coming struggle.

(Churchbells on the right)

WOMAN. The bells of the Holy Virgin.

WOMAN. They're celebrating a solemn mass for peace.

(Bells on the left)

MAN. Bravo! The bells of the Sacred Blood!

MAN. They're celebrating a solemn mass for victory.

(Martial music)

CROWD. The army!

(Four ragged soldiers, led by a brilliant general, march in and about)

MAN. Look at him: the hero of Huachacalla with his dreaded Bullies of the Pampas!

MURMURS. The hero of Huachacalla.

GIRLS. And our soldiers, our sons, our lovers, our brothers, our husbands, our fathers.

(They throw flowers on the soldiers and kiss them helter-skelter)

GIRL *(leaping on a platform)*. For the duration: two dollars flat for any man in uniform!

(Soldiers cheer)

(Enter the modest virgins of La Paz, almost naked, in chorus line)

VIRGINS.   We are the modest virgins of La Paz,
              All daughters of good families (alas).*
              Our thoughts on holy wedlock used to dwell,
              But this is war, let's kiss and go to hell.
              So don't forget us, lads, on your next spree:
              We daughters of good families come free.

(The soldiers cheer again)

GIRL *(furious)*. Scabs! Amateurs!

NEWSHAWK 1. The women of Bolivia in scenes of personal commitment!

(The virgins dance away, waving; the marching soldiers march after them)

(A little boy, dressed in a white sheet, appears)

BOY. Halt!

GENERAL. Halt!

(One soldier keeps marching)

GENERAL. Halt, I said!

(The others make him halt)

SOLDIER. He's deaf in the second ear, sir.

GENERAL. At ease! *(To the boy)* Oh sublime vision! Say, what art thou? And whence? Thou seemest to shine upon our countenances like a phantom out of the deepest time to be!

---

*The "alas" is piped by a solo voice.

CROWD. Yea, thou seemest.

BOY. Kneel, soldiers, kneel, general, kneel, oh people of mother Bolivia. I am none other than the vision of the future generations for which you are about to die. Ah, let me take pride in you. Upon you all my watchful gaze is resting: do not fail me in the hour of danger; do not weaken; do not falter, Bolivians! The world knows that you do not raise the standard of liberty for mean and selfish purposes, for petty greed and low private ambitions. The world knows that you are laying down your lives for the future generations. We of the future generations thank you in advance. If you die for our sakes, we feel that you shall not have died in vain, but rather for the worthiest of all causes: us. (*He vanishes to gentle music*)

GENERAL. Sweet vision, do not go. Remain yet awhile. Alas, it is no more.

SOLDIERS. We see it no more.

CROWD. It is gone for aye.

MAN. But not from our memories.

GENERAL. All right, men, get off the bloody gravel and look smart. Form ranks! Shoulder arms! Forward, hup two three four . . .

(*Crowd cheers*)

FIRST SOLDIER.

Three square meals each goddam day,
Cabbage, beans and coffee on our tray —
We're cannon fodder like the feller said,
But cannon fodder must be fed.

SECOND SOLDIER.

Our work ain't seasonal, we're always wanted,
We don't go home, not us, just 'cause the
                              flag is planted,
No ma'am, the soldier's job is steady,
When one war's over the next one's getting ready.

THIRD SOLDIER.

The pay ain't much, so what, there's plenty of fresh air.
Fresh air ain't much, but busses is half-fare.
Half-fare ain't much, but who should grouse?
Plenty of women on the house!

FOURTH SOLDIER.

Course if you goof or play it dumb
Or show the foe your trembling bum,
With ten bullets in your belly you're retired,
But man you're in the army and you can't be fired.

GENERAL.

>And don't forget the opportunity for travel
>At speeds that is a bloody marvel.
>Every limb flies first-class on its own
>When a bomb lands in your bloody zone.

FIRST SOLDIER (*pointing to second soldier*).

>Thank God, the man what's gonna die ain't me,
>   it's him,
>'Cause some has got to sink, but I'm the boy
>   who'll swim.
>That's why don't bug me, man, with no disloyal
>   gripes.
>I'm gonna die in bed with sergeant's stripes.

(*The last stanza is repeated by all four soldiers, each pointing at the other*)

GENERAL (*who has been listening to the last chorus with tender attention*) Keep in step, you sons of bitches! Look smart! Rodríguez, blow your nose. In your hanky, goddamit. Hup two three four . . . Back to the barracks, men. Hup two three four . . .

OLD MAN. Hup two three four. Let every able-bodied man enlist! I'm too old to go, but I ain't too old to stir up others to go.

WOMEN. Think of us!

MAN. Our land is free! Our arms are strong!

(*Major Cucuchabaz appears as the army departs; he leaps on the platform*)

MAJOR. And our cause is just!

VOICE. Viva Major Cucuchabaz, hero of Camarones! (*Cheers*)

NEWSHAWK 2. The unexpected appearance of Major Cucuchabaz galvanized the patriotic masses.

MAJOR. Our cause is just. Yes, old veteran, I embrace you. Here is my sword, riddled with wounds but gallant yet. Here is my rusty breast, a shield for my country against the enemy. We shall carry peace into the heart of the Chaco with a flaming brand. But citizens, will you renounce your quarrels and reaffirm your Bolivian solidarity with a single voice? You, for instance, you, what party do you vote for? Speak up, don't be afraid.

MAN. I'm a Liberal, major.

MAJOR. And you?

MAN. Radical Liberal.

MAJOR. And you, sweetheart?

WOMAN. Liberal Democrat.

MAJOR. And you, my good fellow?

MAN. Christian Radical.

MAJOR. And you, dear?

GIRL. Free Democratic Union Liberal.

MAJOR. And you, dad?

MAN. Vegetarian Technocrat.

MAJOR. Now all of you, hug one another. Again, again! Ah sweet war, that brings neighbor and neighbor together. The enemy looks, and is confounded. United we stand.

NEWSHAWK 1. Major Cucuchabaz' moving words made an effect upon the people unparalleled in recent Bolivian history. As if caught by a fever of solidarity, they broke spontaneously into the song of Wartime Love.*

CROWD.   When peace dwelled in the land
             We were so mean, so low, so bad —
             He played the boss — She bit my hand —
             I caught your cold — And I was glad.

             When peace dwelled in the land
             We cut each others' throats all year.
             He took my job — You said be damned —
             She stole my man — He kicked my rear.

             When war came to the land
             We cried — Shake here — Dear friend —
                                     My dove —
             United by our war we stand,
             Filled with sweetest wartime love.

(Enter two brawny young men carrying posters: FARMERS FOR THE CHACO: LET'S DIG IN and BOLIVIAN RADISHES IN THE CHACO)

MAJOR. Our farmer lads! Join us, join us! My sword and your plough. Come into the shadow of the flag with me.

GIRL. What do the posters say? I can't read.

MAN. "Farmers for the Chaco: Let's Dig In," and "Bolivian Radishes in the Chaco."

WOMAN. Can a girl feel your biceps, farmer-boy?

FARMER 1. Here. Some potato, hey?

WOMEN. Oooooh!

FARMER 2. Mine too. Feel them. The left one's even better 'cause I'm a lefty. I can pitch twice the load of hay in half the time of any Paraguayan, lemme tell you.

WOMEN. Oooooh!

MAJOR. Young Bolivian manhood.

*The song is in part ensemble, in part solos.

GIRL. Young manhood hell! Draft-dodgers is what they are!

MAN. Thass right.

FARMER 1. What did you say? Just say that again!

GIRL. They took my man away. Why aintchoo in uniform?

MAJOR. Children — solidarity —

FARMER 1. For half a turnip I'd shovel up your ugly snout.

MAN. Listen to that flour-sack! Are you picking on a girl is it?

FARMER 1. Come on, I'll pick on you and anything else that grows in this here slum.

MAN. Oh yeah? Cowhand. Go rassle a milkmaid in the daisies.

FARMER 2. He's insultin' us that feed the likes of him.

(He tries to hit the man with his placard)

MAJOR. Children! Bolivians!

MAN. You think you're gonna hit a defenseless bystander? Gimme that flag somebody!

GIRL. Take it. Go on. Stick it into the draft-dodger.

FARMER 2. He struck me with the sacred emblem — I'm bleedin'!

MAJOR. Our emblem!

FARMER 1. I'm comin' to the rescue!

MAJOR. Keep them apart. Get them reconciled! Give me that flag, you there! *(Swinging his sword, he manages to conquer the flag)* Embrace, my lads, unite against the common enemy.

FARMER 1. My pal's bleeding.

CROWD *(they have been holding the combatants down)*. Go on — have a beer instead — all three of you — etc.

FARMER 2 *(to the girl)*. Did you call me a draft-dodger too?

CROWD. No she didn't. Go on, go on with the others.

VOICE. And take your spuds to the Chaco.

FARMER 2. Who said that?

CROWD. Nobody!

(They are hustled off the stage. The flag is replaced)

NEWSHAWK 1. So great was the popular fervor that here and there a good-natured commotion occurred, quickly dissolved in a renewed outburst of public togetherness.

NEWSHAWK 2. At every moment the spirited crowd was treated to another manifestation of civic enthusiasm.

GIRL. Look who's coming!

(Enter four men carrying the foreigner on their shoulders)

FOREIGNER. Mon cœur plein d'amour pour la Bolivie . . .

MAN. A lousy foreigner!

MAJOR. No! He is the Foreign Volunteer!

(Crowd cheers. The foreigner is carried off)

NEWSHAWK 2. In a gesture of spontaneous affection and loyalty to their adopted land, the foreign colony of La Paz contributed a splendid corps of volunteers to the armed forces.

RADIO. We interrupt our native rumba to bring you a news bulletin. At dawn today a force of two thousand Paraguayan infantrymen, supported by heavy mortar fire, mounted a surprise attack on the Bolivian fort of Pitiantuta. Our heavily outnumbered garrison is staging a heroic defense against the brutal invader.

RADIO PARAGUAY (in the auditorium).* It's a lie! This is Radio Paraguay, the Voice of Truth. The Paraguayan military command categorically denies that its forces have launched an attack on Fort Pitiantuta or at any other point in the Chaco. This is yet another in the long series of vindictive, malicious and futile lies spouted by Bolivian provocateurs and warmongers, whose imperialistic designs on the Paraguayan Chaco are known to the entire world.

RADIO BOLIVIA. Another bulletin from Radio Bolivia! The outnumbered Bolivian forces manning Fort Pitiantuta have compelled the enemy to raise his siege, and dramatically reversed the military situation. Our army is once again in full control. Paraguayan casualties are heavy. On our side it is reported that one Bolivian private suffered minor scratches in a cactus patch while pursuing the Paraguayan cavalry. According to the latest dispatches, the enemy is falling back in a disorderly rout.

RADIO PARAGUAY. The Bolivian propaganda machine cranks on! But the truth cannot remain concealed for long. Our troops have captured Fort Pitiantuta. We are in undisputed possession. Three hundred exhausted and undernourished Bolivian soldiers have fallen into our hands, and have requested political asylum. The Chaco — (static, roars, silence)

MAJOR. Jammed at last. There is no power on this earth so strong as the naked truth. Listen, my friends, to the guilty silence of Radio Paraguay.

RADIO BOLIVIA. We resume our program with a selection of patriotic sambas.

GIRL (worried). Is the war really on?

WOMAN (to a friend). I'm gonna lay in a few pounds of sugar. (Off)

CROWD (waving flags, dubiously). Hurrah???

NEWSHAWK 1. Declaration of President Salamanca, extra, extra: "We are determined to make a last effort to secure a peaceful and honorable settlement of the issue which divides our two nations. Our ambassador to the United Nations, Dr. Fortunato Concepción Urubamba, has instructions to explore every possible avenue of conciliation

---

*During the exchange which follows, the crowd will turn their heads to and fro to listen to the speakers.

which does not imperil our national security."

MAJOR. And now, citizens, attend. I give you Fortunato Concepción Urubamba, the flower of Bolivian diplomacy! *(Enter Urubamba, carrying a briefcase and raincoat; he is accompanied by aides)* Sir: the people of Bolivia and I, hero of Camarones, greet you, and wish you God's speed in the difficult task that awaits you in New York.

(Cheers)

URUBAMBA. Thank you, Major Cucuchabaz. Friends and citizens, I pledge myself to work unremittingly for the good of our country.

MAN. Tell the Yankees we're buying an atom bomb from the Rooshians.

MAN. Tell the Bolsheviks the Americans are promising to give us the good old hydrogen bomb.

MAN. Bring back grants and corn flakes and weapons and experts and whiskey.

MAN. Tell 'em a passel of lies!

URUBAMBA *(shocked)*. Lies? Lies, my friends?

MAN. I meant for the good of the country — not lies, really, but the right kind of lingo, you know —

URUBAMBA. The Holy Virgin defend me. I thank God that our country needs no lies, as some others do.

MAN. Damn right. We can jam their radio any time.

URUBAMBA. I have studied the old border dispute, my good people. Our cause, I am happy to report, is just. Otherwise I would not represent it. And, given time enough and the efforts of good men, right always prevails in the world, along with freedom, democracy, and justice. And now, allow me to get through — the airplane is waiting for us. Remember, my conscience is satisfied.

MAJOR *(privately)*. A diplomat with a conscience, Dr. Urubamba? This could be dangerous to the land.

URUBAMBA *(benevolent)*. Tut tut, major. You will not part me from my conscience. I don't go anywhere without it. Well —

MAJOR. Wait. What do you propose to tell them when the Paraguayan shows his map of 1620?

URUBAMBA. I reject the map of 1620, I annihilate it with my Charter of 1583, which proves that the Chaco lay within the jurisdiction of the Bolivian Court District.

MAN. What about that lousy Soler-Pinilla Protocol of 1907?

URUBAMBA. A protocol is a protocol, my friend; it is dignified but it has no legal standing. Gentlemen, have faith, I ask you. I intend to bring you back a favorable vote in the World Assembly and major concessions from Paraguay.

CHOCOLATE MAN. Dr. Urubamba, I would like to offer you a chocolate bar as a gift from the common people.

URUBAMBA. Thank you, my good man. But an official is not allowed to accept gifts. Thank you. I really must be on my way. Farewell. *(Cheers; he leaves with his aides)*

MAN. Urubamba will show those horsethieves who's in the saddle!

MAJOR. A lovely man. And honest as my mother's milk.

(Urubamba returns)

URUBAMBA. One more thing. Don't for God's sake overthrow the government while I'm up there pleading our cause.

MAJOR *(moved)*. We won't, Dr. Urubamba. Not this week. Allow me to assure you — *(He follows Urubamba out)*

(A moment of silence. Then a man leaps to the flag)

MAN. From border to border
Joy and disorder!
Rumba, samba,
Urubamba!

(The crowd goes wild. The radio blares, the newshawks shout, the crowd yells and dances, the boy reappears selling flags, the soldiers and farmers reenter, general enthusiasm and amity)

NEWSHAWKS. War imminent — Final peace efforts — Urubamba confident — Vickers of England pledges to strengthen Bolivian army — United front — Is Paraguay trying to distract its people from home troubles by its imperialistic adventures? — French war profiteers sign contract to beef up Paraguay with fighter planes — Urubamba declares "honesty is the soundest policy in the final analysis."

BOY. Patriotic tunes, five cents a sheet! Cut-rate flags! Paraguay dolls with two-weeks supply of pins! Loyalist buttons! Pictures of Bolivian generals in three volumes!

CROWD. Oh happy happy happy we
To quell the foreign infamy!
And when our fist the alien quells,
We go on quelling someone else!

(Crowd leaves. Only the newshawks, dancing arm in arm, remain)

NEWSHAWK 1. And when our fist the alien quells,
We go on quelling someone else!

Noble words!

NEWSHAWK 2. Say you so, brother newshawk?

NEWSHAWK 1. I do. But as for being your brother newshawk, I'm not so sure.

NEWSHAWK 2. Why aren't you sure?

NEWSHAWK 1 (*tearing off his mask*). That's why.
NEWSHAWK 2. Blodgett! The Industrial Magnate! (*Tears off his mask*)
NEWSHAWK 1. Pimpkin! The Labor Leader!
(*They fall into each other's arms*)
PIMPKIN. Good old war-monger!
BLODGETT. Dear old hate-peddler!
PIMPKIN. Great days, what?
BLODGETT. I'll say. Brace the nerve.
PIMPKIN. Stiffen the bowel.
BLODGETT. Production rate is soaring.
PIMPKIN. Wages are up.
BLODGETT. Price index rises.
PIMPKIN. Wages are up.
BLODGETT. Stock average climbed 18 points overnight.
PIMPKIN. Wages are up.
BLODGETT. You old labor agitator, where's the class war now?
PIMPKIN. The what war? Listen to the Song of Industrial Peace.

> There's no class war in a first-class war —
> Owners, workers pull together.
> There's money in the air, so roar roar roar
> For bloody thundering weather.

BLODGETT.
> Our stock, from bullet to atomic pile,
> Is wrapped up for delivery.
> We'll quote you with a cheerful smile
> The going price of victory.

TOGETHER (*saluting the flag*).
> Drive out the foe, but slowly please,
> Don't jostle the production rate.
> Give us a hundred costly victories,
> Oh generals, to celebrate.

BLODGETT. Which leaves us only with Urubamba to worry about, our peace-loving delegate to the United Nations. Shall I discredit him in the press? There's a picture of him at dinner in the same room with a Paraguayan only nine years ago.
PIMPKIN. Oh I don't know, Blodgett. I think you're unfair to the man. Is Urubamba a thief?
BLODGETT. I didn't say that.
PIMPKIN. Then he won't rob us of our hopes. Is he a killer?
BLODGETT. Oh no.
PIMPKIN. Then he won't stab our war effort. Is he dishonest?
BLODGETT. Dishonest he is not.

PIMPKIN. Then he won't cheat our expectations.

BLODGETT. Say you so, brother?

PIMPKIN. Take it from me. Goodbye now, I'm off to inspire the masses.

BLODGETT. And I, to hearten the business community. (*They shake hands and part*)

(*Silence on the empty stage. Then the hideously wounded soldier stumbles in and falls before the flag*)

WOUNDED SOLDIER (*ultimate terror*). Mother — I was the first one — who died!

(*Wild cacophony of music and crowds on the radio, in the midst of which:*)

RADIO BOLIVIA. Bulletin: Dr. Fortunato Concepción Urubamba has landed in New York.

(*Music resumes*)

SCENE TWO

(*The United Nations. A few delegates, white, yellow, and black, are sitting and half-listening. One plays a surreptitious yo-yo. One emits an occasional snore. A number of empty chairs. Onesto Morales, the Paraguayan delegate, is nearing the end of his speech. Above him sits the President of the Assembly. Among the delegates, Urubamba is listening in very visible discomfort, and frequently mops his brow and nibbles his knuckles*)

MORALES. . . . As for their so-called possession of the Chaco, it is an uncontroverted historical fact that the last official Bolivian attempt to penetrate into that territory occurred in the sixteenth century, when Captain Andres Manso, a Bolivian adventurer, was boiled alive by the outraged Indians whom he sought to baptize. Bolivia lost interest, and retreated behind the fortifications of the Andes. The rest is a story of occasional private interlopers, shabby incursions and shabbier setbacks. Until your government, Dr. Urubamba, was ignominiously beaten away from the Pacific Ocean by Chile in 1883, and until your government, Dr. Urubamba, began to suspect the existence of oilfields under the Chaco — until that time your government took less interest in the Chaco than we do in Alaska. I could distribute maps drawn by as many "experts" as my esteemed colleague has been pleased to call upon for his side; I could exhibit Royal Charters, Privileges, Decrees dating back to the days of Pizarro himself! But what are ancient maps against fact? Fact tells us that

Paraguay has held the Chaco for three and a half centuries. Held, gentlemen, settled, colonized, ploughed, policed. It is we who impose and collect taxes on the ageless legal principle that he who owns a land taxes it, and he who taxes a land owns it. And to us fell the difficult tasks of converting the Indians to the Christian faith and of wiping them out — both privileges stemming directly from the King of Spain, as stated in the royal decrees of January 23, 1765 and July 15, 1769, of which you have received copies. Come, Dr. Urubamba, do you deny these facts? Or do you claim that we Paraguayans have been squatting illegally upon your land since 1580, without so much as a protest from your side for three hundred years? But my Bolivian colleague is feebly waving his copy of that excellent Charter of 1583, which calls the Chaco a portion of the Bolivian Court District. He has given each one of you a photostat of this interesting document. I remind you that I never denied its authenticity. The truth will never find a more ardent supporter than the government of Paraguay. But Paraguayan exhibit number 462 — and I ask you to glance once more at the photostats I have distributed of *our* documents — Dr. Urubamba, will you oblige me with another glance? — this exhibit is, it seems to me, a decisive one. 1581. Observe the date. 1581. The seal of King Philip II, of revered memory. "Let it be known to our beloved Viceroy in La Paz that whereas the Law Court residing at Sucre and La Paz shall sway under God from the Ocean to the Argentines, the authority of the executive bodies, of the administration, and of the constabulary forces shall be confined to the land lying West of the Chain of the Andes." I read no further. The truth has burst into full view. What Bolivia never held in fact it never held in law. All that remains to me is to call upon Dr. Urubamba, whose integrity is well known to this Assembly — I need only recall his splendidly impartial decisions as arbitrator in Puah-Puah at the time of the Fifilese uprisings — and to call upon the people of Bolivia, whom we embrace as brothers in spite of these differences of ours; to call finally upon the government in La Paz to heed the voice of reason and the claims of justice: join us, I say, join the people of Paraguay in seeking the flower of peace under the jagged stones of controversy. I thank you.

(He regains his seat. Hand-clapping. The President hems, shuffles papers. His aide whispers at him now and then)

PRESIDENT. We have just heard — indeed — the delegate from — from — hem — Paraguay — ah yes — the forty-first crisis of the season — the session. The issue being debated — the Chaco — we shall put a suitable motion — after preliminary procedural dispositions — the roll call of course — unless a veto —

AIDE *(whispering)*. You must call on the Bolivian delegate, sir. Article 126, as amended.

PRESIDENT. Ah yes — there *is* always another side, isn't there? I daresay that is why God gave us two ears. Where are the documents? *(He confers in a low voice with the aide)*

DELEGATE A *(low)*. Shall we see you at the Japanese Grand Ball tonight, Ossip?

DELEGATE B. You joke! We are launching the fishing boat crisis this afternoon.

DELEGATE A *(appalled)*. Before the Grand Ball? Is that the action of a mature state?

PRESIDENT. I've got it now. Dr. Fortunato Concepción Urubamba. Please take the floor and let us hear the other just side. Dr. Urubamba? Are you with us?

URUBAMBA. I am, Mr. President, I am. *(He rises painfully and walks slowly to the rostrum, where he remains speechless)*

DELEGATE C *(waking up suddenly)*. Huh. What's the silence? I'm frightened.

EVERYBODY. Sssh. For shame.

DELEGATE D. Urubamba is about to speak.

DELEGATE C. Oh, the Congo again. Good night. *(Instantly falls asleep again)*

URUBAMBA. Fellow delegates to the United Nations. As the delegate of the Republic of Bolivia, I am called upon to — it is my duty — my instructions — in brief, my instructions are to instruct you in the — to point out the justice — in short, to speak. In the past forty-eight hours, I have had greater leisure to restudy the claims — that is to say to review the Chaco problem once more — I have given the documents presented to the Assembly by my honorable colleague and I may truly say, my friend, Dr. Onesto Morales, the delegate of the Republic of Paraguay, who has been addressing this Assembly, and who, you will recollect, has appealed to our sense of honor, of justice, of reason — claims which touch me personally — deeply — indeed — deeply, for he did not allude in vain to these principles, which govern, I hope, the actions of all our governments, and of their representatives, among whom I have been numbered these three years and two months — not unhonorably, I think, as indeed Dr. Morales was good enough to note when he referred to the difficulties in Puah-Puah, and — aaah —

PRESIDENT. Do you require an interpreter, Dr. Urubamba?

URUBAMBA. No thank you — thank you kindly. In short, the evidence is all too clear — the documents — the Royal Charter of 1581 — not to mention the facts — in a word — *(He draws a deep breath)* Paraguay is right, we haven't a leg to stand on, and there it is.

(The delegates have sat up. Gasps)

DELEGATE D *(nudging Delegate C in vain)*. Wake up, wake up!

DELEGATE A *(dazed)*. President, a word, a point of order . . .

PRESIDENT *(who has dropped his gavel)*. Excuse me, Dr. Urubamba, but I think we failed to catch your meaning. May I ask you to repeat?

MORALES *(choking)*. Yes — repeat.

URUBAMBA *(drawing another deep breath)*. My country is in the wrong. Our documents are worthless. I suspect we forged two or three of them. Ah, so did Paraguay —

MORALES. An open insult!

URUBAMBA. But Paraguay was right anyway. *(Crying out)* The Chaco belongs to Paraguay! I must care for my soul!

(General panic)

DELEGATE E. His soul!

PRESIDENT. Shocking! Offensive!

DELEGATES. This is outrageous — A scandal here, here of all places! — Indecent exposure — A maniac! — I refuse to be a witness — Hear hear — Shame! *(The cry is taken up)* Shame! Shame!

DELEGATE F. In view of the circumstances, this delegation boycotts the meeting. Make way please!

DELEGATE A. Us too. Positively shameful. Excuse me.

DELEGATES. With your permission — allow me — excuse me please — may I, MAY I?

MORALES. Wait — wait —

(Rush to the exit)

PRESIDENT. The meeting is adjourned and struck from the record!

MORALES. Wait everybody!

DELEGATE C *(waking up in the rush)*. Hey, hey! *(Catching somebody's coattails)* What happened?

DELEGATE B *(pointing to Urubamba)*. Honesty! *Honest* honesty!

DELEGATE C *(suddenly commanding)*. Keep the reporters out! *(He runs away with the others)*

MORALES. Wait everybody! My government utterly rejects and disavows — wait . . . *(Left alone with Urubamba)*. They're gone. Fortunato my boy, why have you done this? Are you ill? Lean on me. What made you give in?

(A reporter rushes in. Morales jumps away from Urubamba)

REPORTER. Dr. Morales, do you have a statement for United Press?

MORALES *(thundering)*. I do! The Paraguayan delegation denounces the Bolivian move as a desperate device which will deceive no one. This maneuver, whose transparent goal is to cause Paraguay to relax its vigilance, will be met with renewed firmness and resolution. My country intends to fight all such peace moves to the death!

REPORTER. Thank you, sir. *(Rushes off)*

MORALES. Fortunato, speak to me! I'll call the delegates back! There's time yet for a retraction. Denounce me a little, for God's sake!

URUBAMBA. I can't — Onesto — something here . . .

SCENE THREE

(Cabinet meeting in La Paz. Members attending: President Salamanca, Ministers of the Exterior, Interior, Defense, Transportation, Commerce, and Information. With them: a couple of aides, and a nurse who is giving pills and glasses of water to the Cabinet. General despondency. Now and then a noise of clamoring multitudes in the distance)

SALAMANCA *(to the nurse).* What's the idea of giving me only two pills, like the others? Am I the President of this jackass republic or what the hell?

NURSE. I am ever so sorry, President Salamanca. *(She gives him extra pills)*

(A cabinet member sobs)

COMMERCE. My country, my Bolivia.

DEFENSE. Disgraced.

TRANSPORTATION. And the people — outraged — humiliated — listen to them, our heads may fall.

ALL. Ooooh. *(Their hands go out for more pills)*

EXTERIOR. Couldn't you call the army out to defend us, Carrión?

DEFENSE. Don't give the army ideas.

SALAMANCA. It's dangerous to be defended too much.

INFORMATION. Is Urubamba still in the waiting room?

AIDE. Yes, sir.

INFORMATION. Guarded?

INTERIOR. Three policemen are supposed to be sitting on him.

SALAMANCA. Just wait till I bring him to trial. I'll try the pudding out of him, I'll try him from the end of a rope. A man I trusted like a brother . . .

TRANSPORTATION. He seemed so honest, I can't understand it . . .

(Silence. Sighs, a sob or two)

INFORMATION. Listen to that mob. Lousy rabble. *(Pulls out a pistol, puts bullets in it)*

COMMERCE. My dear Gómez!

INFORMATION. As Minister of Information, I know a loaded argument when I see one. *(Replaces the pistol in his pocket)*

EXTERIOR. What do we do, President Salamanca?

SALAMANCA. Until the messenger arrives, we'll be firm and do nothing.

INTERIOR. I have seen plumbers and charwomen weeping in the streets.

COMMERCE. Bolivia, Bolivia, I shall die of grief and shame . . . *(He slumps)*

SALAMANCA. Come on, Alessandro, buck up. A little grief is good for your circulation.

DEFENSE. Ortiz, I say, what's the matter with you? Nurse!

NURSE. Dr. Ortiz! *(Examines him)* He's dead of grief and shame.

SALAMANCA. I'll be damned!

EXTERIOR. A shining example to us.

INTERIOR. Only yesterday I was playing tennis with him.

SALAMANCA. Ayala, as Minister of Transportation — a sad duty —

TRANSPORTATION. Me? Well, I suppose — *(He and an aide carry out the Minister of Commerce)*

SALAMANCA. My heart's near breaking too, and our country shown up for a weakling. When I think of our past — who had the right to sneer at us up to this moment? Every year a conquest, a noble massacre, a crushing defeat — because you get credit even for a defeat — a defeat is good honest work too — every year a hundred forceful declarations, accusations, challenges, denials, protests as good as any country can show — we've been called brutal aggressors as far away as Denmark — and now our heads are bowed —

EXTERIOR. All up in smoke — in one evil minute.

(The Minister of Transportation reappears)

TRANSPORTATION. News! The messenger is arriving at last!

SEVERAL. At last! The messenger!

SALAMANCA. Nurse, leave us now. Remove these pills. What will he bring us? Santa Maria dolorosa, what will he be telling us?

AIDE *(flinging open the door)*. The messenger!

MESSENGER *(entering to the sound of trumpets)*. Bolivia, I bear tidings of glorious events!

(He is a creature from a fairy tale: a vision of gold and silver, blue and pink resplendance; brocades and sequins, satins and laces, a shimmer of cascading yellow hair, a coruscating train held up by a cherub, and a wand in his right hand)

SALAMANCA. Speak, Messenger; we had almost lost the will to live.

MESSENGER. Bolivians, behold, I bring you comfort, high pride, and sweet replenishment. The honor of our ancient realm is secured: the war has begun.

ALL *(coming to life)*. Ah!

SALAMANCA. I knew it, I sensed it.

EXTERIOR. My spirit never flagged.

INFORMATION. Trust the noble people of Bolivia.

SALAMANCA. Speak on, Messenger, tell us all you know.

MESSENGER. My tale is brief. No sooner had the traitorous Urubamba received his sudden dismissal from the post he darkened with infamy than his successor rose before an expectant Assembly of the potentates of this earth to preconize the sacred claims of mother Bolivia to the Chaco its child. Conscious of high and bloody destiny, he cast his indignant challenge at the Paraguayan bosom, and, filling with his voice the shivering silence of the appareled hall, he confirmed our historic determination that the Chaco, which must be ours, by the just heavens shall be ours!

SALAMANCA. A sage.

INTERIOR. A patriot at last.

MESSENGER. The Paraguayan delegate shed tears and perspiration in vain. Suddenly the powers nodded. The ballots were cast. Eighty-seven voices crushing one dissenting vote gave the world's decision, which I am charged with reciting to you: "The Assembly of the United Nations expresses its support for a just settlement of the dispute which has arisen over the Great Chaco." This audacious and stunning vindication of the Bolivian cause has given our people new heart. And already Colonel Rojos has uttered the fatal command. Our troops have moved. Colonel Rojos has occupied Fort Masamaklay. Already our valiant blood, and the cowardly blood of the enemy, has flowed. Already our history is adorning itself anew with the glorious sacrifices of the battlefield. History, take up thy pen! Begin, oh Muse, to inscribe the matchless record of the War of the Great Chaco! (*The trumpets blow, and the messenger leaves*)

SALAMANCA. We did it! Thanks to my foresight. Gentlemen, let's get to work. Where do we start?

TRANSPORTATION. Start with Urubamba, by God and by Satan.

THE OTHERS. To it! Bring him in! Good idea! Blood! etc.

DEFENSE. The quicker and quieter the better.

INTERIOR. We give him a fair trial in three minutes and hang him this afternoon.

TRANSPORTATION. I know just the lamppost.

INFORMATION. Gentlemen, gentlemen, what is this? I'm simply shocked.

SALAMANCA. You, Gómez?

INFORMATION. Yes, I. You are planning a gross injustice, a gross, gross injustice, and I raise my voice against it.

SALAMANCA (*worried*). What injustice are you talking about? It's a regular hanging.

INFORMATION. If you hang Urubamba, you'll be admitting to the world that we stupidly sent a traitor to represent us at the United Nations.

A pretty picture of us! Well, I call this conception of Bolivia a gross injustice to our nation.

EXTERIOR. It's a good point, but how can we help it? It's all been in the open, you know, and the harm's done.

SALAMANCA. He's right, Gómez. Your scruples do you honor, but we're stuck with Urubamba.

INFORMATION. Not necessarily. I propose that we redeem him.

(General surprise)

SALAMANCA. But how? The man's plainly a traitor.

INFORMATION. No. The man is plainly — insane.

(Silence. Effect)

SALAMANCA. A stroke of genius!

DEFENSE. An idea altogether worthy of you, Gómez.

EXTERIOR. By Saint Barabbas, this will wipe the grins off the diplomatic set. We'll be able to hold up our heads at cocktail parties again.

TRANSPORTATION. A coup, Gómez, an absolute coup.

INTERIOR. Bring in the rascal at once.

SALAMANCA (to an aide). Tell the guards to get off Urubamba and have him come in.

(Exit aide)

SALAMANCA. Compose your faces, my friends, into a mask of indignant hostility.

(The Cabinet do so)

INFORMATION. But at the same time, may I suggest a relaxed expression? Give me permission to question him and to humor him into a confession. Relax, gentlemen, look friendly.

(Faces relax)

SALAMANCA. I leave him to you, Gómez.

AIDE (appearing). Dr. Fortunato Concepción Urubamba.

(Enter Urubamba, his clothes in shreds)

URUBAMBA. President Salamanca, members and friends of the cabinet —

INFORMATION. Your appearance, sir —

URUBAMBA. The people, Alfredo — I mean Dr. Gómez — a strange misunderstanding of my motives.

INFORMATION. Ah, your motives?

URUBAMBA. Yes. The common people failed — I don't know — they are not capable of judging fine moral points — they failed to understand — my honesty — my — they tore my clothes, called me vile names —

SALAMANCA. You don't say.

URUBAMBA. But here — intelligent men, thank heaven — my own peers, so to speak —

SALAMANCA. Ha!

URUBAMBA. President Salamanca, you and I were students together — in

Professor Arvieja's law seminar — Fundamentals of Justice — and
you — San Martín — in the consular service — in short —

INFORMATION. In short —

URUBAMBA. You understand me.

INFORMATION. And?

URUBAMBA (a momentary flash). You will reinstate me.

INFORMATION. Perhaps. But will you first submit to a brief, though
formal, interrogation? Merely for the record.

URUBAMBA. I'll answer anything.

INFORMATION. The questions may seem strange to you. I'll be open with
you, Urubamba; you've behaved in an unorthodox manner in New
York.

SALAMANCA. The United Nations may never recover.

INFORMATION. And we want to look into — well — frankly —

URUBAMBA. My mental condition.

INFORMATION. Yes.

URUBAMBA. I'll answer all your questions, Alfredo.

INFORMATION. Good. (He goes to a door, and opens it) Will you come in,
sir?

(Enter the CIA man, a figure robed in black from head to foot. The
cabinet members are startled and frightened. They creep nearer to
one another. Urubamba is surprised)

SALAMANCA. Who is that?

INFORMATION. Don't you recognize him, President?

SALAMANCA. Recognize who? Come on, Gómez, what's the story?

EXTERIOR (crosses himself). Sweet Jesus . . .

INFORMATION. I've simply called in an undercover agent to conduct the
interrogation.

URUBAMBA. A CIA agent?

SALAMANCA. What in holy damnation is the CIA?

CIA MAN. The Committee on Insidious Agitation. Maybe.

INFORMATION. I'm dumbfounded, President Salamanca. The CIA is the
highest security branch of the Bolivian administration.

SALAMANCA (bawling). Then why haven't I been told about it?

CIA MAN. We're fabulously secret. The fact is, I am possibly not a CIA
man at all.

SALAMANCA. What does that mean?

CIA MAN. I might be a woman disguised as a man. Or a man disguised
as a woman impersonating a man. Even I'm not supposed to know.

SALAMANCA (squealing). But I'm the president of this asstail republic!

INTERIOR (timidly). How about us? I'm Minister of the Interior.

INFORMATION. You, Prado, will be so kind as to take notes of the proceedings. That is, President, assuming we are ready to proceed.

SALAMANCA. Go on, don't mind me. As long as you get Urubamba, that's all.

CIA MAN. Dr. Urubamba, a simple question: how many ten-cent coins were situated in your pocket last Tuesday at nine o'clock in the evening?

URUBAMBA. Is this a game, sir? I mean —

INFORMATION. This is deadly serious, Urubamba. It is nothing less than psychology. And remember, we haven't got forever.

DEFENSE. There's a war going on.

URUBAMBA. A war? Oh God, did the war break out?

CIA MAN. The question, please. How many ten-cent coins were in your pocket last Tuesday evening?

URUBAMBA. This is absurd. I don't know. How should I know?

CIA MAN. Thank you. Take note, Dr. Prado. Dr. Urubamba has lost his memory for the simplest recent events of his own life.

INTERIOR (puzzled). Yes, of course.

URUBAMBA. This is outrageous. I have *not* lost my memory! What childish game is this?

CIA MAN. Thank you, Dr. Urubamba. We appreciate your cooperation. Next question. How much is 8.37912 minus 6.9716 plus 3.4599342076? A few seconds should be ample.

URUBAMBA. I protest. This is a monstrous —

CIA MAN. It is not a monstrous, Dr. Urubamba. Kindly answer the question.

URUBAMBA. How can a man answer that kind of question? And without even a pencil.

CIA MAN (solicitous). Would you like a pencil?

URUBAMBA. No! I won't lend myself to this farce.

CIA MAN. Thank you. (Signals to Prado) Dr. Urubamba cannot add and subtract figures under 10 without a pencil.

URUBAMBA. This is grotesque — a trap — let me go!

INFORMATION. Cristóbal, kindly help Dr. Urubamba back to his seat. Thank you.

URUBAMBA. Heaven cries out —

SALAMANCA. Damn it, Fortunato, leave heaven upstairs. What are you complaining about? Are we pulling your nails out? Are we burning you with cigarettes? Are we threatening you? You ought to thank us.

URUBAMBA. I'm sorry . . .

CIA MAN. It's only a routine check, Dr. Urubamba. Now I want to ask you, who has an inch-long scar two inches above his right nipple?

URUBAMBA. This is torture, I say! But I defy you! I don't know and I don't want to know! Scars, nipples, coins — is this a madhouse?

Yes — that's it — I've gone mad!

SALAMANCA. Ha!

CIA MAN. Please enter, Dr. Prado. Did not recognize even at close quarters a person he has known seventeen years.

URUBAMBA. What person?

CIA MAN. Your friend, Dr. Ayala.

TRANSPORTATION (*raises his hand to his breast*). By God, it's true, by God.

CIA MAN. I hope you don't deny that you have known Dr. Ayala for seventeen years. Holy Cross College for Boys. Little Ignazio Ayala trips over a loose shoelace. Falls against your geography book.

TRANSPORTATION (*remembers*). My left hand hits the wall.

CIA MAN. Your right hand. We have the photos. (*To Urubamba again*) You help him up. He introduces himself.

URUBAMBA. Mad, utterly mad . . .

INTERIOR (*writing*). "Mad, utterly mad . . ."

CIA MAN. Dr. Ayala, is it not true that you have a scar of that description?

TRANSPORTATION. Yes, it is. Allow me. (*He exhibits the scar to all*) I was exercising in the club's gymnasium ten years ago —

CIA MAN. Eleven.

TRANSPORTATION. That's right, eleven . . .

CIA MAN. Thank you. Now tell me, Dr. Urubamba, on what latitude and longitude does your house stand? Be honest, sir, and give us a fairly accurate answer.

URUBAMBA (*shouts*). Monster, I don't know! (*Breaks down*)

CIA MAN. Thank you. That will do. Dr. Urubamba does not know the whereabouts of his own domicile. President Salamanca, members of the cabinet, it appears from a confidential routine check that Dr. Urubamba's mental stability is seriously impaired. He has lost his memory, he cannot make simple additions and subtractions, he does not recognize persons he has known since boyhood, and he does not know the location of his own house. Furthermore, he has admitted that he is subject to fits of madness, as is shown by the minutes of the interrogation. This, however, is as far as the CIA's responsibility goes. The secular arm must do the rest.

(*As he goes, all huddle away from him*)

TRANSPORTATION (*crosses himself*). Mother of God . . .

SALAMANCA. Hey, you're walking into the wall!

(*But the wall opens, the CIA agent vanishes, the wall returns to normal*)

URUBAMBA. I protest!

TRANSPORTATION. Did you really know nothing about — about *them*, Salamanca?

SALAMANCA. Oh, I wouldn't say that. You can never tell. I may have pretended . . .

INTERIOR (*dreamily*). Maybe I'm one myself.

DEFENSE. You never know.

INFORMATION. Gentlemen, shall we?

SALAMANCA. Right. Back to Urubamba, all of you. Gómez, take over again.

INFORMATION. Will those who favor the motion that Dr. Fortunato Urubamba is insane raise their hands and say aye?

ALL. Aye!

URUBAMBA. Nay!

INFORMATION. As the object of the motion, you are naturally disqualified from voting. President?

SALAMANCA. Dr. Urubamba is insane.

URUBAMBA. Let me go! You'll murder me next!

DEFENSE. Delusions of persecution.

URUBAMBA. Oh God, oh God, I am in your hands now.

EXTERIOR. Delusions of grandeur.

SALAMANCA. Fortunato Concepción Urubamba, stand up! On grounds of legal and illegal insanity, you are stripped of all your posts, dignities, civil rights, and emoluments. Your birth certificate is rescinded. Your labor permit is revoked. Your passport is recalled. You become an individual without legal footing and standing, except for your inalienable right to be taxed.

INFORMATION. As Minister of Information, I shall issue a public release at once. (*He leaves*)

URUBAMBA. And still I say: Bolivia was wrong.

SALAMANCA. The patient has lost touch with reality.

SCENE FOUR

(*Family scene at the home of the Urubambas. Urubamba, Mrs. Urubamba, their little son Pepe — with a bandaged head — the father-in-law General Cochón, and Aunt Urubamba. Mrs. Urubamba is holding her son and sniffling. General Cochón is patting her hand*)

COCHÓN. My daughter, this won't do. The Cochóns don't give way.

MRS. URUBAMBA. But how can I bear —? This morning the butcher refused to sell me veal cutlets. And look at Pepe.

PEPE. They knocked my head to pieces in school because daddy betrayed his country they said.

(*Groans and weeping*)

COCHÓN. Child, child, this curse will stunt your growth. Better if I strike you down at once and spare you a life of suffering.

MRS. URUBAMBA. Father! Put back your sword!

COCHÓN. You women have no pride. But for myself, the alternatives were clear. Either I turn in my sword, or I go to stretch my body on the field of honor. I didn't turn in my sword.

MRS. URUBAMBA. Father!

AUNT. It's easy for you men. But what about us women: unmarried women especially. What field of honor are we going to stretch our bodies on?

COCHÓN. You're only his aunt, Miss Urubamba.

AUNT. Only his aunt! I was on the Reception Committee of the Library and Museum Association, and now they've put me in the back room licking envelopes. Only his aunt! And under a weak bulb, too.

MRS. URUBAMBA. I'm sorry, auntie.

(Urubamba turns away, as if to leave)

COCHÓN. Stop, sir. You do not leave this house without making reparations. Who owns the property? the automobile? the securities?

MRS. URUBAMBA. I'm too delicate to listen to these horrors. Let me go.

AUNT. So much refinement, and such suffering . . .

MRS. URUBAMBA. Pepe, come with me.

PEPE. They say that daddy is a scum in the earth.

(They leave)

AUNT. There you are, Fortunato. Look at your handiwork. You're killing your wife, you've ruined your innocent babe, and I don't even talk about *us*.

COCHÓN. To the point. *(He takes a piece of paper out of his wallet and places it on the table. Urubamba signs without reading it. He removes a ring from his finger)*

URUBAMBA. Two diamonds.

(General Cochón places the signed document and the ring in an envelope, seals it, and returns it to his wallet. Aunt Urubamba breaks down)

COCHÓN. Miss Urubamba, control yourself!

AUNT. If I could only change my name, if I could only go away! Saying on a platform the Paraguayans are right and we are liars! What did we ever do to him? General Cochón, he was always a good boy!

COCHÓN. Of course, Miss Urubamba.

AUNT. And I who refused a dozen offers to devote myself to the family, little thinking the day would come I'd do anything to bear another name, even marry a man.

(Martial music outside)

COCHÓN. The Ninety-fourth Cavalry. My old outfit. Hearts and hooves beating in unison. Bugles, fifes, pennons in the wind. *(Reenter Mrs. Urubamba and Pepe)* My child! I go to my last battle, my moustache erect to the end. May the blood of a Cochón cover the foul stain on the name of Urubamba. *(Gives her the envelope)* Keep this. The property is yours. And remember your father. He sought the bullet that found him.

MRS. URUBAMBA. Oh father! I'm proud of you. I'll visit your grave twice a year. *(They kiss. Cochón kisses Pepe)*

COCHÓN. Pepe — be brave. Miss Urubamba, the horses neigh, and I go. I kiss your hand. *(He leaves)*

(Mrs. Urubamba and Pepe run to the window and wave)

PEPE. Granddad! Granddad! Kill a lot of Paraguayans!

(Urubamba leaves through the back door)

SCENE FIVE

(A park, a bench, gray weather. A beggar is sitting on the bench, shivering and playing on a ruined guitar)

BEGGAR. It has been a long war, war, war. We call the Chaco the Green Hell. Hard to believe in this cold and damp, but in the Chaco it's hot, hot, hot. You dig fifty feet into the tough earth for water, and when you get there there isn't any, the flies crawl over you when your hands are busy with your rifle or your mattock, when you die a million white butterflies fall on you to suck you dry, you're just a bloody cocktail lounge as far as the butterflies are concerned, and in the last battle I was at, that was the battle of Zenteno, we lost 8,000 men who croaked of heat and thirst in the retreat, and the Paraguayans who were the winners alack and alas lost 9,000 men in the advance, serves them right for winning, besides the 25,000 men who were done for fair and square by gunfire, and the 90,000 who've pooped their guts out in the scrub, and all the rest of us down to one loaf of bread a month, and the women alone in their beds and getting frantic, I've got six wives in town myself out of sheer patriotism, and although we hanged President Salamanca from a lamppost for allowing General Pfundt to lose the battle of Nanawa, all we got for it was total mobilization, hospitals included, under President José Luis Tejada Sorzano, that's when they mobilized me out of my chocolate store, I went to the front where I fought like a tiger until I came down with typhus and they sent me back here because they don't want any weaklings in battle, it looks bad in the photographs, but what's the use, my chocolate store is ruined and nobody can afford to buy chocolate anyway, and if they could, where would I find chocolate to sell? No, a businessman like me, who worries, is better off at the front. *(He sings)*

> Soldiers march, soldiers sweat,
> Soldiers shoot and soldiers die.
> Let news be good or news be bad,
> The casualties are high.
> Above the ragged battlefield
> The happy vultures fly.

They're having a good time too; it's an observed fact.

> Above the bloated battlefield
> The happy buzzards fly,
> Appraising all that human meat
> With an impartial eye.
> The birds don't ask you "What's your side,
> Where d'you come from, when and why?"
> They eat alike Bolivian boys
> And lads from Paraguay.

No identification required, the birds are a tolerant, democratic, liberal bunch.

> They love alike Bolivian boys
> And lads from Paraguay.

And that is the Song of the Beggar with a Ruined Guitar. Look who's coming. The War Veteran; and over there Honest Bamba, the shoeshine boy. Join me, join me, fellow revelers.

(Enter, from different directions, the ragged war veteran, using a crutch, and Urubamba, unshaven and shabby, with a shoeshine kit. They converge on each other for lack of anything else to do)

URUBAMBA *(to the beggar)*. Shine, mister?

BEGGAR. Them isn't shoes, Bamba, just cardboard and an old army shirt I tore in two. *(To the veteran)* You wouldn't be interested in a serenade though, would you? One dime.

VETERAN. Sure I would, being as I'm a music lover from way back, but first I gotta get the money to pay you with. *(To Urubamba)* You got a dime for a wounded war veteran, old pal? Don't hold back on me.

URUBAMBA. I do have a dime. Here it is.

VETERAN. Thanks, old pal. Okay, troubadour, shoot the serenade.

BEGGAR.

> A shepherd by a stream did stray
> And gently breathed his amorous tune,
> The while his sheep did gently play
> And frolic 'pon the grassy dune.

"Aminta," went his piteous moan,
"O cruel maid, why dost thou flee,
And leave me with these tears alone
To bear me humid company?"

VETERAN. Jesus that was pretty. Sent a goddam shiver through my crutch. Here's a dime.

BEGGAR. Thank you, sir. Are you at liberty to give me a shine now, honest Bamba?

URUBAMBA. Certainly, sir. *(He shines the beggar's shoes, with many a flourish of his brush and a professional regard for the cardboard and the army shirt)* I'm afraid it isn't the old shoe polish, sir. They thicken it with ratgut nowadays.

BEGGAR. Well, do your best, Bamba. *(To the veteran)* So how's the leg?

VETERAN. I know it's there, and a man shouldn't be thinking he's got a leg.

BEGGAR. Better than thinking he hasn't got one. Where was it they shot you?

VETERAN. At Boquerón. Only I wasn't shot. Y'see, I was kicking a sick prisoner when I missed him and kicked a rusty nail instead. Serves me right for taking my duty serious. Now I get them lousy stinging pains every time the sky's overcast.

BEGGAR. Bad.

URUBAMBA. Here you are, sir.

BEGGAR. A bit more on this flap. That's right. Thanks. Here's a dime.

URUBAMBA. Thank you, sir. *(Off)*

VETERAN. There's prosperity in that man. Now that he's got a dime, maybe he'll buy me a drink outa this cold. *(Turns up his collar and hobbles out after Urubamba)*

BEGGAR. It keeps the economy rolling.

(Enter the Ministers of the Exterior and Information, the latter holding an umbrella, both in overcoats)

EXTERIOR. Let's sit down a minute, Gómez. The park's the only place where they can't come after a man with a telephone.

INFORMATION. Good idea, though it's going to rain any minute.

(They sit next to the beggar)

INFORMATION *(glaring)*. Hrmph.

BEGGAR. Serenade, gentlemen? Springtime lyric of youthful love, one dime.

INFORMATION. No thank you. You'll find an audience by the pond.

(Beggar doffs his cap and leaves)

EXTERIOR. Is your watch still on its chain, Gómez?

INFORMATION. It is. I had my finger on it.

EXTERIOR. You can't be too careful. It's become totally sickening.

INFORMATION. What do you expect? The country is aswarm with cripples, paupers, bums, orphans; even the widows are becoming dangerous. I don't allow my wife to leave the house any more, and I'm waiting to have my throat cut any afternoon for saying no I don't want a serenade.

EXTERIOR. Oh God, dear God, who would have guessed the Paraguayans were going to get stubborn about that patch of dust? And suppose it doesn't yield any oil after all? Meantime prices are going up — paper money — pha!

INFORMATION. Somebody lifted the pacifier right out of our baby's mouth while Nanny had her back turned.

EXTERIOR. They'd steal the cracks off the sidewalks.

INFORMATION. Day before yesterday I went to the Café de la Paz to meet Cucuchabaz — remember? Of course, I draped my overcoat over the back of my own chair — you can't hang up a coat any more. Well, I got up, put on my coat, and guess what — somebody had made off with all the buttons!

EXTERIOR. The buttons!

INFORMATION. Plastic buttons.

EXTERIOR. Incredible. *(Silence; then confidentially)* Speaking of buttons, Fernando, what about General Pfundt?

INFORMATION. What *about* General Pfundt?

EXTERIOR. Well — is he or isn't he?

INFORMATION. At the front?

EXTERIOR *(impatient)*. At the front! You know what I mean. I mean is he getting the Grand Cross of the Condor of the Andes?

INFORMATION. He is getting it.

EXTERIOR. I thought as much. It's disgusting. Look what they're saying about him in London. *(Shows Gómez a newspaper)* "General Pfundt, the German military expert imported by the Bolivian government to carry out the war according to the latest scientific methods, has proved to be the most brilliant innovator of the century in the art of surprise retreats. He has indeed been known to organize highly effective evacuations of territories not even threatened by the enemy." And so on. They also know about these blasted fourteen-year-old infants he's been using in the artillery. While you and me sit here day after day doing the dirty work now that Salamanca has left us *(he crosses himself)* and get nothing but stones in our faces.

INFORMATION. You don't understand, San Martín, and you're all steamed up about nothing. If we give Pfundt the Grand Cross, people will suppose he's getting it for winning battles, won't they? It's good for morale.

EXTERIOR. It's not good for mine. I've been working my ass to the bone for two years without a medal.

(Enter Urubamba)

URUBAMBA. Shoeshine?

INFORMATION. How much?

URUBAMBA. Ten cents.

INFORMATION. It's going to rain in a minute.

URUBAMBA. Only five cents, in that case. On request of the customer I also enumerate the provinces of Brazil or Argentina, each with its capital.

EXTERIOR. Good heavens, what for?

URUBAMBA. A little entertainment, sir. The effect of competition in the shoeshine enterprises.

INFORMATION. Well, we'll see about the provinces. Start shining anyhow.

URUBAMBA. Yes, sir. *(He shines the shoes)*

EXTERIOR. How is it you're still charging ten cents, my friend?

URUBAMBA. Because, to tell you the truth, Dr. San Martín, although everybody is charging twice the price, I feel that our shoe polish is not as good as it used to be —

EXTERIOR. How do you know I am Dr. San Martín?

URUBAMBA *(to Gómez)*. The other shoe, sir. *(To San Martín)* I see your picture in the papers, sir. And that of Dr. Gómez too.

INFORMATION. How about those provinces, my good fellow? Let's have a rundown on Brazil.

URUBAMBA. Yes, sir. Alagoas, capital Maceió. Amazonas, capital Manáos. Bahia, capital San Salvador. Ceará, capital Fortaleza. Espírito Santo, capital Victoria. Goyaz, —

INFORMATION *(laughing)*. Stop, that's enough! I'll take your word for the rest. Clever businessman, that's what he is. Here is your five cents. Come along, San Martín.

URUBUMBA. Thank you, sir.

EXTERIOR *(as they are going)*. Have you checked for your watch and purse?

INFORMATION. Everything's in place, I've got my finger on them.

(They leave, but Gómez has forgotten his umbrella)

URUBAMBA *(sniffing the shoe polish as he is putting his kit together)*. Pah! How can a man do a decent job with this? Cracks right on the shoe. Well, that's war for you. *(He notices the umbrella)* What now! Gómez left his umbrella behind. Hm, I even remember *it* from the old days. I wish *I* had an umbrella to keep my bones dry. *(Calling)* Dr. Gómez, your umbrella!

INFORMATION *(off stage)*. What's that? Oh! My umbrella. *(Both he and San Martín return)* Yes, that's it. Thank you, my friend.

EXTERIOR. Heart-warming, really heart-warming.

INFORMATION. I don't know where my thoughts are any more. Thanks again, and here — here is the other five cents, rain or no rain. *(His hand on Urubamba's shoulder)* I wish there were more honest men of your kind in this country.

EXTERIOR. Amen to that. I admire you, my good man.

INFORMATION. Come along, San Martín, it's beginning to drizzle.

(He opens the umbrella and they leave arm in arm)

URUBAMBA. Thank you, sir. *(Alone, he takes out a small bag and places the coin in it)* Almost three-quarters of the way to a pork chop. *(He sits on the bench, his collar up. He covers his head with a newspaper, then changes his mind and protects the shoeshine kit instead)* And now, accompanied by the beggar with the ruined guitar, I am going to sing the song entitled, "The Whole World Loves an Honest Man." *(The beggar has entered)* Ready?

BEGGAR. Wet but ready.

(There is a period of complete silence, then the curtain slowly falls)

THE END

LIVING ROOM WITH 6 OPPRESSIONS

CHARACTERS

MATTHEW AVAILABLE: *38 years old*

NANNY: *60 years old*

THE WORKER

THE NEGRO

THE INNOCENT BYSTANDER

THE CAPITALIST

THE PUERTO RICAN

THE POLICEMAN

(The action takes place in Matthew Available's comfortable living room. One of its doors leads directly to the street, another one leads to the kitchen. Matthew wears a lounging robe)

MATTHEW. Sunday afternoon. Fair weather, my pulse regular, all my rhythms in order, my mind alert, informed and compassionate. *(He sits down with a ledger and rings a little bell)* Nanny!
(Nanny appears)
NANNY. You rang, Mr. Matthew?
MATTHEW. Yes I did. Bring my coffee, will you? And half a muffin with cinnamon.
NANNY. It's all ready in the kitchen; I'll just heat the muffin a bit.
MATTHEW. Fine. Don't burn it, though. *(Exit Nanny. Matthew turns to his ledger)* Let's see. Twenty-five dollars for the Cancer Society. Fifty for the Orphanage. Forty for the blind. Poor people. I'd rather be deaf, dumb, anything. Another twenty for the Greek refugees. Twenty-five, fifty, forty, twenty — that makes a hundred thirty-five. I should be able to do better. I'm a bachelor, damn it, and Nanny doesn't cost much. I'll slow down buying books and use the library instead. There's been another earthquake in Sicily, an invasion in Yemen, a massacre or two in Indonesia, and here I am with my steady pulse and my slippers. Come to think of it, I've got my shoes on. On a Sunday afternoon! Nanny! *(Impatient)* Nanny!!
NANNY *(from the kitchen)*. What now?
MATTHEW. Why haven't I got my slippers on?
NANNY. The muffin will burn if I go for your slippers now!
MATTHEW. All right all right. *(To himself)* Always ready with an excuse.
(Enter Nanny with a tray)
NANNY. I'll get your slippers in a minute, but I've got to look —
MATTHEW. Damn damn damn. I've told you a million times — damn! Look at that lump of sugar.
NANNY. Well? I'm looking.
MATTHEW. It's wet!
NANNY. A bit of coffee spilled into the saucer.
MATTHEW. I *know* a bit of coffee spilled into the saucer! And yet I've told you a million times to bring me the sugar in a bowl. Do you know what I mean? A bowl, a crystal bowl, the way it's done in every bloody civilized household on earth.
NANNY. But why? Always the same story! Why all the fuss? You've been taking two lumps in your coffee for the last twenty years, Mr. Matthew, and you were taking two lumps in your hot milk when you were four years old, so what's the use my carting in a bowl full of useless lumps of sugar?

MATTHEW. The use is that the sugar won't get soggy. I hope it's not too much to expect — two dry lumps of sugar picked up with a pair of sugar tongs. Now what? What's this? What's going on?

(The entrance door is flung open, and the Worker rushes in, more on all fours than on his two feet. He is bloody, abject, emaciated and exhausted)

WORKER. Help me, hide me, he's going to kill me!

MATTHEW. Who? What? Who are you?

NANNY. Get out of here, this is Mr. Available's private house!

WORKER. I'll explain later — Mr. Available — I'm beggin' you — save me — have a heart — I'm an honest working man and the owner is after me, I smashed his machine.

NANNY. Well! I advise you —

MATTHEW. Shut up, Nanny! Here, give me your hand, here's a closet —

WORKER. Too late! Oh Jesus!

(The Capitalist rushes in)

CAPITALIST. Where's the swine?

WORKER. Protect me!

MATTHEW. Now wait a minute!

NANNY. This is private property!

CAPITALIST. *I* am private property. Don't hide behind chairs, you slum-bum, I'll rip you to pieces, striker, machine-breaker, drunkard, collective bargainer —

MATTHEW. Now wait a minute! This man is under my protection.

CAPITALIST. Who are *you*?

MATTHEW. What do you mean? This is *my* house. Kindly take your capitalist hide out of here, skinflint, blood-sucker, gouger, golf-player.

WORKER. That's tellin' him.

CAPITALIST. Hold it, feller.

MATTHEW. Nanny, show the gentleman the door.

NANNY. I keep telling you to lock that door of ours, Mr. Matthew.

MATTHEW. Never. Let nobody say that he found Matthew Available's door locked in his face. Good day, sir.

CAPITALIST. Good day my pink toe. I'll have that bolshevik gangster in manacles before I leave the house. Out of my way!

MATTHEW. What did he do to you?

CAPITALIST. He smashed my machine.

WORKER. I smashed his machine.

NANNY. Why, look at him. He's so weak he couldn't smash an egg-shell.

WORKER. I smashed it all the same, and I'll keep smashing it till I get a living wage.

CAPITALIST. Scum! Ten years in the clink is what you'll get! Come out of there! *(To Matthew)* Let me go, or I'll slug you too!

MATTHEW. Stop bawling. You bloated oppressor, how much longer are you going to live off the work of the poor?

CAPITALIST. As long as I can, you bet your life. I've smashed six unions in my time. And I'm not bloated, I'm well fed.

NANNY. Oh the wicked man.

WORKER. It's off of us the likes of him feed their faces. Me and my starvin' wife and my three sick kids, and a paycheck that ain't enough to feed the flies in our stinking two rooms. I wish I'd have smashed *him* instead of his machine.

CAPITALIST. Open threats!

MATTHEW. I'll say. And I'm the man to execute them. (*He takes a poker from the fireplace*) See this? Solid brass. Nanny, give me a hand. (*Nanny grabs a monstrously abstract wooden sculpture*)

WORKER. Hit him!

CAPITALIST. Oh yeah? I'm not leaving without this anarchist in custody.

MATTHEW. Yes you are.

CAPITALIST. No I ain't.

NANNY. Yes you are.

CAPITALIST. Out of my way, granny, I'll have you both up for conspiracy.

MATTHEW. Get out!

CAPITALIST. Get out yourself!

MATTHEW (*To Nanny*). Hold him!

CAPITALIST. I'll knock your teeth into your windpipe.

WORKER. Hit him! Hit him!

(*Matthew hits the Capitalist*)

CAPITALIST. Ouch!

NANNY. Parasite! (*She hits him too and lays him out flat*)

WORKER. That's the ticket! (*He comes out from behind a chair and kicks the Capitalist*) I wish I was stronger.

MATTHEW. Sit down, my poor man. Nanny will give you something to eat. And I'll drag this carcass out.

CAPITALIST (*opens an eye*). What hit me?

NANNY (*shows him the sculpture*). Justice Unbound.

CAPITALIST. Damn. (*He faints away*)

MATTHEW. Give me a hand, Nanny. All that blubber. (*They drag the Capitalist outdoors*) So much for that. The world can stand a little improvement. How are you feeling, Mr. —?

WORKER. Smiggins. Josh Smiggins. And real grateful to the both of yous.

NANNY. I'll fix you something to eat, Mr. Smiggins. You look like you're about to become extinct.

WORKER. Gee, I'd appreciate a little somethin. Just anything will do, ma'am; I ain't used to much.

NANNY. Leave it to me. (*She goes to the kitchen*)

MATTHEW. It's about time somebody stood up to these robbers.

WORKER. Without you I'd a been in jail by now, Mr. Available.

MATTHEW. Well, I did my best. I may be an intellectual, but you don't find *me* playing a harp in an ivory tower.

WORKER. Doin' what?

MATTHEW. I mean, refusing to fight.

WORKER. Refusin' to fight? You? Don't you believe it. That poker o' yours coulda laid out five of him. Boy, if I wasn't a wreck —

MATTHEW. Nanny! Hurry up!

NANNY (*within*). Coming, coming!

WORKER. I don't want to be no trouble to you.

MATTHEW. Trouble? I ought to apologize to you for living in ease and comfort while you — and your wife — and those poor children — God, it makes me choke —

WORKER. Me too. This sure is nice lodgins you got here. A reglar nest, bless you all.

(*Enter Nanny with a tray full of bread, butter, cold cuts and cheeses*)

WORKER. Oh gee, thanks, thanks a million. I'm so hungry, I can't hardly keep my head up.

MATTHEW. Heartbreaking. Here, eat, make yourself at home.

WORKER. Mmmm. Good.

MATTHEW. More butter, Mr. Smiggins?

WORKER. Good idea. What do you know! I'm feeling stronger already.

MATTHEW (*to Nanny*). It's a pleasure to watch him.

NANNY. Why don't I put something in a paper bag for your children, Mr. Smiggins?

WORKER. Gee, would you? They'll be real happy, the poor kids.

MATTHEW. Let's hope that your children will see a brighter future. No exploitation, a decent wage, a good education.

WORKER (*his mouth full*). You said it. Boy oh boy, do I feel better! Lemme wash this down with a cup of coffee, do you mind? Smells great. "Good to the last drop." Yes, sir, I'm gonna put the kids through college, right along with the board of directors, the jet set, Mr. Rockefeller, and everybody.

MATTHEW. Let them read Sophocles, study the sciences, hear chamber music.

WORKER. You bet. I'll see them at the top o' the heap if I ever get half a break at my lousy job. Gee, this here ham is the best I ever ett. Thanks for the bag, granny.

(*While eating, the Worker has become remarkably stronger, larger, ruddier*)

MATTHEW. This meal has really propped you up, Mr. Smiggins. I hope today will mark a new beginning — and you know you can always count on me. Well now, listen to this!

(*Music outside*)

WORKER. What's that?

MATTHEW. I don't know. Nanny, why don't you take a peek outside.

NANNY. I will. (*She goes out*)

WORKER. Sure sounds foreign to me.

MATTHEW. I think it's Puerto Rican.

WORKER. Oh yeah?

MATTHEW. Chamber music, Mr. Smiggins. I realize that this sounds a bit remote to you, but it's what your children will need. The best that civilization has to offer, once the bonds of slavery are broken, once men become true brothers. Go on, my friend, have another sandwich.

WORKER. I dunno. Them foreigners upset my appetite.

MATTHEW. I don't see why. (*Nanny reappears*) Well, Nanny?

NANNY. It's the Virgin of Guadalupe's birthday, and they're all coming this way, bless 'em, dancing and banging on things.

WORKER (*roars*). I don't like foreigners!

MATTHEW. Mr. Smiggins! We're all Americans here. Remember the melting pot.

WORKER (*roars*). I don't like foreigners!

NANNY (*aside to Matthew*). We gave him too much to eat.

MATTHEW. Mr. Smiggins, all kinds of people went to the building of this nation — the English, the Poles, the Swedes, the Chinese, the Mexican —

WORKER (*roars*). I don't like lousy foreigners! They grab our jobs for half pay and what do they do? They take a plane back home first chance they get, and jabbering away jabber jabber in their lingo that ain't even white. (*At the door*) Cut out that noise! Jesus, lemme take a crack at them!

MATTHEW. Wait, hold it, hold it!

WORKER. Out o' my way! This place is for hundred percent Americans and union labor! I ain't gonna stand for no heathen celebrations!

MATTHEW. Nanny, help me!

WORKER. I'll moider em!

NANNY. Watch the gueridon!

MATTHEW. Mr. Smiggins!

(*The Worker has thrown Matthew off and flings himself into the street. Loud Latin music outside. Suddenly the music stops. Sounds of a fight, curses, trumpets blaring off-key. Then a Puerto Rican rushes into the house, more on all fours than on his two feet. He is mauled, enfeebled, astonished and terrified*)

PUERTO RICAN. Help me, hide me, Jesus Maria, he's going to kill me, the

Yankee has gone mad!

MATTHEW. Close the door, Nanny, quick!

NANNY. Can I lock it, Mr. Matthew?

MATTHEW. Never! Here, sir, here, sit down, you're safe, believe me, we'll protect you. Here's a handkerchief.

PUERTO RICAN. Thank you, señor, thank you. Oh I can't breathe, I'm dying.

MATTHEW (to Nanny). Get him a glass of wine, hurry. Gently, my friend, you're not dying, you're only scared. My name is Matthew Available. You're safe under my roof, and I am going to give you all the help I can.

PUERTO RICAN. Mucho gusto. My name is José García. I don't even know what happened. It's the feast of the Virgen de Guadalupe today. (He crosses himself) Thank you, señora, kind lady. (He drinks) She is our holy guardian. We were singing and dancing. I was one of the men chosen to carry her on my shoulders.

NANNY. I don't see how you could carry a statue, Mr. García, you're so thin and weak I could break you in two by throwing a glance at you.

MATTHEW. Nanny!

PUERTO RICAN. There were six of us carrying her, señora, before that wild bull fell on us. Who was he, anyway? Why did he start knocking peaceful people down?

MATTHEW. Hm — I don't know. Lack of education, I'd guess.

PUERTO RICAN. I thought I saw him coming out of here.

MATTHEW and NANNY. Oh no.

PUERTO RICAN. We weren't doing anything wrong.

MATTHEW. I should say not. It's marvelous to see so many of you keeping faith with your traditions and beliefs. It's beautiful.

NANNY. Oh yes.

MATTHEW. Look at your history — Ponce de León — Sir Francis Drake — Morro Castle — Mr. García, I'm proud to have you as a guest in my house. Did you know that Puerto Rico had a sugar mill in 1548?

PUERTO RICAN. Wonderful.

MATTHEW. It was operated by oxen.

NANNY. Speaking of oxen, I think Mr. García would enjoy a ham and cheese sandwich.

PUERTO RICAN. Oh no. Please. You've both been too nice. The Virgen will bless you, but I'd better go now. (He tries) I can't.

NANNY. I knew it.

MATTHEW. That does it. Bring some food, and plenty of coffee.

PUERTO RICAN. You shouldn't . . .

MATTHEW. Nonsense! On your way, Nanny.

NANNY. Good thing it's Sunday only once a week. (She goes)

MATTHEW. Relax, Mr. García. If there's anything I can't abide, it's national prejudices. Imagine one people thinking itself better than another. I know you're not feeling well.

PUERTO RICAN. Oh yes . . .

MATTHEW. No no, you're shivering.

PUERTO RICAN. A little, maybe. Nerves.

MATTHEW. We'll put you on your feet again. If only people could understand the idea of brotherhood, regardless of race, religion, nationality, and what not. I try my best as an individual. I contribute, I sympathize, I join, I fight — literally fight, you know — look at this bruise.

PUERTO RICAN. Caramba.

MATTHEW. Fighting a brutal capitalist, defending a poor workingman.

PUERTO RICAN. You mean the one who almost killed me?

MATTHEW. Maybe he was the one. I couldn't stop him, Mr. García.

PUERTO RICAN. You did your best, amigo.

MATTHEW. It takes time. Generations.

PUERTO RICAN. Centuries.

MATTHEW. Aeons.

PUERTO RICAN. Eternity?

MATTHEW. But I keep fighting. Decency. Human decency, you know; nothing startling or exceptional. Nanny! Damn her! Where's the food? How long are you going to keep us waiting?

NANNY. Coming, coming! (She enters with another tray) This is the best I could whip together.

PUERTO RICAN. I'm —

MATTHEW. It's perfectly all right, Mr. García. Eat, get some strength, and pay no attention to us.

PUERTO RICAN. Delicious. My compliments, señora. I'm already feeling much better.

NANNY. Don't eat too fast.

MATTHEW. Café con leche?

PUERTO RICAN (laughing). Si, amigo. Muchas gracias. Oh yes, you're right, it's tough to be a small downtrodden people, Mr. — — ?

MATTHEW. Available. I know it must be.

PUERTO RICAN. What are we Latins next to you Yankees? Midgets. And besides, here in America we're second-class citizens. If it wasn't for a few decent nice people like you and the señora —

MATTHEW. Don't mention it.

(The Puerto Rican is beginning to look stronger)

NANNY. You're beginning to look stronger, Mr. García.

PUERTO RICAN. Thanks to you both. I'll say a prayer for you. Oh look! Your door is moving. If it's that worker, I'll smash his face.

MATTHEW. Don't excite yourself, Mr. García. It was only the wind,

I'm sure.

NANNY. I'm not so sure. Lookee.

(In fact, the door has been opening slowly. On the floor we see the head of a Negro, followed by its body: dusty, shriveled, sweating and defeated)

NEGRO. Help, good people . . . *(He speaks with an Oxonian accent)*

(Matthew flings himself toward the door)

MATTHEW. Come in, in God's name, come in, my brother!

NANNY. Another lunch coming up.

PUERTO RICAN *(glumly, to Nanny)*. This is a relative? This?

NANNY. Oh no, Mr. García, only a visitor.

PUERTO RICAN *(indignant)*. A visitor!

MATTHEW *(bending over the Negro)*. What's the matter? Are you injured? Don't worry, you're safe in this house. Nanny, give me a hand, damn it!

NANNY. Sure, sure.

NEGRO. I can't speak. . . . Whoever you are, if there's any pity left . . .

MATTHEW. Come on, let me help you get on your feet. *(To Nanny)* Take the other arm. One, two, three! Here we are! To the leather chair. There now. Easy, easy. My God, he's bleeding in the neck.

PUERTO RICAN *(aside)*. Troublemakers. Monkeys.

MATTHEW. Feeling better?

NEGRO. A bit better. Whoever you are, thank you, thank you. But you must hide me; there's a lynching mob on my trail!

PUERTO RICAN *(aside)*. Muy bien.

MATTHEW. I thought as much. But no lynching mob is going to cross my threshold.

PUERTO RICAN *(muttering)*. Musta raped a white virgin.

MATTHEW. Did you say something, Mr. García?

PUERTO RICAN. Nothing, amigo, I was belching.

MATTHEW. Nanny, don't forget our guest while I attend to Mr. — —

NEGRO. Nguyo Lubumbo. Ambassador of Zimbustan.

MATTHEW. Ambassador of Zimbustan! I don't know what to say. How did you — how did this — ?

NANNY. Here's a cup of coffee, Mr. Lubumbo. I'm honored. Welcome in my country's name.

PUERTO RICAN *(between his teeth)*. Nigger.

NEGRO. Thank you, but really, you must conceal me somewhere, I implore you. I'm too weak to fight back. If they find me I'm done for.

MATTHEW *(to Nanny)*. Take a quick look outside.

NANNY *(looking out)*. Nothing yet. A bit of dust in the distance, that's all.

NEGRO. It must be them! Oh my God, if only I had strength enough to blow this whistle. *(He has a whistle around his neck)* Nobody is going to help me.

MATTHEW. Of course we're going to help you. You're in the house of Matthew Available —

NEGRO. Delighted.

MATTHEW. — who will fight for the downtrodden till the last flake of his body turns to dust. But tell me, Mr. Lubumbo, why this vicious mob is hunting you.

NEGRO. I hardly know.

PUERTO RICAN (*under his breath*). I bet.

NEGRO. I was standing on a streetcorner with the Cultural Attaché of the Cameroon, reminiscing about our days at Trinity, when a pretty girl walked by in front of us.

PUERTO RICAN (*setting his lunch tray down and standing up*). White?

NEGRO. Yes. I laughed and said, "What a pretty girl." A policeman happened to overhear me. He yelled Rape! and suddenly it seemed as if the entire population was down on us, howling, shaking sticks, spitting, throwing stones.

NANNY. How did you get away?

NEGRO. Tom Boyo, my Cameroonian friend, had his open sports coupé parked at the curb. He jumped in and drove off. This diverted the mob long enough for me to run the other way. I ran, I ran, I ran, and now I'm almost dead, I can't even blow this whistle.

MATTHEW. Why the whistle?

NEGRO. To rally my people.

PUERTO RICAN (*aside to Matthew*). Are you gonna stand for this?

MATTHEW. No, Mr. García. We'll all defend him against that mob.

PUERTO RICAN (*roaring*). That ain't what I meant!

MATTHEW. What's the matter, Mr. García? You look mighty upset.

PUERTO RICAN. Sangre de Dios! He don't even knock to come in, he's steaming hot after raping a white virgin, he talks about whistling for his Africans —

MATTHEW. Gently, amigo, we're all equal, black, white, and, if I may say so, brown, like you.

PUERTO RICAN. Brown? Brown? Who's brown? I'm pure Spanish, I'm Andaluz, white, pure white, you're slandering me.

MATTHEW. All right, Mr. García, you're any color you choose. Nanny, go to the kitchen. I want you to fix a good solid lunch for Mr. Lubumbo.

NANNY. I hate to tell you, Mr. Matthew.

MATTHEW. What?

NANNY. All I've got left is a few steaks in the freezer, and it'll take two hours to thaw them out.

NEGRO. My dear, dear lady, I assure you I don't need a thing. Just hide me, or let me die in peace.

MATTHEW. Nonsense; there's going to be a fight, and we must fatten you up for it. There's enough left on Mr. García's tray for two lunches.

PUERTO RICAN. That's *my* tray!

MATTHEW and NANNY. Mr. García!

PUERTO RICAN. *My* tray!

MATTHEW (*trying to seize the tray*). If you don't mind.

PUERTO RICAN (*roaring*). No nigger is gonna eat offa my tray!

MATTHEW. May I point out —

PUERTO RICAN. Who they think they are? Go back to Africa! This country is for white men!

MATTHEW. And here I thought that you Latin Americans were free of these prejudices.

PUERTO RICAN. Sure, prejudices is for Yankees. We're not allowed to have 'em.

MATTHEW. You're getting offensive, Mr. García, now that I've fed you. Give me that tray.

PUERTO RICAN. Over my dead body. I don't like niggers and I don't like nigger-lovers! Wait! I'll call that mob myself! And let the blacks stay where they belong. Under *us*. D'you hear? Down on their knees, up in the trees, back to the plantations!

MATTHEW. Give me that tray and shut up.

PUERTO RICAN. Back to slavery!

NEGRO (*feebly*). We'll kill you all.

PUERTO RICAN (*flinging himself on the Negro*). Like hell you will! Hijo de puta!

NEGRO. Help! He's killing me!

MATTHEW. Nanny, help!

NANNY. Mr. García, you're a Christian!

PUERTO RICAN. Damn right I'm a Christian! That's why I'll murder the voodoo heathen!

NEGRO. Arghhh!

MATTHEW (*fighting the Puerto Rican*). Take your hands off my guest! (*They exchange blows*) Nanny, he's bloodied my eye!

NANNY. Watch the gueridon!

PUERTO RICAN. Ouch!

MATTHEW. We'll see.

PUERTO RICAN. Ouch! White nigger!

MATTHEW. Nanny, hit him with the Justice Unbound!

NANNY. I will. (*She does so and lays the Puerto Rican out flat*)

MATTHEW (*staggering to a chair*). Fighting for the oppressed is no holiday.

NEGRO (*feebly*). Jolly good work, Mr. Available. If only I could have helped.

MATTHEW. Don't mention it, Mr. Lubumbo. Nanny, give me that glass of wine.

NANNY. I'm bleeding too.

MATTHEW (*bathing his eye*). My robe is torn.

NEGRO. I can only apologize for the untimely intrusion.

MATTHEW. Oh no, I assure you, I'm honored to have you in my house, Mr. Ambassador.

NEGRO. You are an honor to your country, to your race, and to mankind.

NANNY. What'll we do with Mr. García?

MATTHEW. The ruffian. Let's drag him out. Is he still breathing?

NANNY. I'm afraid so.

(*They pull him out*)

MATTHEW. Come on, Nanny, do your bit for a change, will you?

NANNY. Sorry, Mr. Matthew, my arm hurts. May I lock the door now?

MATTHEW. Never. Go on, feed our guest.

NANNY. I don't know that we should, Mr. Matthew.

MATTHEW. Why not?

NANNY. Do I have to remind you what happened when you fed the others?

MATTHEW. Isn't that just like you? Egotistical old maid. Nothing counts for you except your own hide. I don't know why I'm even answering you. Now, Mr. Lubumbo, can we induce you to take a little refreshment?

NEGRO. The mob, Mr. Available, the mob. Won't you try to hide me in a cellar or an attic?

MATTHEW. The mob has no earthly reason to stop at this particular house. But if they do, I'll beat them back, don't worry. Come now, take some food. You said yourself you needed strength to blow your whistle.

NEGRO. True.

MATTHEW. Of course, I'd gladly blow it for you.

NEGRO. Oh no! That's for me to do. I *will* have a bite after all. Very good of you.

(*He begins to eat*)

MATTHEW. Nanny, stop fiddling with your wound and prepare some fresh coffee.

NEGRO. Oh, splendid.

(*Exit Nanny*)

MATTHEW. I recommend this Port Salut.

NEGRO. Excellent. I feel the vital spirits starting to course again in my veins.

MATTHEW. You are here on a mission, Mr. Lubumbo?

NEGRO. *Dr.* Lubumbo. Yes, I am. My country is seeking military aid — the usual hardware, I'm afraid — aircraft — tanks — one day, you know, we shall have to exterminate South Africa. A dreary business. Oh my, I'm still very weak. Quite dizzy and all that.

MATTHEW. Nanny, hurry the coffee!

NANNY (*from the kitchen*). Coming up!

MATTHEW. Another slice of ham will help, Dr. Lubumbo. You know, it's simply thrilling to think of all these proud new independent nations. Only a few years ago, you were smarting under the boot of the white colonials, and now here you are, Malawi, Cameroon, the Congo, Gabon, Zambia, Botswana, and so on, I love to roll the exotic names off my tongue.

NEGRO. You are a well-informed man, Mr. Available. (*Nanny has come in with the coffee*) Thank you so much, my good woman. Two lumps, that's it. Smashing lunch. What was I saying? Oh yes, that you are a well-informed man.

MATTHEW. I try to be.

NEGRO. And well disposed toward us.

MATTHEW. Indeed I am.

NEGRO. Ours is a hard struggle.

MATTHEW. But a splendid one too. Already, I'm sure, free Zimbustan has doubled, tripled, quadrupled its resources.

NEGRO. Not quite, perhaps. But today, when a Zimbu starves, at least he starves at the hands of another Zimbu.

MATTHEW. Tremendous.

NANNY. I don't call that much of an improvement.

MATTHEW. Don't meddle in what's beyond you, Nanny. *I* think it's encouraging.

NEGRO. Most encouraging.

NANNY. What about that posse that's out looking for you, Mr. Lubumbo? Ain't you afraid of it anymore?

NEGRO (*fingering his whistle*). Dr. Lubumbo. No, I'm no longer afraid. (*He has grown noticeably larger and stronger*)

MATTHEW. You do look remarkably improved, I'm happy to say.

NEGRO. Perhaps I'd better go. You've been most helpful, and I shan't forget it.

MATTHEW. Please don't mention it. Nanny, take a look outside again to make sure those maniacs have scattered.

NANNY. Sure. (*She looks outside*) I guess you'd better hide Mr. Lubumbo in the wardrobe. There's a mob closing in on us. They're banging on doors and raising the devil.

MATTHEW (*grabbing the poker*). Here's the wardrobe, Dr. Lubumbo.

NEGRO. That won't be necessary anymore. I believe I can manage now. (*Shouts outside*)

A VOICE. If he's anywhere in town, that's where he's got to be, fellers. Egghead House.

VOICES. Let's go in and get him out. Lynch the nigger! Bash in the door!

NEGRO. Steady on, Mr. Available. Courage, madam. I shall manage.

NANNY. There's a sturdy oak tree in front of the house, Mr. Lubumbo; that's what scares me.

NEGRO. I'm glad you mentioned it, my dear; I intend to make good use of it.

VOICE. Easy there, don't jostle, one guy is all we need. Go on in, Officer Slotnik.

(Violent entrance of a burly Policeman)

POLICEMAN. Where's that — ? *(He sees the Negro and shouts to the people outside)* Don't nobody need to foller me. I got him. I got him good. *(Uproar outside. The Policeman whips out a couple of pistols)* Okay, mister, come out quiet, no use puttin up a fight. You got a date with a noose.

MATTHEW *(standing in front of the Negro)*. Over my dead body.

POLICEMAN. I'll sure be glad to oblige.

NANNY *(screams)*. No!

NEGRO *(moving Matthew aside)*. Let me handle this. Here I am, officer. Remember I enjoy diplomatic immunity, but I'm ready to follow you.

VOICE. What's going on in there, Slotnik?

VOICE. Need any help?

POLICEMAN. Relax, boys, lemme handle this my own way. *(To the Negro)* All right, black boy, get your black ass out through that door, and we'll converse about your diplomatic unity from the end of a rope.

MATTHEW. Officer, for God's sake! This is the Ambassador of Zimbustan!

POLICEMAN. If he's the Ambassador of Bustown, let him call his pals out.

NEGRO *(in the doorway)*. That is precisely my intention. *(He blows his whistle)*

POLICEMAN. Whadda ya think you're doin? Calling a fucking taxicab? Come and get him, fellers! Here he is!

(He shoves the Negro out, leaves after him, slams the door. Uproar outside, shots)

VOICE. Don't shoot the guy before we've strung him up!

VOICE. Smith, hold the rope!

VOICE. We got us a nigger!

VOICE. Yippee!

VOICE. No more white girls for the black bastard!

(Other shouts ad libitum)

MATTHEW. I'm sick. What can we do? Call the police! Oh God, that *was* the police! Nanny, I can't, look out the window, tell me what's going on.

NANNY. Oh Jesus Christ, oh Jesus Christ, save him, they've bound his wrists, they've torn off his necktie. Now what? Merciful God! What's this? What's this? Mr. Matthew, oh oh oh oh, come here, quick —

MATTHEW. I can't . . .

NANNY. Come here I tell you! Dozens of blacks running to the rescue! Hundreds! Thousands! Millions!

(Matthew rushes to the window)

MATTHEW. Ha! The whistle! Nanny, the whistle did it! Hurrah!

NANNY. Don't go out, Mr. Matthew, please!

(A new kind of uproar outside)

VOICE. They're comin down from every side!

VOICE. Run for your lives!

VOICES. Shoot! Shoot! Don't wait!

VOICE. Hold it!

VOICE. Africans! Forward! Lynch 'em! Don't let the white bastards escape! Shoot into the groins! Shoot into the eyes!

(Shots)

VOICES. Help, help! Stop!

NANNY. They're stringing up the policeman!

POLICEMAN (outside). Men, they're lynchin me. Call out the National Guard! Aaargh . . . (Shouts of triumph. More shots. Matthew's windows are shattered)

VOICE. Destroy the white man!

NANNY. Behind the sofa, Mr. Matthew! Oh Jesus Christ, the world's coming to an end!

(Enter Lubumbo. He smashes all the furniture)

NEGRO. Nothing personal, you understand.

NANNY. The gueridon!

NEGRO. Personally, I'm most grateful to you both. (He knocks down a last vase and leaves)

VOICE. How many are swinging, men?

VOICE. Fifteen!

VOICE. Down with white imperialism!

VOICE. Freedom!

VOICE. Power!

VOICE. Dignity!

VOICE. Fifteen in a row. Ain't they handsome!

VOICE. Here's another one!

VOICE. Don't let him get away! Fire!

NANNY. Don't move, Mr. Matthew!

VOICE OF VICTIM. Not me! (A shot, and then a white man's body is tossed into Matthew's house)

NANNY. Oh Jesus Christ!

MATTHEW. I think they're finished, Nanny.

(The roars have diminished. Presently all is silent. Matthew and Nanny *come out of hiding and examine the body)*

MATTHEW. Is he dead?

NANNY. Must be.

MATTHEW. Let's place him on the table. Maybe we can still help. Oh God, what a Sunday afternoon!

(They lift the body to the table)

MATTHEW. Careful with all those splinters.

NANNY. He won't mind, poor man. Oh, Mr. Matthew, there's a card in his vest pocket.

MATTHEW. Let me see it. "Innocent Bystander." What do you make of that?

NANNY. I think it's odd.

MATTHEW. I don't know. I'm beginning to feel, I don't know, as if I'd made a mistake somewhere.

(The Innocent Bystander sits up)

INNOCENT BYSTANDER. I'm glad to hear you say that, Mr. Available. *(He shakes hands with Matthew and Nanny)* How do you do. How do you do. I hope I haven't been too much bother.

MATTHEW *(dazed)*. No-no . . . Lunch?

INNOCENT BYSTANDER. Most certainly not. I only dropped in, so to speak. But now I'd better be on my way. No need to see me out, thank you. Oh yes. After I'm gone, I suggest — *(he makes a gesture)*

NANNY. Lock the door?

INNOCENT BYSTANDER. Uhuh. *(He lights a cigarette)*

MATTHEW. My door?

INNOCENT BYSTANDER. Your door.

MATTHEW. And then? What then?

INNOCENT BYSTANDER. Bang bang. Somebody knocks. Who's there? You take a look through the peephole. Another look. And then another look. And then maybe you open sometimes a little.

MATTHEW. And the lunches?

INNOCENT BYSTANDER. Small lunches. So long, my friends. *(The handle comes off the door; he tosses it away)* Beautiful junk heap you've got here. Tut tut.

(He leaves. There is a long pause. Matthew hesitates. He looks at Nanny, who is beginning to take in the shambles, then he goes to the door and locks it)

MATTHEW. We'll replace the doorknob and fix the windows. *(Nanny picks up the gueridon and begins to cry)* It's a junk heap all right.

NANNY *(crying over the gueridon)*. Your mother and me bought it together.

MATTHEW. There, there now.

NANNY *(sobbing)*. And look at the commode, Mr. Matthew, your grandad's it was, lousy Victorian he always called it, every leg broken.

Look at our clock. Look at the glass doors. Look at these chairs. Look, look, look. I can't believe it. All your things, Mr. Matthew, every day for thirty-five years I dusted everything.

(Matthew is staring at Nanny)

MATTHEW *(in a small voice)*. You're bleeding.

NANNY *(still crying)*. I don't care. They even ripped the carpet.

MATTHEW. Sure you care, with all that dust and dirt.

NANNY. I've got a clean handkerchief.

MATTHEW. Give it to me. *(He bandages her)* But you've got to stop crying.

NANNY. I'll try.

MATTHEW. We have to pick up the pieces, you and me.

NANNY. Thirty-five years of work wasted.

MATTHEW. Maybe not. Who can tell? You promised to stop crying, though.

NANNY. I'll stop, Mr. Matthew.

MATTHEW. How's this for a bandage?

NANNY. Fine.

MATTHEW. We should have used iodine.

NANNY. I don't care.

MATTHEW. Sit down a bit. You've had a rough day. Sit down.

NANNY. Me?

(He stares at her)

NANNY. Anything the matter with you, Mr. Matthew?

MATTHEW. Why?

NANNY. You're looking at me as if you'd never seen me before.

MATTHEW. Nanny . . .

NANNY. Yes, Mr. Matthew?

MATTHEW *(in a very small voice)*. What's your name?

NANNY *(dumbfounded, remembers)*. Bertha. Bertha Robbins.

THE END

NOTE: In another version of "Living Room With 6 Oppressions," printed in "Drama & Theatre," the Puerto Rican was a Mexican. The personnel of hatred is infinitely flexible, and by making a few judicious and tactful changes in the text, directors in other places and other times can and should keep it up to date — until such time as universal love shall have made it irrelevant once and for all. Meantime, for productions West and Southwest of New York, the Mexican can be restored by altering the dialogue on p. 102 as follows:

MATTHEW. Look at Mexican history — Aztecs, Olmecs, Toltecs — architecture — calendars — the arts. Mr. García, I'm proud to have you as a guest in my house. I own several books on Mexican murals you might be interested in looking at.

MEXICAN. Wonderful. Mexican what?

NANNY. I think he'd rather look at an American ham and cheese sandwich.

A SPLITTING HEADACHE

(Conceived During the Memorable War Between Istria and Friuli)

CHARACTERS

HANS GROPIUS

THEOBALD GRIGGS

MRS. GRIGGS

FREDDY GRIGGS

THE SIGN PAINTER

MR. WIKKLE

MARTHA WIKKLE

JIM WIKKLE

STANLEY CLOVER

PHILIP O'TOOLE

GENERAL CULPEPPER

SENATOR FLOOGLE

SENATOR SALLOW

CORPORAL BLETTERMAN

PRIVATE DUPONT

PRIVATE GRIGGS

PRIVATE STEIN

A CAPTAIN

Scene One

(A miserable room in a miserable dwelling. Mr. Theobald Griggs is lying sick on a cot. His wife is darning a sock. A clock is ticking. Mr. Griggs wheezes and coughs painfully)

MR. GRIGGS. I don't feel my right leg no more.

MRS. GRIGGS. Sure you do.

(Silence)

MR. GRIGGS. What time is it?

MRS. GRIGGS *(patiently)*. Same time it always is this time of day.

MR. GRIGGS *(angry)*. What time is it?

MRS. GRIGGS. Four o'clock and some. Does that make you feel better?

MR. GRIGGS *(after another coughing spell)*. Where's Freddy?

MRS. GRIGGS. Drink some more water. Maybe Mr. Gropius will be coming soon. Today's Tuesday I think. Sure. Sunday was day before yesterday. I don't know why you can't be more careful with your socks.

MR. GRIGGS *(angry)*. Where's Freddy?

MRS. GRIGGS. You know where he is.

MR. GRIGGS. I mean why ain't he home yet.

MRS. GRIGGS. Drink some more water. Here. You know it's an hour's walk to town. Then to the haberdasher's, another fifteen minutes. And then to the pharmacy, another fifteen minutes, maybe more. And then back home, another hour. Unless somebody gives him a ride, a truck maybe, or Mr. Gropius if he happens to catch sight of him.

MR. GRIGGS. The haberdasher! Ain't we high and glorious today!

MRS. GRIGGS. The boy needs a sweater, Tib. The boy needs a sweater, that's all. He ain't strong and this is October already.

MR. GRIGGS. He'll outlive us both.

MRS. GRIGGS. He needs a sweater.

MR. GRIGGS. I need them pills! I'm the support of this family!

MRS. GRIGGS. Freddy's buying the pills too.

MR. GRIGGS. Yeah, but it's the haberdasher first, the haberdasher first, I heard you.

MRS. GRIGGS. Maybe it'll be the pharmacy first. I was only talking. This first or that first. It don't matter none that I can see.

MR. GRIGGS. It matters to me. It's my twelve dollars. I dug trenches for it for the goddam army.

MRS. GRIGGS. And look where it's got you.

MR. GRIGGS. Gimme a cup of coffee.

MRS. GRIGGS. Wait till Freddy comes back with the pills, then you can take the pills with your coffee. We're down to the last of the sugar, too.

MR. GRIGGS. I can't hardly feel my right leg anymore. Here, touch it.

MRS. GRIGGS. Sure you can.

(A knock at the door)

MR. GRIGGS. Somebody at the door.

MRS. GRIGGS. Who is it?

HANS *(outside)*. It's Hans Gropius!

MRS. GRIGGS. Come in, come in! *(She opens the door)* Welcome to you, Mr. Gropius, God bless you, I was just saying it's Tuesday today.

HANS. How are you, Mrs. Griggs. Close the door quickly, it's getting awfully chilly. Here, take this. *(He gives her a large paper sack)*

MRS. GRIGGS. Thank you, Mr. Gropius. Thank you. *(She takes various comestibles out of the sack)* Look, Tib, fresh tomatoes, Mr. Gropius remembered! And here's a can of condensed milk!

MR. GRIGGS. We appreciate your help, Mr. Gropius, even if I can't swallow a morsel the way I'm sick.

HANS. Not feeling any better, Mr. Griggs?

MR. GRIGGS. Worse. I won't be around much longer, though I'm only forty-two.

MRS. GRIGGS. Go on!

MR. GRIGGS *(half rises)*. Forty-two, and look at me! Worn out at forty-two! But I'm only a working man, so who cares? God damn it, I remember the day the members of the Board come walking down the factory aisle on their inspection tour. Yeah. I remember their white hands, same as yours. One of 'em had a carnation in his lapel. Closer and closer they came. I was holding a heavy wrench in my hand, and it made my palm itch, I tell you. "Lemme take a crack at one of them rich bastards," I kept telling myself. "Lemme present one of 'em with a widow and a couple orphans." Course I didn't. They was born to drink champagne, right? and I was born to be laid off and to die my stinking death.

MRS. GRIGGS. Oh shut your mouth, Tib.

HANS. You should try to keep calm, Mr. Griggs. Getting angry only makes you worse.

MRS. GRIGGS. He was always like that, violent.

MR. GRIGGS. And if there ain't enough pheasant to go round for everybody, let everybody take turns, God damn it, let everybody take turns. *(He coughs furiously)*

HANS *(sadly)*. I agree with you, Mr. Griggs. I wish I could really really help. I wish I could start from zero and build something decent.

MRS. GRIGGS. How can you talk like that, Mr. Gropius? You're an angel sent from heaven.

MR. GRIGGS. You're okay, Mr. Gropius. I didn't mean you. You're okay.

MRS. GRIGGS. Look at all that meat, Tib.

HANS. Don't mention it, Mrs. Griggs. People like me — we're like paper towels trying to soak up a flood. Has your boy gone for the medicine?

MRS. GRIGGS. Yes, he has. He should be right back.

HANS *(aside to her)*. And the sweater too, I hope.

MRS. GRIGGS. Oh yes. *(Taking a few coins out of her pocket)* Look, there's even forty-five cents left.

HANS. When is the government check coming?

MRS. GRIGGS. Early next week, I hope. *(She sees Freddy through the window)* Here's my boy now. And he's got a package under his arm! *(She opens the door)*

MR. GRIGGS. Sure, it's Christmas.

MRS. GRIGGS. Look at him! Look at that grimy face! Let me wipe it.

HANS. Hello, my boy.

FREDDY *(looking glum)*. Hello, Mr. Gropius.

MRS. GRIGGS. What's the matter with you? You got your sweater, didn't you?

FREDDY. Yes, mom.

MRS. GRIGGS. Lemme see. *(She opens the package)*

HANS. Very nice. *Very* nice. *(He feels it)*

MRS. GRIGGS. Isn't it? We saw it months ago, didn't we, Freddy? And we figured brown's the best color, being that dirt don't show on it so bad. Try it on, Freddy, come on, try it on. The poor boy's tired, look at him, he's been perspiring too.

MR. GRIGGS. What about my pills?

MRS. GRIGGS. Give him the pills, Freddy, your dad needs 'em.

HANS. I'll make him take a couple while you're trying on the sweater.

FREDDY. I haven't got the pills.

MR. GRIGGS. What?

MRS. GRIGGS. They was out of pills?

FREDDY. No, they wasn't out.

HANS. Come on, my boy, don't be afraid to tell us.

MR. GRIGGS. He forgot! He plumb forgot! Sure, it's Christmas, ain't it? I'll kill you!

FREDDY. I didn't forget.

MRS. GRIGGS. Don't just stand there! What happened? I'll give you a hiding you won't forget if you don't tell us the truth.

(Freddy hands Mrs. Griggs some money)

MR. GRIGGS. He forgot! I told you! He don't care if I die on this cot tonight!

MRS. GRIGGS. That's only a dollar sixty-five, Freddy. The sweater was six dollars. I gave you twelve.

HANS. What happened, Freddy? Did you really forget?

MR. GRIGGS. Belt him for me! That'll make him talk.

(Freddy starts crying)

HANS. Come on, come on, sit down, fella, give the boy a chance, Mr. Griggs. Did you stop to buy something else, Freddy, some candy?

MRS. GRIGGS. Did you, Freddy?

FREDDY. No, I didn't. The sweater was ten twenty-five, mom, we musta made a mistake. I went in —

MR. GRIGGS. Ten twenty-five! You're outa your mind! Take it back! I'll beat the daylights out of you before I let you keep a sweater that costs eleven dollars.

MRS. GRIGGS. Shut up! Shut up! Let the boy tell his story.

MR. GRIGGS. I don't want to hear it!

MRS. GRIGGS. Shut up!!!

HANS. Go on, Freddy. What store was it anyway?

FREDDY. Mr. Wikkle's haberdashery. The one near the station.

HANS. All right. Then what? You went in.

FREDDY. He said to me —

MRS. GRIGGS. Who said?

FREDDY. I don't know. I guess it was Mr. Wikkle himself. He said the sweater cost ten twenty-five.

MR. GRIGGS. And all you could say was fine, great, is that all, and you handed him the money.

MRS. GRIGGS. Let the boy finish!

MR. GRIGGS. I'm a sick man! What you both gonna do when I'm in the grave? Tell me that! Live on air? You gonna marry Mr. Gropius?

FREDDY. I was all set to go for the pills, dad. But when the man said the sweater was ten twenty-five I thought maybe we'd made a mistake.

MRS. GRIGGS. No we didn't. I didn't, Mr. Gropius. The price tag was on it as clear as daylight. They took advantage of the boy.

HANS. That's what it looks like. I'm going to take care of this right away.

FREDDY. There wasn't enough money left over for the pills.

MR. GRIGGS. Don't come near me! I'm through with all of you.

HANS. I'm going to drive into town this minute, Mr. Griggs. Leave it to me. I'll make that shopkeeper whoever he is return the difference to you.

MRS. GRIGGS. Give Mr. Gropius the sweater, Freddy.

HANS. The fool must have thought, "Here's a child, I can make a large extra profit. His parents must be poor. They won't know what to do." I've seen it too often, Mrs. Griggs. They call it charging what the traffic will bear. All right, Freddy, you're coming with me.

FREDDY. Are you gonna return it to him, Mr. Gropius?

HANS. No, my boy, that sweater is yours no matter what.

MR. GRIGGS. What about my pills?

HANS. You'll have them by tonight. Leave everything to me.

MR. GRIGGS. Tell that bum your father was a senator.

MRS. GRIGGS. Won't the store be closed by now, Mr. Gropius?
HANS. I'll kick it open.
(He and Freddy leave)

Scene Two

(Street and shop. A signpainter is standing on a ladder finishing a large sign which reads DANGER. Enter Hans, holding the sweater, and Freddy)

HANS. Excuse me up there.
SIGN PAINTER. Yes?
HANS. I'm looking for Wikkle's Habersdashery.
SIGN PAINTER. You mean old Cash-on-the-line Wikkle?
HANS. Is that what they call him?
SIGN PAINTER. Who is they?
HANS. Well — people.
SIGN PAINTER. Some does and some doesn't. I do. What's in your package?
HANS. A sweater I'm returning.
SIGN PAINTER. Overcharged you? A rip in the sleeve? Color come off in the wash?
HANS. He overcharged us.
SIGN PAINTER. Well, don't be hard on Mr. Wikkle. He's got to pay off the mortgage, you know. On the ten-room villa up the hill. That's his shop over there.
HANS. Thank you.
FREDDY. Why does that sign say DANGER, mister?
SIGN PAINTER. Because it's a useful thing to say, sonny.
HANS. Come along, Freddy.
(As Hans reaches the shop, the sign painter comes down the ladder and follows out of curiosity. He will listen at the door after Hans and Freddy have entered. Hans tries the door but finds it locked. He looks at his watch, decides he has arrived after business hours, and knocks. He has to knock several times before an answer is heard)
WIKKLE (inside). Who is it?
HANS. You don't know me. Open the door.
WIKKLE. It's after five o'clock. I'm closed for the day.
HANS. Open the door or I'll call the police!
(Wikkle opens the door. He is an old man dressed as a Boy Scout leader)
WIKKLE. What do you mean, call the police? What is this, anyway? Who are you?

HANS. I'll tell you who I am in a minute, Mr. Wikkle. But first, do you recognize this?

WIKKLE. Looks like the sweater I sold this boy today. What's going on?

HANS. My name is Hans Gropius.

WIKKLE. Gropius?

HANS. That's right.

WIKKLE. Come in, sir. Surely this isn't —

HANS. No, this belongs to one of the families I try to look after. I don't know you, Mr. Wikkle, but I'm going to be blunt with you. Here's a six-dollar sweater you sold for ten dollars and twenty-five cents today. Is this correct, or did the boy lie to me?

WIKKLE. He lied to you.

HANS. Oh?

FREDDY. I didn't, I didn't lie!

WIKKLE. This is a ten twenty-five sweater which I sold for ten dollars and twenty-five cents. It *was* a six-dollar sweater. Once upon a time.

HANS. Once upon what time? This morning?

WIKKLE. No, Mr. Gropius. Two weeks ago. Here's another sweater just like it, only in beige. Please read the price tag. If you'd like to exchange —

HANS. How did this wonderful leap come about, Mr. Wikkle? Seventy-five percent! Simply because there's a war on?

WIKKLE. Speaking with due respect, I don't owe anybody an explanation. I don't care whose son you are, Mr. Gropius.

BOY'S VOICE. Mr. Wikkle! We're waiting for you!

WIKKLE. I'll be out again in a minute, boys! Do the half-hitch a few more times, let Jim show you how!

BOY'S VOICE. Okay, Mr. Wikkle!

WIKKLE. We're learning how to tie knots. Like I said, Mr. Gropius, I don't mean to be disrespectful, but I've been serving our community for well-nigh forty-five years. There's not a speck of dust on my reputation. I'm a Boy Scout leader. I love children. But —

HANS. If you love children, you might have noticed that here was a child in bitter need. (*He puts his finger on Freddy's rags*)

WIKKLE. There's a war on, Mr. Gropius. Maybe there won't be any woollen goods at all to be had in another two months, and then where will I be? People are buying up everything in sight, pins, buttons. I could have sold that boy's sweater three times over this afternoon for fifteen dollars. And what about the prices *I* got to pay to keep going? What about the relatives I got to feed that fled from the border?

HANS. Sure, sure.

WIKKLE. Martha! Martha!

MARTHA (off). Yes?

WIKKLE. Come here a minute!

(Enter Martha Wikkle, wiping a cup)

MARTHA. What's the matter, honey?

WIKKLE. Who is living with us up on the hill these days? The gentleman would like to know.

MARTHA. You mean Ben, the children, and everybody?

WIKKLE. Yes. Tell him why they're here.

MARTHA. The war, of course. We're giving them shelter, sir. Is anything wrong? Something wrong with their papers?

WIKKLE. No, no, everything is all right. You can go back to the kitchen, don't worry. (He shoos Martha out)

HANS. Fine. You've convinced me that you're kind to your relatives. But not that you aren't cruel to strangers. There's a shortage of woollens. Granted. So you double the price. Economic law. But when a ragged boy stands before you, and you're a Boy Scout leader, why don't you duck economic law for five minutes?

(The sign painter barges in)

SIGN PAINTER. Because he's a greedy pig, that's why!

WIKKLE. Who are you? Get out of here! I'm closed!

SIGN PAINTER (waving his brush). I'm nobody but I ain't leaving. I been listenin' to your crud and I've had all I can take. Greed, nothin' but lousy greed. The house on the hill, that's who he loves. (To Hans) You and your boy! Are you kidding? He'll let that boy starve in the gutter before he'll clip a dime off of his price. Boy Scout leader! He makes me sick! But I'll let you in on a little secret, Mr. Wikkle. We've got your name. The name of Wikkle will be remembered when the day of reckoning comes, and that'll be sooner than you think, the way your rotten war is going.

WIKKLE (tremulous). Get out of here! I'll call the police! Get out! Martha, call the police!

HANS. You'd better leave.

SIGN PAINTER. Okay, okay, as long as we know who the bloodsuckers are. Just remember, Wikkle, there's eyes watching this place day and night. (He leaves)

(Martha has entered meantime; she and Wikkle hold each other)

BOY'S VOICE. Grampa!

(Wikkle does not hear it)

MARTHA. Who was that? What's going on? Somebody tell me.

WIKKLE (pale). I don't know.

HANS. I don't either.

FREDDY. It was the sign painter who told you where the shop was, Mr. Gropius.

WIKKLE. Why did he tell you? How did he know?

HANS. Whoever it was, I hope he's given you something to think about, Mr. Wikkle. Exploitation can go too far, and then the smashing begins.

WIKKLE. I don't exploit nobody. That's political talk. I work day and night, seven days a week.

HANS. Let's go, Freddy. You see, Mr. Wikkle was right to charge you whatever he could get away with. He was only obeying the law of supply and demand, which says that some people have a right to villas on the hill and others have the right to be cold in winter.

WIKKLE. You're unfair to me, Mr. Gropius.

MARTHA. What did he mean about eyes watching this place day and night?

WIKKLE. They're giving me a bad name. Why don't you take on the textile people? Who am I, anyway? Small fry. When the pressure comes from the top, I've got to raise my prices same as everybody else.

HANS. Blaming somebody else is too easy, Mr. Wikkle.

MARTHA. Why don't you show him the letter?

WIKKLE. I didn't want to.

MARTHA. Don't be proud. Everybody can be caught short, it's no crime.

WIKKLE. All right. Where is it?

MARTHA. You put it in the drawer. Here.

WIKKLE. Give it to me.

(Martha hands him a letter, which he gives to Hans)

WIKKLE. It's from my supplier, Ultra Textiles.

HANS (reading). "Dear Mr. Wikkle: May we draw your attention to the fact that your payment for Shipment No. 44 is now one month overdue. Circumstances beyond our control compel us to depart from our peacetime policy and to require prompt and full remittances in order to insure future deliveries. In addition, with regard to your current order, we are obliged to request a prepayment of 25% of the full amount before said order can be shipped. We sincerely regret" etc. etc. etc. Signed Ultra Textiles.

WIKKLE. Am I supposed to sell my house? Every merchant in town was hit by this. Everybody rushed to the bank, and the bank says, All right, we'll have to charge you 12% interest for this loan, you people are working without a safe cash margin, you're charging unrealistic pre-war prices for your merchandise.

MARTHA. It's not in our interest to overcharge. But how else can we raise the cash? And keep our own heads above water?

HANS (softly). You could sell your house.

WIKKLE (staring). Am I supposed to become a poor man so as to help strangers? Where is it written I'm supposed to be a saint?

MARTHA. We didn't make the world.

WIKKLE. We're plain people who worked hard, never took a holiday, and finally made it. This is a crime?

(Jim Wikkle comes running into the shop from the backyard)

JIM. Grandma!

MARTHA. What's the matter, sweetie?

JIM. Dave splashed some juice on my sleeve, look, we tried to wash it off but we couldn't.

MARTHA *(kissing him)*. It's just a tiny nothing of a spot. Come to the kitchen, I'll get you spanking clean in a jiffy.

JIM *(noticing Freddy)*. Who's this, grandma?

MARTHA. A little boy who bought something from us.

JIM *(whispering to Martha)*. He's awful dirty.

MARTHA. Hush! Come along! *(They leave)*

WIKKLE. Isn't he cute? *(To Freddy)* Here, my boy, here's a dime for you, buy yourself some candy on the way home.

FREDDY. Thank you, sir.

WIKKLE. Why don't you go and complain to Ultra Textiles, Mr. Gropius? They're the ones you should blame, believe me.

HANS. I'll go to Ultra Textiles.

BOY'S VOICE. Mr. Wikkle! We can't do nothin' without you!

WIKKLE. Coming! Coming! *(He sees Hans and Freddy out, locks the shop door, and vanishes through the back door. Hans and Freddy are in the street. Hans takes Freddy's hand)*

HANS. Let's go buy your dad's medicine, Freddy.

FREDDY. Can I buy a chocolate bar with my dime on the way, Mr. Gropius?

HANS. Sure. *(His hand goes to his skull as the headache is born)*

FREDDY *(looking at the coin)*. He was a nice man.

(They shuffle out, after Hans has paused to look at the sign)

Scene Three

(The office of Stanley Clover, vice-president of Ultra Textiles)

HANS. Let me have a glass of water, will you?

STANLEY *(jumping up)*. Excuse me, old pal, I forgot all about pouring you a drink. Absorbing confabulation causes dereliction. What can I offer you?

HANS. Nothing, Stan. I really meant water. I've got a headache.

STANLEY. Oh, all right. *(He gives Hans a glass of water. Hans takes a couple of aspirins)* That sweater story of yours is very touching, but you know, your do-goodery from one end of the country to the other is going to conduct you from headaches to outright ruin.

HANS. Maybe.

STANLEY. Of course, when I say from one end of the country to the other, I mean what's left of it.

HANS. I've still got 10,000 shares in your lousy company.

STANLEY. Ultra Textiles is no lousy company, old pal. And don't forget that your dad was one of the founding fathers. Memory certified on brass plaque. Besides, we're keeping our boys warm, including my own brother by the way, while they're up there fighting in the mountains.

HANS. At huge profits to yourselves.

STANLEY. Are you starting *that* again?

HANS *(jumping up)*. Somebody has to be guilty!

STANLEY. Take another aspirin. *(The buzzer sounds)* Who is it? Oh fine. Ask him to come in. *(To Hans)* It's Phil O'Toole, the union representative. He's coming in to get my signature on the settlement.

(Enter Philip O'Toole)

O'TOOLE. Hi. I'm not disturbing, I hope.

STANLEY. Not at all. Phil, I want you to meet Hans Gropius, college chum and noble soul.

O'TOOLE. The senator's son.

STANLEY. Right.

O'TOOLE. Glad to know you, Hans. Your dad was a true friend of the working man. I've seen him picket with the boys against his own company.

HANS. How do you do.

STANLEY. Got that piece of parchment, Phil?

O'TOOLE. Sure thing. *(To Hans)* Look at him now. Grinning from ear to ear. Two weeks ago at the bargaining table you should have heard him bark and fume that another raise was going to break Ultra Textiles. How come I don't see anything broken around here, Stan? Matter of fact, I met your Lamborghini Amphibian parked in the lot, so I don't suppose you've had to sell it to support your old mother.

STANLEY *(laughing)*. Gimme that historical document, you bastard. *(He signs it)* If you guys hadn't kept that last meeting going till past my beddy-bye time — on top of which the coffee machine broke down — hey, I don't suppose one of your boys sabotaged that coffee machine?

O'TOOLE *(laughing)*. Sure!

STANLEY *(holding up the contract)*. Look at this. Dental insurance!

O'TOOLE. Shocking, isn't it? A working class without cavities! All right, Stan, hand it over.

STANLEY. And this. Now this is really too much. "No more than three percent — "

O'TOOLE *(suddenly serious)*. Hold it, Stan. That's not — you know what I mean.

STANLEY. Not for public disclosure. I know. You haven't read this morning's papers, I guess.

O'TOOLE. You leaked it out!

STANLEY. Me? I doubt it. Maybe one of the typists.

O'TOOLE. Jesus! Talk about integrity! Give me that telephone.

STANLEY. Help yourself.

HANS. Let me see that, may I?

O'TOOLE *(after dialing)*. Pete! Get me Pete right away! It sounds worse than it is, Mr. Gropius. Where the hell is he?

HANS *(reading)*. "No more than three percent of the total working force in any given calendar year shall consist of employees of non-Caucasian origin."

O'TOOLE. Your dad would have understood, Mr. Gropius. Pete! Where you hanging out? Never mind. Yeah. I just heard. Listen carefully. When the newswires call, you issue a categorical denial. That's right. O'Toole states unequivocally etc. etc. I'll talk to you later. *(Hangs up)*

STANLEY. You see? No harm done.

O'TOOLE. You son of a bitch.

STANLEY. Management fought tooth and nail against that clause.

O'TOOLE. Why not? A tractable cheap labor force that's not going to move into the mansion next door. Why shouldn't management be broad-minded about it? Besides, you can afford to be holy because you know there's no danger of succeeding. And it gives you a chance to blacken *our* faces.

STANLEY. Watch your language.

(Both laugh)

O'TOOLE. Seriously though. We in the leadership didn't like that secret clause any more than they did.

HANS. You didn't like it, they didn't like it, but here it is.

O'TOOLE. The men insisted on it. And you can't really blame them.

HANS. Why not?

O'TOOLE. Let's put it this way. They're a group; a cohesive group; it began with their grandfathers, or even before; they've fought as a group to get where they are now; and suddenly they see a flood of outsiders coming in to compete with them. Outsiders with dark faces. They react by instinct, like threatened animals.

HANS. Like animals. Exactly.

O'TOOLE. You expect them to react like saints? All right. If you expect them to react like saints, then they're to blame. But they're human. That's the way they were brought up. Go blame their parents. Go blame society. Go blame the stupid chromosomes. I'm not trying to apologize for them, you understand. But when they tell me, "We've got hold of something and we're not giving it away," what can I answer?

HANS. That they're not giving anything away. They're only taking somebody into their cohesive group whose skin has a different color.

O'TOOLE. There's only so many places in that group, Hans. You let in a stranger, you've got to keep out a member of the family.

HANS. What family? What family? It's all the human family!

STANLEY. Beautiful!

O'TOOLE. You're talking above their heads, Mr. Gropius. I tell you they're not saints. You and I have reached another stage maybe, but that doesn't give us the right to spit in the faces of those that haven't. Give them five hundred years to catch up and then we'll talk again.

HANS. Here's your document, Phil. I'm glad you're personally a liberal. I suppose you're one of those who'd even be willing to marry one of them.

O'TOOLE. Quite a joker, aren't you?

STANLEY. Ha, ha, ha.

O'TOOLE. I — well, gentlemen, I'll be on my way. See you around, Mr. Gropius. So long, Stan.

STANLEY. So long, Phil. Don't forget our golf date.

(Exit O'Toole)

STANLEY. That was a funny joke, a very funny joke.

HANS. What was a funny joke?

STANLEY. About being willing to marry one of them.

HANS. Why?

STANLEY. Because he did.

HANS. Oh no! Where's that glass of water? (He takes another aspirin)

STANLEY. She's a nice girl, but we're keeping it a secret, all of us at the top. Otherwise he'll be picking lint in the basement. And that's something we don't want to see happen. Phil is a man we can work with. Although that settlement really puts the squeeze on us; no fooling, Hans. It's their fault if that sweater of yours went up to ten twenty-five.

HANS. They're not driving Lamborghini Amphibians. You are.

STANLEY. You want me to donate my car and my salary and stock options to Freddy Griggs?

HANS. They should be forced from you.

STANLEY. Remedy more fatal than disease. Poverty is ugly, but a gun is uglier.

HANS. Cut your prices then! Cut your profits!

STANLEY. The stockholders own this company, Hans! Lots of *us*, I admit, but a gaggle of mothers and orphans too. You've read about those mothers and orphans. They really exist. And don't forget your ten thousand shares.

HANS. Or your fifty thousand.

STANLEY. If I'm deprived of my fifty thousand shares, I'll quit, and your downtrodden friend Mr. Griggs will have to replace me. If he botches the job, the business will sink, the workers will be laid off, and a new Freddy Griggs will be cold. If he doesn't botch the job, the fifty thousand shares will go to him — they'll call it something else, of course — and we'll be back where we started, only with new personnel. *(A siren sounds)* Here goes again. Come on, Hans, maybe today the bombs will do the job for you. Ultra Textiles will be blown to the skies and justice will have been done.

HANS. By the unjust.

STANLEY. To do justice requires force. Force is violent. Violence is unjust. Hence it is unjust to do justice. As all revolutions prove.

HANS. Aren't we taking shelter?

STANLEY. Only if you want to. But as a man with a certain responsibility, I like to set an example. Besides, who'd want to blow up a textile plant? First come the refineries. *(The siren has stopped)*

HANS. And I don't care whether I'm alive or dead.

STANLEY. Oh come on now! Even your Mr. Griggs wants to live.

HANS. Why couldn't you have extended credit to Mr. Wikkle, so he wouldn't have had to raise his prices?

STANLEY. I *told* you.

HANS. I know, I know. But I'm not an economist, I'm a man who suffers. The strike, wages, lost output, the government —

STANLEY. Let's try again. We're hit by a strike, the payroll shoots up ten percent, retroactive to sixty days ago. Last month our army lost Gorizia when it was supposed to hold it till the morning after doomsday. Now we suddenly have to go overseas for our raw wool, at three times the cost, provided the ships aren't sunk to the bottom. Meantime we're contracted to the government —

HANS. I know. At prices set half a year ago —

STANLEY. In the merry merry springtime.

HANS. Give up your salaries! You, the directors, the vice-presidents!

STANLEY. A drop in the bucket. No, my lad, nothing can save us. Grim reaper besets large textile firm. Two plants must be shut down, fifteen hundred workers sent home to their famished infants. Is that what you want?

HANS. No.

STANLEY. One alternative remains. We duck under the tidal wave by collecting on all outstanding debts without playing favorites; which seems fair enough.

HANS. And a boy who can't afford ten dollars for a sweater pays ten dollars for a sweater.

(Explosions in the distance)

STANLEY. Why blame us? Blame the war. Prices are going up like kites in spring. If it weren't for the silly war, that sweater would still be costing six dollars.

HANS. I must find where the chain begins.

(The buzzer sounds)

STANLEY. Yes? Oh fine. Splendid. Thanks for telling me, Miss Durville. (To Hans) Our workers refuse to take refuge in the shelters. They are staying at their benches.

(More explosions)

HANS. Is General Culpepper still in town?

STANLEY. No. I was on the plane with him about a week ago. He told me he was leaving for the front almost immediately. If he could find it.

HANS. I'll go look for him.

STANLEY. Why?

HANS. There is poison. There's a fang that delivers the poison. There's a head that holds the fang. I must find it. And when I find it — (He slams the desk with his fist)

(More explosions)

SCENE FOUR

(The front. The artillery is going full blast. In a protected position, General Culpepper is entertaining Senators Floogle and Sallow. Corporal Bletterman is pouring coffee)

CULPEPPER. I always take my Rosenthal set to the front. It gives me a feeling of continuity and reminds me of my wife.

FLOOGLE. It's quite a thrill for us to be at the front, General Culpepper. Your men are performing miracles of valor.

SALLOW. What are you shelling just now, general?

CULPEPPER. Everything in sight.

(A shell burst almost knocks the cup out of Sallow's hand)

SALLOW. Oops!

CULPEPPER. This is not the Senate floor, my friends. You've got to expect a few rough moments. Sand flying in your eyes.

FLOOGLE. I should hope so.

CULPEPPER. Especially with the enemy coming on as strong as he is.

SALLOW. Death on every side.

CULPEPPER. Or flight. Let's be realistic, off-the-record, eh?

FLOOGLE. That famous sense of humor! However, when you say "flight" you happen to remind me of the question some of us in the Senate have been wanting to raise with you.

SALLOW. Same here.

CULPEPPER. Before you go on — Corporal Bletterman!

CORPORAL. Yes, sir.

CULPEPPER. Tell Lieutenant Williams to silence Battery A for half an hour, will you?

CORPORAL. Yes, sir.

FLOOGLE. That's mighty considerate of you, general.

CULPEPPER. Well, it's hard to carry on a conversation.

CORPORAL. What about the soldiers' deputation, sir? Should I tell the men that you can see them now?

CULPEPPER. How long have they been waiting?

CORPORAL. A couple of hours, sir.

CULPEPPER. And how many are they?

CORPORAL. Three, sir.

CULPEPPER. Tell them from me that's six man-hours lost to the army. They could have been stacking shells instead of sitting on their asses. That's all, Corporal. I'm busy with the senators.

CORPORAL. Yes, sir.

CULPEPPER. On the other hand, the moment Mr. Gropius arrives, have him join us and bring some fresh coffee. Make sure it's piping hot.

CORPORAL. Yes, sir. *(He leaves)*

SALLOW. Is that Hans Gropius you're expecting?

CULPEPPER. Yes. His dad and me were army buddies.

FLOOGLE. That was one of the best men we ever had in the Senate. A warm friend to commerce and industry.

CULPEPPER. Well disposed to the army too. It was his vote for the S-4 tank that carried the appropriation, when was it, two years ago, just before he passed on.

FLOOGLE. Don't you think, general — and by the way, I've been talking — informally, of course — with General Stillitoe and General Bancroft —

CULPEPPER. I respect their opinions.

FLOOGLE. They seem to feel that front-line reports have become a shade too optimistic recently.

CULPEPPER. Say, that's interesting.

FLOOGLE. I don't know if you've been keeping an eye on the legislature.

CULPEPPER. I'm pretty busy here, you know. Every day another retreat. The layman thinks that in a retreat you just pack up and leave. But the fact is that retreats take a lot of brainwork on the part of commanding officers. On top of that, the men are griping and whining like a flock of bloody Girl Scouts. Excuse me. You were saying.

FLOOGLE. Only that last Thursday Senator McAllister stood up on the Senate floor with a bulletin issued from this very sector.

CULPEPPER. He did, did he?

FLOOGLE. And he said — I don't recall his exact words — but he said, in effect, that on the basis of your reports we might as well slow down on the TSF-111 program.

CULPEPPER. Oh?

FLOOGLE. It was your opinion, apparently, that under present conditions the artillery was better able to cope with the enemy than the Air Force.

CULPEPPER. Did I really say that? Son of a gun! Well, what was the reaction?

FLOOGLE. I raised the question that since we're being forced to retreat, what was meant by "coping with the enemy"?

CULPEPPER. You've got a valid point there, Senator Floogle. But on the other hand, for us military men coping may mean clobbering the enemy, coping may mean standing still, or coping may mean retreating a little. It depends on the overall strategy.

SALLOW. Overall strategy — that's the key to the problem.

FLOOGLE. But the nub of the matter is that we're retreating. Are we or aren't we, General? I'm asking as a friend.

CULPEPPER. As a friend, I already told you, we are retreating.

FLOOGLE. So I pointed out in the Senate. I suggested that what we needed was more TSF-111's, not less.

CULPEPPER. Good idea. I'm all in favor. How did they react to you, Senator?

FLOOGLE. Hard to judge. But it didn't help — I'm being frank with you, General — as open as a child — you don't mind, do you?

CULPEPPER. Mind? I appreciate it, believe me.

FLOOGLE. Because I'm under heavy pressure in my constituency. A lot of fine people out there are interested in the TSF-111. Billions are at stake. And I don't get elected to flush billions down the drain, if you know what I mean.

CULPEPPER. Sure.

FLOOGLE. So that when you report that the TSF's are being shot down at a "dramatic" rate over enemy lines —

CULPEPPER. I see what you mean, Senator, but you're doing me an injustice.

FLOOGLE *(apologetic)*. Oh!

CULPEPPER. Frankly, I thought to myself, "If I report how many TSF's are lost every day, what the hell, they'll have to step up production to replace 'em and Floogle will be happy." But I guess that was a booboo.

FLOOGLE. I appreciate the idea, even if it miscarried. The Senate is volatile.

SALLOW. And meantime there's an election coming up.

CULPEPPER. I'd forgotten about that. Thank God, we don't go in for elections in the Army. Corporal Bletterman!

(Enter Corporal Bletterman)

CORPORAL. Yes, sir.

CULPEPPER. Tell Lieutenant Watkins to silence Battery B, will you? It's so noisy here, a man can't think constructively.

CORPORAL. Yes, sir. What about the soldiers' deputation, sir?

CULPEPPER. Can't you see I'm still busy? Clear out.

CORPORAL. Yes, sir. *(He leaves)*

CULPEPPER. Sassier every day.

SALLOW. What do they want, General?

CULPEPPER. Who knows? Maybe they want elections too!

SALLOW and FLOOGLE. Ha, ha, ha.

CULPEPPER. Or their coffee in Rosenthal cups. Anyway, to get back — oh yes, those bulletins of mine. I guess I'd better rethink them. How are Stillitoe and Bancroft handling the problem?

FLOOGLE *(producing some papers)*. Here.

CULPEPPER *(reading)*. True, true. Five to one aircraft kill ratio in air-to-air combat . . . Gun systems to be optimized by next spring . . . Obsolescence of the XQ-12 . . . Oh? The XQ-12 is obsolescent?

FLOOGLE. Unquestionably. Read what it says about its low muzzle velocity, or the trouble at long slant ranges.

CULPEPPER. Well, well. They ought to know. I'm glad you brought this down with you, Senator. I guess I ought to tone down these reports of mine a bit.

FLOOGLE. A little less brisk, in the national interest.

CULPEPPER. Maybe I've been overrating the artillery. Corporal Bletterman!

(Corporal Bletterman enters)

CORPORAL. Yes, sir.

CULPEPPER. Pour the senators some more coffee and tell Lieutenant Vogel to give Battery C a rest.

CORPORAL. Yes, sir. *(He opens his mouth again)*

CULPEPPER. Tell 'em to wait!

CORPORAL. Yes, sir. *(He leaves)*

CULPEPPER. Might as well economize a bit. I've been firing so long, I think I've permanently lowered the land level a foot or two. Considering it's our own land . . . Anyway, now we can really talk.

SALLOW. Actually it's an idyllic day.

CULPEPPER. What's left of the landscape is at its best this time of year. I want you to use my binoculars, Senator Sallow, and look at that patch of goldenrod — there — over to the left, where the burned-out oak trees are.

SALLOW. Beautiful. As soon as they rebuild those farmhouses it will look like a picture postcard again.

FLOOGLE. Is your aunt Ursula still active in the Nature Club, General Culpepper?

CULPEPPER. Active? She *is* the Nature Club, Senator!

FLOOGLE. That's wonderful.

SALLOW. Just wonderful.

FLOOGLE. When I think of what she's done to keep our country beautiful, the times she's gone to jail for tearing billboards down —

CULPEPPER. She's beautified the jails too.

FLOOGLE. And so many indifferent people, so much inertia to overcome, so much downright cynicism, not to mention the scarcity of funds.

CULPEPPER. Who wants to support nature clubs nowadays?

FLOOGLE. Some of us want to, General, and some of us do.

CULPEPPER. Everybody knows you're a giver, Senator Floogle.

FLOOGLE. I'd like to prove it now, General. Maybe this isn't the ideal time or place for a donation to the Nature Club —

CULPEPPER. Oh, I don't know.

FLOOGLE. Then you wouldn't actually object if I asked you to remit a small sum to your aunt? A personal heartfelt contribution. We all know the club is non-political.

CULPEPPER. I don't see why Aunt Ursula would object.

FLOOGLE. What's *your* opinion, Senator?

SALLOW. Who wouldn't want to support our wonderful goldenrod?

FLOOGLE. I won't bother you with a check here at the front, General.

CULPEPPER. It's not exactly the place to open an account, is it?

FLOOGLE. Ha, ha, ha. That unfailing sense of humor! (*He gives Culpepper a pile of bills, which the General promptly places in a briefcase*) You'll give Miss Ursula my very personal and confidential regards.

CULPEPPER. Leave it to me. She'll be delighted, the dear old body.

SALLOW. Do you hear that cuckoo in the distance? As I look at these beautiful fields, I can't help thinking how good it would be if our country were at peace again.

CULPEPPER. Sure. But now that the Istrians have crossed the river —

SALLOW. Granted, granted. But couldn't we look at the bright side of that crossing?

CULPEPPER. What would it be?

SALLOW. Enemy advances. Country worries. The young demonstrate in the streets. Shortages. Casualties. High prices. Why not seek an understanding with Istria? Why not find a formula? Before you know it, a peaceful settlement could be achieved, the enemy would go home, and the farmer would be happy again.

CULPEPPER. Oh yes, the farmer.

FLOOGLE. You don't want to forget, General, that Senator Sallow feels for the farmer.

SALLOW. And the farmer is dejected, General.

CULPEPPER. Why? Doesn't the Army eat bread?

SALLOW. It does. But what about farm machinery? Four times or five times what it cost a year ago. Replacement parts can't be found for love or money. And I won't even mention chemical fertilizers.

CULPEPPER. You mean you can't fertilize our fields with our native dung?

SALLOW (smiling). General Culpepper! Chemicals! Dung is passé.

FLOOGLE. And the chemicals come out of Finland.

SALLOW. From which we are cut off.

CULPEPPER. What can I do about it? I've just promised Floogle here to request more TSF-111's. And I'm a man of my word, Senator.

FLOOGLE. With a formula there's always a way out.

SALLOW. Suppose your reports — suppose you said in your reports — that the situation is alarming; we ought to look for a settlement; but on the other hand we must negotiate from strength, the national honor demands it.

CULPEPPER. I get it.

SALLOW. Because, between ourselves — this is strictly classified, General —

CULPEPPER. Go on!

SALLOW. You tell him, Floogle.

FLOOGLE. Sallow and I have been adding up the figures of your weekly reports of enemy casualties. We do it in my office, curtains drawn, after the secretaries have gone home. You've wiped out 112% of the enemy male population, Culpepper, and the war isn't even a year old.

CULPEPPER. It must be my inborn optimism. I get carried away.

SALLOW. That's it. If you could shade the picture a little. Emphasize our losses, release a few gory photographs, and suggest to the President that we might come to terms with Istria —

FLOOGLE. Always from a position of strength.

CULPEPPER. Plenty of planes on one side.

SALLOW. And peace on the other.

FLOOGLE. You see, life can be perfect.

CULPEPPER. I'm thinking of Aunt Ursula too. That dear old heart of hers is longing for peace.

SALLOW. A great womanly figure. Of course, we farmers can't compete with the industrial interests —

CULPEPPER. Nobody could expect you to.

SALLOW. But if Miss Ursula wouldn't snub a modest —

CULPEPPER. Snub? Aunt Ursula? She wouldn't snub a fly off the honey pot!

SALLOW (taking out a bundle). Still, I apologize —

CULPEPPER (snatching the bundle and inserting it in the briefcase). Nonsense. Don't say another word. My only concern, gentlemen, is over what I can personally accomplish.

FLOOGLE. Oh, of course, Stillitoe and Bancroft will support you; and others; there are many patriotic voices, though yours is one of the most important.

CULPEPPER. Corporal Bletterman! (Enter the corporal) You might tell Vogel, Watkins and Williams to resume shelling at 16:04. And clear the table, will you?

CORPORAL. Yes, sir. Mr. Gropius arrived a few minutes ago. Shall I tell him to wait till the deputation has met with you, sir?

CULPEPPER. You'll do no such thing. Tell Gropius to join us here. And let the shelling go till 17:04.

CORPORAL. Yes, sir. (He leaves)

FLOOGLE. What does young Gropius want, General?

CULPEPPER. I don't rightly know.

(Enter Hans, carrying a tattered sweater)

HANS. Peace, General, peace. I want peace. The country wants peace.

CULPEPPER. Hans! You look like some kind of apparition! You're not sick, are you, boy? Peace is exactly what we've been talking about here. Hans Gropius. Senators Floogle and Sallow. Inspecting the front lines.

FLOOGLE. We both knew your father well, Gropius. A genuine patriot.

SALLOW. A friend to the farmer.

CULPEPPER. What brings you down here, my boy? Are you trying to enlist? And what are you doing with that frazzled sweater?

HANS. This is a bribe for you.

ALL THREE. A bribe!

HANS. Take it, and in exchange for it — you're an influential man, Culpepper — I want you to tell the civilians to make peace, so we can begin from the beginning, down to zero, you understand, down to zero and then up again, but something decent this time, food and shelter for every human being.

CULPEPPER. What's he saying? Hans, you're not well. I ought to call our medic. I don't want your sweater. What's it all about?

HANS. I found it in the last village coming here. A dead boy was holding it lying in a shell-hole in the street. I've brought it to you. The clues have led me here. This is where it begins. You three. I know you. The gravediggers.

FLOOGLE. Mr. Gropius!

HANS. Where you go, ruin follows with happy fangs.

CULPEPPER. Give me that sweater. Bletterman!

(Enter the corporal)

CULPEPPER. Throw that thing away.

CORPORAL. Yes, sir. *(He leaves)*

HANS. Throw it away, Culpepper, but we demand peace. I am here to cry out against abomination.

SALLOW. Mr. Gropius, I happen to be here on the same mission as yours. These gentlemen will bear witness.

HANS. Who are you?

SALLOW. I speak for the farmers. The farmers want peace too.

HANS. You tell me. Isn't there enough and plenty on this earth? Enough and plenty of meat, enough bread, enough fruit for every man, woman and child? Basically?

SALLOW. Basically, yes. Science —

HANS. And enough and plenty for a roof over mankind? And enough for a sweater when a child is cold? And medicines when a man is sick? Basically?

SALLOW. Sure. Science —

HANS. Then why are they cold? sick? hungry? Somebody is guilty! And it's you, Culpepper, you! I have found you.

CULPEPPER. Hey! My uniform! Easy!

HANS. Silence the artillery!

CULPEPPER. I did!

HANS. Ground the planes! Send the men home! Bury the guns!

CULPEPPER. Hans, remember where you are! This isn't a college campus! I'm conducting a serious war here. Grow up, kid. I thought you wanted some favor or other. Always ready to oblige in memory of your dad. But I've got no time for games.

FLOOGLE. You seem to be forgetting that the Istrians attacked *us*, my boy.

SALLOW. That's right, I'd forgotten. An unprovoked attack.

FLOOGLE. They've occupied 35 percent of our land.

CULPEPPER. And that was yesterday, God damn it. Was it my fault they started a war? I was headed for retirement, God blast it, and then bang they dropped a load of bombs on Taipana when nobody was looking, killed two hundred people —

FLOOGLE. And ruined the goddam Gothic cathedral, Byzantine mosaics and all.

HANS. But you're making money in it! All of you!

SALLOW. Not me.

HANS. You too. I smell money around here. Victory or defeat, it's all the same. Deals. Profits.

CULPEPPER (*hand on briefcase*). What about yourself?

HANS (*producing a bundle of papers*). Ten thousand shares of Ultra Textiles. Here. Here. Here. (*Tears them up. Exclamations*)

CULPEPPER. The boy's gone blotto. Bletterman! Corporal Bletterman! (*Enter the corporal*)

HANS. I'm sane! That's why I'm crazy! Stop the war!

CULPEPPER (*bellowing*). We're losing it! We're running! Tell Istria to stop the war! They started it! Go to the bloody Istrians!

HANS (*beside himself*). I will! (*He starts to climb over the earthworks*) Somebody is guilty!

CULPEPPER. Stop him, Corporal, he'll get killed!

HANS. I don't care! Hands off!

BLETTERMAN. I can't, sir.

(*Bullets whizz and Hans is out of sight*)

CULPEPPER. Stop, you fool! Listen! Gropius! Turn back! If we hadn't torn their guts out with the Treaty of Klagenfurt twenty-five years ago — do you hear me? — they wouldn't have started this war! You know it as well as I do! It's not their fault either! (*Hans reappears*) Sit down, Hans, you're overwrought. Have a cigarette.

HANS. Thanks. Give me a glass of water, somebody. (*He swallows three aspirins*)

FLOOGLE. We'll take him away with us, General.

SALLOW. Maybe a cup of coffee . . .

HANS. Let me go. (*He tries to get up, but falters*) I'll sit down five minutes. Go ahead. I interrupted your deals. Go on with the war. Make money.

CULPEPPER (*aside to Hans*). Not in front of the Corporal, Hans, after I saved your life. Bletterman, why don't you tell that deputation I'll see them now.

CORPORAL. Yes, sir. (*He leaves*)

FLOOGLE. We ought to be on our way, General.

CULPEPPER. Don't hurry. (*Aside to them*) A couple of witnesses might come in handy.

(*Enter the three privates, accompanied by Corporal Bletterman. They salute and stand at attention. All three are armed*)

CULPEPPER. At ease, men. Glad to see you, and always ready to hear any legitimate complaints in my division. Bletterman, take down the proceedings. First your names.

FIRST PRIVATE. Dupont.

SECOND PRIVATE. Griggs.

HANS. Griggs?

GRIGGS. Yes, sir.

HANS. You're not related to Theobald Griggs, are you?

GRIGGS (surprised). Yes, sir. He's my cousin. How would you know the likes of him, sir? He's a loser if there ever was one.

HANS. My name is Gropius. Hans Gropius.

GRIGGS. Oh, Mr. Gropius. I should have known. The way they carry on about you, you're the raft in a shipwreck to them. (He shakes Hans' hand)

HANS (moved). Thank you, thank you.

CULPEPPER. All right, Griggs.

CORPORAL (to the third man). Your name?

THIRD PRIVATE. Stein.

CULPEPPER. Okay, Griggs, Stein and Dupont. On with it. The shelling resumes at 17:04.

DUPONT. Sir, we've been elected by the men to petition you. Military Code, Article 68, paragraph C.

CULPEPPER. Okay. Go on.

DUPONT. Number one, sir, considering as it's almost winter, the men would like to be issued winter boots. (He shows one of his heels) You see what happens to these, sir. They're not made for this here climate where it's wet most of the time. The men are suffering real bad and morale is low.

CULPEPPER. Have you got that, Bletterman?

CORPORAL. Yes, sir. Shall I say he showed his heel?

CULPEPPER. Sure, it's the evidence. Number two.

DUPONT. Number two is the food, sir.

CULPEPPER. I thought so.

DUPONT. The officers —

CULPEPPER. Leave the officers alone! If the officers eat steak, that's their lookout. What's the point of being an officer if you can't eat steak?

STEIN. But it doesn't seem fair —

CULPEPPER. You're not in the Boy Scouts, Private Stein.

GRIGGS. Well, sir, the men are sick of dry biscuits, that's all. You can't fight forever on dry biscuits.

CULPEPPER. What about the beans?

GRIGGS. Dry biscuits and beans. There's a lot of dysentery too because the water is dirty.

CULPEPPER. So you don't like the food! You're unhappy because the Ritz doesn't operate a restaurant at the front! You ought to blush your three heads off. And in front of the senators. Every word you say is going to be repeated on the Senate floor. With your names attached. To tell you the truth, Griggs, I thought you men were going to petition for more ammunition. Now *that's* a grievance I sympathize with. The supply convoys have been slow and unreliable. And it wouldn't have surprised me if this had caused a raised eyebrow or two in the ranks. Instead you come to me chattering about boots and biscuits like we were sent here for a Sunday picnic. But I'm willing to listen. I'm not like some others who'd have you up for mutiny the moment you let out a squawk. I don't even *use* the word mutiny. Did you hear me say mutiny? Not General Culpepper! All right then, let's get on with number three.

DUPONT. Well, sir, last week Captain Baxter took out a patrol at night, and then he decided on his own to take a look at an Istrian gun emplacement at close quarters.

CULPEPPER. Yes, I know the story; only two men came back. Tough, but didn't the captain get killed too? You can't say he didn't do his bit. What's your point?

DUPONT. The men feel that they should vote on missions.

(Culpepper looks speechlessly at the senators and Hans)

GRIGGS. Not emergency missions, sir; but routine missions.

CULPEPPER. You're insane. Everybody's going berserk today! Bletterman, did you take that down? Vote? You've got the cheek to stand here and use the word "vote" before an Army man?

STEIN. It's our lives.

CULPEPPER. What else? Don't stop now! Abolish ranks? Elect your officers? Stop saluting?

DUPONT. Yes, sir.

(Culpepper nearly suffocates)

CULPEPPER. They're under arrest! Call the MP's! Five years in the stockade!

DUPONT *(yelling)*. We're through with this war!

(Hans rises excitedly; but at that moment a captain comes running)

CAPTAIN. The Istrians are all over the place! Who's the moron who stopped the guns? They took advantage of the lull, they're over-running our positions!

(Shooting is heard)

FLOOGLE. Where do we go?

CULPEPPER. Everybody stop! I'm in command!

SALLOW. What do we do?

STEIN. Raise the blue flag! Stop the war!

DUPONT. Nobody's fighting!

GRIGGS. Alert the 7th and the 13th! On the telephones!

CAPTAIN *(to Culpepper)*. Stop them, for God's sake! *(Aside)* It's the subversives, I know them, make concessions, you numbskull, it's only words.

VOICES OFF STAGE. Fire! Fire!

CAPTAIN *(towards the wings).* Don't give an inch! General Culpepper is taking personal command!

(The three privates are in a corner consulting)

VOICES OFF STAGE. Raise the blue flag! Fraternize!

HANS. Nobody's fighting! Griggs! Take charge!

CULPEPPER. Men! Your demands are granted! No more saluting! Election of officers! I'll sign! Winter boots! Steaks! Now go back there and fight!

DUPONT. Like hell. *(The three privates point their weapons at all present. The corporal follows suit)*

CULPEPPER. You too, Bletterman!

CORPORAL. Hands in the air, all of you. *(He catches hold of the captain and pins him down. Culpepper has whipped out his pistol)*

CAPTAIN *(to Culpepper).* Shoot, you cretin!

CULPEPPER. I'm a general, I don't know how to shoot. *(He throws the pistol to the ground)*

DUPONT. I'll go spread the word. Don't let the pigs escape.

STEIN. Get Jones in the 7th and Stevens in the 13th!

DUPONT. I know what to do. *(He leaves)*

VOICES OFF STAGE. Hold your fire!

HANS *(hands in the air).* Hold your fire! Raise the blue flag! Hallelujah!

CULPEPPER. Traitor, you bastard of a traitor! And I saved his life!

GRIGGS. He's one of us, fellas.

CORPORAL. I know. Pick up that pistol, Mr. Gropius, and join the gang. *(Hans does so)* The rest of you don't move.

HANS *(embracing Griggs and Stein).* I'm one of you. We'll start from zero.

(While the men embrace, Culpepper, Floogle and Sallow dash away)

CULPEPPER. Run! Run!

CORPORAL *(who is holding on to the captain).* Get them!

(General outcry ad libitum. The captain tries to free himself, and Bletterman knocks him down. Stein and Griggs start shooting. The two senators escape. But Culpepper has made a small detour to pick up his briefcase, and as a result Hans brings him down with a single shot. Roar of satisfaction)

STEIN. Culpepper is down!

CULPEPPER. Bastard! *(He dies)*

GRIGGS. Culpepper is dead!

CORPORAL. Long live the revolution! Summon the Soldiers' Council!

STEIN. Raise the blue flag! Culpepper is dead! The war is over!

(Bletterman and Stein leave)

(Griggs is disarming the captain, who is lying unconscious on the ground. Now he examines Culpepper's body)

GRIGGS. Cripes, that was a clean kill, Mr. Gropius. Cover the captain till I come back, will you? You're going to be needed here. *(He leaves)*

(Hans opens the briefcase and sees the money. He drops all the bills over Culpepper like a shower of leaves. The captain groans. Hans helps him)

CAPTAIN. Thanks. Oh my head. What happened? *(He sees the body)* Jesus! Who shot the general?

HANS. I did.

CAPTAIN. Jesus Christ! *(He kneels beside the body, clears the paper money from it, puts his head to Culpepper's chest)* He's gone all right. Killing out of uniform is murder, my friend. What are you after? His money?

HANS. Fool. I shot him for mankind.

CAPTAIN. *(stupefied, looks up into Hans' face)*. For who?

HANS *(shouts)*. For mankind!

CAPTAIN *(as one who sees the light)*. Oh. That's different. *(He leaves)*

HANS *(still shouting)*. Nobody can blame me!

SCENE FIVE

(Same as Scene One. But this time it is Mr. Wikkle who is lying on the cot and coughing, while Martha darns a sock)

MARTHA. Don't be bitter, dear. What's the use? A revolution is bound to be nice for *some* people.

WIKKLE. But this is too much — the Griggs Brothers, Haberdashers for the New Society! *(Laughs bitterly)* In neon!

MARTHA. I wish you'd never gone to look.

WIKKLE. Never gone to look! After two years in jail, and my lungs in shreds, God knows how much longer I've got —

MARTHA. Don't say such things.

WIKKLE. And working in the sewers, me, at my age *(he coughs)* — I'm not long for this filthy earth. So I went on a pilgrimage. I wasn't going to miss it. The Griggs Brothers! And you never told me.

MARTHA. Take a little more tea, dear.

WIKKLE *(violently)*. I hate tea! I want my coffee!

MARTHA. There isn't any, love. Since the last war scare it's been ever so scarce and expensive. Please drink a little more tea, do it for my sake.

WIKKLE *(drinking)*. Ha, ha, ha, Haberdashers for the New Society!

MARTHA. Hush! Don't take it to heart. Hush baby, go to sleep now.

(She sings softly)

WIKKLE *(relaxing)*. Why don't you read to me again?

MARTHA. I will. What would you like me to read?

WIKKLE. The book Mrs. Appelbaum lent you. I like it.

MARTHA. I'll begin where I left off last time, all right?

WIKKLE. All right.

MARTHA *(she has a little trouble with the French and the hard words)*. "Don't overlook the restaurant La Tour d'Argent, where a most particular kind of duck is served, called Pressed Duck. The duck is squeezed until it quacks Uncle —"

WIKKLE. Ha, ha, ha! That's good.

MARTHA. "And cooked before your eyes in a super-rich sauce flavored mainly with its own blood — a grand manner, if you have the stomach that can take dissection, dismemberment, and hearty squeezing by a heavy Iron Maiden."

WIKKLE. What's an Iron Maiden?

MARTHA. I don't know, dear.

WIKKLE. Turn my pillow around, would you? There's a rip on this side.

MARTHA. All right like that?

WIKKLE. Ah-hah.

MARTHA. "You may not like duck; you may detest duck; but if you visit Paris and fail to try the pressed duck at the Tour d'Argent, for the rest of your life, I warn you, you will have to explain to friends who will infallibly ask you if you have tasted pressed duck at the Tour d'Argent." Oh dear. Are you awake?

WIKKLE. Mmmm . . .

(Martha sees that Wikkle has fallen asleep. She takes the teacup away to wash in the sink. The doorbell rings. She opens)

MARTHA. Oh, Senator Gropius! How nice!

(Enter Hans, carrying a bag of groceries. His right hand is bandaged)

HANS. Hello, Mrs. Wikkle. It's a fine day.

MARTHA. Yes, isn't it? The birds are all singing today. Let me take this from you.

HANS. I'll set it down on the table. Mr. Wikkle's asleep?

MARTHA. Yes, he dozed off. A can of pineapple chunks! Isn't that —

HANS. I thought I heard you say you liked pineapple.

MARTHA. You're an angel, senator. I don't know how we'd survive without you. *(She is removing the items from the bag)* Just when we were running out of sugar. And look at this! "Heavenly Chocolate Cookies." That's a treat.

HANS *(smiling)*. Since I'm an angel —

MARTHA. Never mind. You're not a hundred-percent angel, Mr. Gropius. In fact, you're even naughty.

HANS. What have I done?

MARTHA. You keep things from us.

HANS. I do? What have I kept from you?

MARTHA. That you're in the tourist guide!

HANS (uncomfortable). Oh, that.

MARTHA. Don't try to look modest, senator. Mrs. Appelbaum, our neighbor, came running in this morning waving the book in her hand and
shouting, "Your friend the senator is in the official tourist guide!"
And sure enough I put on my glasses and read it with my own eyes:
"On the twenty-eighth of every month at ten to five the right palm
of our hero Hans Gropius bleeds, as if in commemoration of the
glorious day of liberation." I was so excited, I didn't know what to
say. And to remember simple people like us and come here — where
it's not fit for you — and help us out — a celebrity! But it wasn't
nice to keep it from us, was it?

HANS. I'm sorry. It was unimportant.

MARTHA. Unimportant? To be an official hero?

HANS. How is Mr. Wikkle? I pay you a visit and you don't even tell me.

MARTHA. He's so-so. I think he's better. God wouldn't let him down now,
after two years in jail. But he never used to do much physical work,
poor thing, so now, digging in the sewers, at his age, it makes his
cough worse.

HANS. Here are some pills. They should help. What else can I bring to
help him? Please tell me.

MARTHA. Maybe — I don't know.

HANS. Tell me, Mrs. Wikkle.

MARTHA. Maybe you could bring him a sweater. It's cold in the sewers.

HANS. Of course. I'll bring you one the very next time.

WIKKLE (in his sleep). The Griggs Brothers!

HANS. What did he say?

MARTHA. Nothing.

HANS. I thought he said "the Griggs Brothers."

MARTHA. Well, what happened — when we took him from jail last week,
maybe you remember, I asked you to drive the long way around the
park.

HANS. I remember.

MARTHA. It was so as we wouldn't pass in front of our old store.

HANS. Oh, I didn't realize.

MARTHA. But today he took a walk that way after work, and he saw the
new sign. It bothers him a lot.

WIKKLE (waking). Is that you, senator?

HANS. Yes, it's me. You're looking much better today, Mr. Wikkle. In
another week you'll be used to the work, while I try to get you

something more suitable.

WIKKLE. You think so?

HANS. No doubt about it. Come on, let's have a cup of tea together.

WIKKLE. How's your hand, senator? Still —

HANS. Everything's fine. I'm very well. I brought you some pills for your cough.

WIKKLE. Thank you.

MARTHA. And groceries, all we need.

WIKKLE. Did you bring coffee by any chance?

MARTHA. You know the price is out of reach.

WIKKLE. Why is the price out of reach? It's not out of reach for everybody, is it?

MARTHA. I don't know. Everybody's poor in Friuli nowadays.

HANS. We've started from zero, Mr. Wikkle. We're building.

WIKKLE. If everybody's poor, how come I see limousines in the street when I poke my head out of the sewer?

MARTHA. Some of the poor have limousines, that's all.

WIKKLE. Then why can't I have my coffee? I want my three cups of coffee every day like I've always had them since the time I was eighteen years old! Somebody high up is making a fortune holding on to the coffee.

MARTHA. Hush, love, don't get yourself excited again.

WIKKLE. That's what the fella from Ultra Textiles in Cell 304 used to say: Somebody high up is making a fortune in jail uniforms! Say, senator, did I remember to give you regards from the Ultra Textiles gang?

HANS (uncomfortable). Yes, you did, thank you.

MARTHA. You've told the senator several times, dear.

WIKKLE. I guess I'm really getting old. Boy, when they heard that Senator Gropius was picking me up at the gate, they nearly died. Gropius? Hans Gropius? Kiss him on both cheeks for me, says one of 'em, I forget which.

MARTHA. Yes, dear, you told us.

HANS (low). I'll try to bring you a can of coffee next time, Mr. Wikkle.

WIKKLE. Will you, senator? It sounds silly, but after two years of drinking slop, you don't know how I long for it, it's as if it was the last thing I ever wanted on this filthy earth.

HANS (low). I'll get you some, I promise.

MARTHA. Why has it become so expensive, senator? Is it really the war? Mrs. Appelbaum next door and me were asking ourselves. And soap too. Not to mention clothes. Why? Whose fault is it?

HANS. Whose fault?

MARTHA. Who is to blame?

HANS. Who is to blame?

MARTHA. Yes.

(Hans stares at her)

HANS. You see, when God created the world —

WIKKLE *(sitting up)*. What did you say?

HANS. When God created the world —

WIKKLE. What's that got to do with the price of coffee?

HANS. When God created the world —

MARTHA. What's the matter, Mr. Gropius? You're crying!

HANS. I have such a headache . . .

THE END

The VIRGIN And The UNICORN

A Miraculous Drawing-Room Comedy

Characters

UMFREY, *Earl of Dumfrey*

ROBERT, *Baron Theefton*

MARGARET, *heiress of Wyngham, Brigsley, Tuckbetter and Glaswin Epton*

SIR RALF BASSET, *the earl's Master of the Revels*

CLOTILDA BENNYWORTH, *daughter of the earl's late chamberlain*

LEOFA, *the People's Delegate*

PETER, *a servant*

The action takes place in the Earl of Dumfrey's castle, under the reign of King Stephen the Merry.

SCENE ONE

(A large room, warmly and cheerfully furnished, in the ancestral home of the Earl of Dumfrey. A small balcony overlooks the grounds. The curtain rises on a tableau: Peter, the servant, is exhibiting a gored poodle to the Earl of Dumfrey, to Robert, Baron Theefton, and to the earl's Master of the Revels, Sir Ralf Basset, a somewhat older man. Far away is heard the strange trumpeting of an animal. It is the call of the unicorn.)

EARL *(appalled)*. Another one!

BARON. Very strange indeed. I must believe you now, my dear Umfrey. But do pull yourself together.

EARL. How can I? Wherever I turn, nothing but gored poodles, gored kittens, gored cows, horses, sheep, we even found a gored canary. God only knows how it happened. *(The trumpeting again)* Listen to the horrible beast.

SIR RALF *(gloomily)*. Two thousand gored chickens. Our farmers are being pauperized. Whose poodle is it this time, Peter?

PETER. Lady Ann's, Sir Ralf.

EARL. Oh no. My wife's best friend. Has she been told?

PETER. Indeed she has, my lord. Lady Ann is in bed under sedation.

EARL. Oh my God, my God. Take the horrible thing away.

BARON *(who has been examining the poodle)*. A clean penetration through the abdomen. A circular perforation of an inch and a quarter on one side of the poodle, and of something less than an inch on the other. This is no rapier thrust, Umfrey.

EARL. Robert —

SIR RALF *(to the baron)*. My lord, allow Peter to take the poodle away. His lordship cannot bear —

BARON. Oh, of course, of course.

(Sir Ralf motions Peter away)

EARL *(weakly)*. And bring us some refreshments, will you Peter?

PETER. Very good, my lord. *(He leaves with the poodle)*

EARL. So there it is. I'm deadly white from head to toe, my hands are chilly, I'll have grey hair before my time.

SIR RALF *(patting his hand)*. There, there, my lord. A cup of wine will restore you.

EARL *(still weakly)*. Good Sir Ralf. I'm beginning to understand it your way. And mark my words. If all men, bar none, had resembled you in this miserable earldom of mine, the unicorn would never have appeared to make life bitter to me.

BARON. What on earth do you mean, Umfrey? What has Sir Ralf got to do with the unicorn?

SIR RALF. Nothing, my lord.

EARL. No, tell him, let him understand it too.

SIR RALF. It's only a personal view.

EARL. When our common everyday wickedness rises, says Sir Ralf, when people become even less tolerable than they usually are, a kind of malevolence accumulates — like a pressure on the atmosphere — and then — it's happened before, you know — read the chronicles.

BARON. My friends, this animal has really gone too far if it has gored your brains as well.

EARL. You don't understand, Robert — lucky passer-by — you come and pay us a visit — jolly, dressed to kill, swimming in perfume, the song leaping from your lips like a kitten off a windowsill — you don't know the darkness of it all.

BARON. Nonsense. I'm still waiting to hear how this unpleasant unicorn is connected with good Sir Ralf Basset.

EARL. Good Sir Ralf — there's your answer. If we were all as good as he — don't you understand?

BARON. No, I don't.

SIR RALF. Perhaps later, my lord. I am deeply embarrassed.

EARL. Let the wicked be embarrassed, and in the highest places, not you! Wicked deeds, wicked thoughts — greed, ambition, lust, envy — all these gather and push — they become overmuch — no innocence is left except here and there *(taking Sir Ralf's arm)* — and suddenly the unicorn appears, someone sees his long thin horn peering into a farmyard, the alarm is sounded, mothers call their children indoors, everyone is afraid of the dark — and yet the unicorn never kills people, he kills their livelihood, their pets — like the poodle . . .

SIR RALF. He exists because there are people; perhaps that's why he spares us.

EARL. Who knows? But when he arrives, the world becomes unhinged. Wives murder their husbands. People refuse to pay taxes. Rain falls on Sir Ralf's fireworks. Merchants break contracts. I lose at chess. King Stephen asks for levies. Thank God, here's Peter again.

(Enter Peter with refreshments. He serves the earl and the baron)

EARL. Where is my wife, Peter?

PETER. Lady Margaret is in her Garden of Exotics, my lord, but she intends to call on Lady Ann as soon as Lady Ann wakes up. *(He pours water for Sir Ralf)*

BARON. Water for you, Sir Ralf? What sort of Master of the Revels are you employing, Umfrey?

EARL. Let him explain it himself.

SIR RALF. It's not that I'm not fond of wine, my lord; nor that I *am* fond of water. The truth is, I used to press the grape rather too freely, if anything.

EARL. Couldn't bear to see the wicked lot of us, that was why.

SIR RALF. Really, my lord! I simply swore to my poor wife on her deathbed to give it up. It's an old story, not worth telling.

BARON. Very touching, Sir Ralf. I adore principles! Well, Umfrey, let the two of us sinners drink to the downfall of the unicorn. One of your men is bound to catch him sooner or later, and you'll be nailing his horn over your mantelpiece before the month is out.

SIR RALF. A man can never catch the unicorn, my lord.

BARON. Nonsense. And if one man can't, a dozen will.

SIR RALF. Not a dozen, nor a thousand. Only a virgin can.

BARON. A what?

SIR RALF. A virgin. Carrying a mirror in her hand, and walking at random in field or forest. She prays to the Holy Mother of God, and perhaps the unicorn appears. If he does, she turns the mirror to him, his face is caught, and he cannot move away from his image. Then she walks backward, holding the mirror fast to the unicorn, and he follows in fascination. It is the purity of the glass and the virgin's purity he follows, and he follows wherever she goes until she leads him to the men who kill him. But all this happens only perhaps.

BARON. Only perhaps what? Why haven't you sent a battalion of virgins out, for God's sake?

EARL. Oh, the things he doesn't know!

SIR RALF. Only a virgin can catch the unicorn, my lord, but a virgin does not *necessarily* catch him. Do you see the difficulty? You send a girl out, mirror in hand. A girl with a reputation. But suppose she fails to catch the unicorn. Perhaps the time simply had not come. But perhaps on the other hand —

BARON. I see. *(A light comes)* I see!

SIR RALF. Now everybody wonders — is she, or isn't she? Father and mother lose their sleep, fingers are pointed, quarrels break out —

EARL. Besides, the world has gone so foul that half the girls in the realm would take offense if you asked them to go. Who wants to be an official virgin? They'd feel ruined if you asked them, and they'd be ruined if they came back empty-handed. You see, one way or the other —

SIR RALF. One daren't ask any girl — almost — *(The earl looks uncomfortable)*

BARON. I have an idea!

EARL. I'm sure we've tried it, Robert; he's *our* unicorn.

BARON. Don't you want to hear it?

EARL *(wearily)*. Of course we do.

BARON. Why not send out a girl ten years old? It's so simple, and so sublimely obvious, that it probably never occurred to any of you. A ten-year-old girl, carefully chosen, is sure to be immaculate, and would certainly not object to being thought so.

SIR RALF. I'm afraid —

EARL. Poor Robert, do you take the unicorn for a fool? A ten-year-old girl!

BARON. Or nine.

EARL. I'd laugh if I weren't on the edge of a breakdown. Leave me to my gloom. *(Half to himself)* My guilty gloom.

SIR RALF *(low)*. Your idea is astute, my lord —

BARON. But?

SIR RALF. Ten-year-old, or nine-year-old girls have no effect on a unicorn. For him, a virgin is a girl who might be no virgin if she chose. You see the point, my lord: there has to be merit in it. Otherwise it's like asking a cat not to bark.

BARON. I give up.

SIR RALF. Very often I am tempted to do as well. I am the saddest Master of the Revels in Christendom, my lord. The violins are out of tune. My clown stops mid-stage and falls to sobbing. The pheasants are either gored or overcooked. The plums shrivel on the branch. Our juggler lost his right hand while cutting wood. You've heard about my rained-out fireworks.

BARON. Perhaps I shouldn't have come.

EARL. Don't say that, Robert. You're my best friend, you know. We'll go hawking again together.

SIR RALF. My lord —

EARL. Oh God, I forgot, the hawks are gored. As for the foxes . . . I shouldn't have written you at all.

BARON. Tush. I wanted to help. Provide you with ideas. When you sent a message about the unicorn, and about Lady Margaret's favorite greyhound — remember, I have known Margaret forever: we grew up together — I dropped everything, I rushed here with hardly an attendant. I am at your service, Umfrey; the ancient oath, baron to earl, and all the rest.

EARL. Have another cup of wine, Robert.

(He sits down heavily in a chair. Loud boos are heard outside)

EARL and BARON. What's that?

SIR RALF. I'll go see. *(He leans out from a window)* Dear heavens!

EARL. What now? And do I have to know it?

SIR RALF *(reluctantly)*. It's Clotilda. *(The earl gets up as if stung, then doesn't know what to say. Sir Ralf explains to the baron)* The daughter of our late chamberlain.

BARON *(looking out the window)*. Why is that mob booing her? Somebody threw a lump of mud!

EARL. No . . .

BARON. Handsome girl! Look at her! Watch her walking absolutely *through* them! Magnificent! (*Shouting*) Rabble! Umfrey, do something! Wait — I think she's come in at the gate. I can't see her anymore.

SIR RALF. Yes, she has.

EARL. Is she safe? Where's the crowd now? What are they doing?

SIR RALF. They're dispersing, my lord.

BARON. You look petrified, Umfrey. Who was this, who is this, what is going on? I insist on being told.

EARL. I suppose she'll come up here.

(*Sir Ralf looks at the earl, who shrugs his shoulders*)

SIR RALF (*discreetly*). A very sad affair, my lord. Bennyworth, our chamberlain, clamored to have his daughter dispatched to find the unicorn. It was a point of honor for him. Perhaps ambition. And we dispatched her. Lord Dumfrey was most reluctant — most, most reluctant: he has such delicate feelings. He struggled, but to refuse outright was impossible — as bad as expressing an open and official doubt about the Bennyworth family. Well, she was dispatched, and she returned without. It means nothing, you understand, the Immaculate Virgin might have failed too, if I may so express it, but the people do not make fine discriminations — and even in better circles — in short, a few well-bred snickers killed our chamberlain. The mother, thank God, had been dead for years. (*To the earl, whose anguish is obvious*) My lord, calm yourself, I beg you. You are not even remotely to blame; on the contrary, everyone knows how generously, how persistently, you opposed poor Bennyworth.

BARON. It's obvious you did you best, old man. Come on, what's done is done. The storm will blow over; it's always the first —

(*Enter Clotilda Bennyworth. She glides in with a look of mournful reproach, and sits down on a stool in a corner. General silence. Then Sir Ralf rushes over to her and kisses her hand*)

SIR RALF. My poor dear child.

CLOTILDA. Always kind, Sir Ralf. There's a tear in your eye! You at least are a man I can count upon.

SIR RALF. Always, my dear; I consider you as my adopted daughter.

CLOTILDA. For everybody else I am a nuisance, or worse.

EARL (*softly*). Did anyone hurt you, Clotilda?

CLOTILDA. Since when does it matter?

SIR RALF. Shameful, shameful.

CLOTILDA. No one raised his voice to protect me —

BARON. It came and went so fast — I —

EARL. Oh, Robert, Baron Theefton, my oldest friend. Mistress Clotilda

Bennyworth, daughter of our late chamberlain.

BARON. Honored.

CLOTILDA. I am happy to meet you, my lord, I knew you had arrived.

BARON. And I have heard a great deal about you. Look on me, my dear lady, as a champion ready to defend your fair name against any dastardly imputations.

CLOTILDA. Thank you, my lord.

(Another clamor outside)

EARL. What now? What now?

(The baron and Sir Ralf rush to the balcony. Their backs are turned to Clotilda and the earl)

EARL *(who is standing near Clotilda, pathetically)*. Clotilda . . .

CLOTILDA *(fiercely)*. Kiss me.

SIR RALF *(leaning over the balcony)*. What happened? Leofa, Leofa, what happened? I'm holding you responsible!

(Meanwhile the earl, one eye to the balcony, embraces Clotilda with passion and reluctance)

CLOTILDA. Again. Villain! Again. Coward!

SIR RALF. Speak up down there!

(The earl jumps aside)

BARON *(turning about)*. Another killing!

EARL. Another one?

SIR RALF. I am afraid so. The man Leofa is coming up.

BARON *(joyously)*. And here comes my Lady Margaret.

EARL. I don't want to know what happened.

(Enter Leofa, a ruddy man of the people)

LEOFA. She done it again, and here she is, the vamp, and she done it again. Your lordships, I salute you with respeck.

BARON. Who is this oaf?

LEOFA. This oaf is sincerely yours, Leofa, the People's Delegate, and I ain't come to see your worship but the Earl of Dumfrey, head of the legally constitooted government of this here earldom.

EARL *(weakly)*. Well, I insist that you speak courteously to everybody in this room, and "everybody" means "everybody."

LEOFA. In that case and speaking courteously to everybody in this room, I announce that your lady's white foal, my lord, was gored till death ensued a half an hour ago, and standing for the people I say that if it wasn't for the unsavory likes of *her*, *(pointing to Clotilda)* still speaking courteously to everybody, we wouldn't have no bleeding unicorns running through the edibles of the land. The people has spoke.

EARL. The white foal is gored?

LEOFA. Yes, sir. Till death ensued.

CLOTILDA. Is that all you can think of, my lord, a stupid horse, while this baboon stands here insulting me?

EARL. I'm sorry . . .

LEOFA. "Baboon" is undemocratic.

BARON. I'll gladly have one of my footmen thrash him, madam. My position prevents me from doing it myself.

LEOFA. Excuse me, sir, but no stranger has the right to thrash the common people; that's the prevocative of his own dooly elected government.

SIR RALF. All right, Leofa, but you've gone too far this time. What on earth has Mistress Clotilda got to do with the unicorn? You know as well as I do that the unicorn appeared weeks before she — to make a long story short, one thing has nothing to do with the other. I have explained the logic of it a dozen times.

LEOFA. Nevertheless we the people has got a feeling that wickedness and wickedness goes hand in hand.

SIR RALF. What wickedness? For the life of me — use logic, man!

LEOFA. Logic is all right for them what can afford luxuries. The people has got feelings, and the feeling today is that it's time the land was purgated. We demand morality in high places. And there's some in our midst that mutter worse.

EARL. What do they mutter?

LEOFA. I'm not with 'em, mind you, I'm just reporting.

EARL (anxiously). Well, out with it.

LEOFA. Look at 'er smiling while the people manhandle her. Anybody but a witch would have a good cry and run for her life. That's what some of 'em are saying.

CLOTILDA. Will you tolerate this, my lord?

EARL. Certainly not.

BARON. Scandalous!

SIR RALF. This is too much.

LEOFA. I was only reporting, your lordships, and all inside the circle of respeck I owe to one and all.

BARON. The ruffian!

SIR RALF. Here's half a crown, Leofa. Now go away.

LEOFA. You're a sensible man, anyway, Sir Ralf. I meant no harm. Hoo, here's Lady Margaret now.

(Enter Lady Margaret)

LADY MARGARET. Simply incredible!

EARL. We've heard the news, my dear.

BARON. My dear Margaret, I was struck dumb. Your favorite foal. I feel as though a child of mine had been gored. I could weep.

LEOFA. Me too.

CLOTILDA. Please accept my condolences, Lady Margaret.

(Lady Margaret snubs her)

LADY MARGARET *(to the baron)*. Thank you, Lord Theefton. Peacefully at pasture she was, in the innocent blue of the day: then all of a sudden gored to oblivion. Is there a God, I ask you? As for Lady Ann, she has simply taken to her bed. What do you mean to do about it, Umfrey? The cup is overflowing at last.

EARL. I'll call another meeting of the privy council — an urgent session.

LADY MARGARET. I give up. *(She sees Leofa)* And why is this dreary low-life allowed in the house? Mud wherever he has set his boots.

LEOFA. Honest earth, madam.

SIR RALF. That's enough, Leofa. Out you go.

LEOFA. The people condole, madam, but they want a return to morality, and causes removed. Your lordships — *(He leaves)*

LADY MARGARET. Something to drink, if you please. I can't breathe.

(The baron rushes a refreshment to her)

SIR RALF. If only people were a little kinder. I speak in general.

CLOTILDA. If they were kinder to defenseless girls.

LADY MARGARET *(under her breath)*. Hah, this is too much! *(Aloud)* Umfrey, a person doesn't know where to turn anymore. Do you realize that I saw Princess born and that I could practically *talk* to her? It's as if the only creature who ever loved me had died.

EARL and BARON. Come now — really!

LADY MARGARET. Honest animal affection, without deceit, without secrets.

EARL. Still, you have your Garden of Exotics to distract you, my dear. *(He nudges the baron)*

LADY MARGARET. The simple love of an uncomplicated beast.

BARON. I've longed before everything to be allowed a peek at your famous garden, Lady Margaret. These violent plants, these poisonous flowers, these crawling grappling choking vines — what splendid moral lessons they teach us.

EARL. You really must show Robert your garden, my dear. It will take your mind off the tragic event. And the best time is now.

SIR RALF. A very good idea.

LADY MARGARET. Are you really interested?

BARON. Interested — interested —? Lady Margaret, a higher gratification mortal man could not endure.

LADY MARGARET. Very well. Yes . . . ! It *will* distract me a little.

EARL. And by tomorrow noon you will see measures taken. An iron fist —

LADY MARGARET. Yes, dear. Call your council again. Sir Ralf. Come with me, Lord Theefton. *(The two leave)*

(There is a moment of silence. Churchbells ring)

SIR RALF *(glancing out of a window)*. An extraordinary service of prayers against the curse of the unicorn. The good people huddling toward church.

CLOTILDA. The good people. I still shudder at the words I heard. They're ready to burn me as a witch.

SIR RALF. My dear Clotilda, no harm will come to you, believe me. The people are a little excited, of course. But I myself, with my lord's permission, stand between your innocence and the world. And I sincerely hope that Lord Dumfrey is your protector as well.

EARL. Of course, of course.

SIR RALF. My lord, I am going to speak frankly before Clotilda. I am disappointed in — how shall I put it? — in your inaction.

EARL. I am calling a meeting for —

SIR RALF. No, my lord, you know perfectly well that I am not talking about *that* inaction, but about your immobility with regard to my adopted Clotilda. (*The churchbells ring again*) She is being treated rudely — beyond toleration — by the common folk in the streets — and by other persons — of higher rank — in this very room, I'll make bold to say — but, be that as it may, I look in vain for a firmer stand on your part, a public declaration of your faith in the young lady's innocence. Listen to these bells, Lord Dumfrey. Think of your father who wore the cross under the gates of Jerusalem. Think of the founder of your line who baptized the savage Saxons. Think of our faith in you, and then call out to the people, "As you know my virtue and purity, thus shall you believe in hers!"

EARL. Why doesn't lightning strike me now?

SIR RALF. Strike *you*, my lord? Our beloved ruler?

EARL. Stop, stop . . .

SIR RALF. Have I said too much?

EARL. Too much, oh too much! I must speak . . .

CLOTILDA (*frightened*). Umfrey!

SIR RALF (*staring at Clotilda*). Umfrey?!

EARL. Sir Ralf — Clotilda — I warned you many times — it can't be hidden forever! My virtue, my purity! Daggers into my flesh! Sir Ralf: Clotilda and I — I and Clotilda — yes —

SIR RALF. No.

EARL. Thank God, I've told you, of all men. I feel better already, but the unicorn is my fault, I bear the guilt. I know I'm not the only transgressor in the land, but I am the ruler, in me it counts more heavily, what can I do? I am bewitched by the poor girl, I tremble when I see her — love and desire tear me to shreds, I wrong my wife, my innocent wife, but the perfection of her form —

CLOTILDA. Umfrey, this is too much!

EARL (*dragging Sir Ralf to one side*). The perfection of her geometry — madness — but you will see it — Clotilda, don't move! — look at her

— let your eye draw a line from the tip of her magnificent nose —
but what do I care for magnificent noses — or raven hair — or angelic
faces — or expressive hands — or surging breasts —

SIR RALF. My lord — let me go!

EARL. No, you'll stay to the end, I'm emptying my depravity into your
soul — (To Clotilda) Don't move! — Let your eyes draw two lines
from the tip of her nose to her two nipples, then join the two nipples
with another imaginary line, and what is the result?

SIR RALF. Lunacy!

EARL. A faultless triangle! A work of the gods! No, of the devils! Then
continue — join the nipples to the navel — another sublime triangle
— inverted now — and both together forming the masterful lozenge,
the perfect diamond. This in a woman — I become helpless — I see
and know no one else — perfect form made into pulsing flesh — oh
look at her, Sir Ralf, I know I am the most hellridden man of the
kingdom.

CLOTILDA (from the other side of the room). How long must I stand here
like a schoolgirl? Now Sir Ralf knows it all. I hope you're happy.
But what good it will do me I don't know.

SIR RALF. I wish I had died ignorant of this. I who loved and respected
you, my lord. Triangles!

CLOTILDA. Umfrey, really this is going too far. You might at least have
done it behind my back.

SIR RALF. I'm all muddled. My lord, you knew all the time — to put it
mildly — and yet when Bennyworth made his daughter look for the
unicorn, you relented and let her go.

EARL. I had to relent! Or I would have insulted the poor misguided man
beyond recovery. I didn't know then that people would hound her
to the stake with evil suspicions. (Resolutely) Sir Ralf, I have not
told you all this in a fit of weakness. I am going to fight the devil
within me. Tell us both what to do.

SIR RALF. Undo the injustices you have done. Kill the unicorn with justice.
But first, my lord, allow me speak alone with Clotilda.

EARL. By all means; an excellent first step. Clotilda, see that you obey
Sir Ralf, no matter what.

(He leaves. Sir Ralf looks for words)

SIR RALF. Clotilda, have you ever been to Paris?

CLOTILDA. No, Sir Ralf.

SIR RALF. Paris is an extremely remarkable city. Infinitely more diverting
for beautiful young women than our obscure earldom of Dumfrey.
We have heard of Paris, but has Paris heard of us?

CLOTILDA. I don't suppose it has.

SIR RALF. Now as Master of the Revels, I think I can promise you the most

comfortable conveyance to the French capital, and the richest entertainment upon your arrival. You will lodge with Comtesse du Joli-
mot, who is our blood relation there.

CLOTILDA. No.

SIR RALF. Why not? Hers is one of the finest houses in Paris.

CLOTILDA. No, I'm not going, good Sir Ralf.

SIR RALF. Dresses, servants, balls, opportunities for an advantageous
marriage, what more can a girl want? You are an orphan, my dear.

CLOTILDA. I am not leaving the earl.

SIR RALF. This touches me, Clotilda. A charming first love! It is something
I respect and even envy a little, being an old man. What a pity that
love is so often illicit and hate so seldom! You cannot love the earl,
my child, without wounding his wife.

CLOTILDA. His wife! It's a pleasure to wound her, it's my one consolation.

SIR RALF. Isn't she a little jealous of you? Even without knowing? These
are things our instincts feel, so to speak, before our minds are alerted.
But leave Lady Margaret aside. You are harming the earl, you are
harming yourself, and didn't your hidden deeds help bring the curse
of the unicorn on our heads? Because the earl is right. The sins of
the great weigh more heavily. Believe me, my child, you will love
again. It seems impossible to you now, you feel that all you possess
of love has gone irrevocably to his lordship, but you will be surprised,
I promise, one year, two years from now, when you discover that
a new power to love has replaced the old; the dry well has slowly
and imperceptibly replenished itself. Go, my child, leave us for two
months, try, and then we shall consider again what to do.

CLOTILDA. No, Sir Ralf, your words are very beautiful, but I am attached
to the earl; here I am, and here I stay. I have my reasons.

SIR RALF. Something I don't know? Are you — ?

CLOTILDA. No I am not.

SIR RALF. Anything else? This amazing passion —

CLOTILDA. Why amazing? I love the earl, I am all his, he is mad about me,
and I won't budge, I am going to make my way right here.

SIR RALF. Make your way?

CLOTILDA. I mean, love where I love.

SIR RALF. But suppose a terrible scandal breaks out?

CLOTILDA. I don't care.

SIR RALF. How can that be?

CLOTILDA. Please, Sir Ralf, are you pretending to be a child? The earl
loves me so tremendously, and I love him too with all my might,
isn't he bound to do something for me? Even if there's a scandal?
Especially if there's a scandal?

SIR RALF (groaning). Heavenly angels . . .

CLOTILDA. Now you'll go and misunderstand me again. I would die for the earl, I'd do anything for him, I'm sure I can never love anybody again, exactly as you said, but I'm an orphan, you made a very special point of that yourself. Who knows what would happen in Paris — the earl might forget me — no — I don't like to gamble.

SIR RALF. Whereas here you hold a trump in your hands.

CLOTILDA. Here I know the rules of the game.

SIR RALF. What are you hoping for?

CLOTILDA. As the earl's mistress —

SIR RALF. Brazen girl!

CLOTILDA. I don't care. I have my dreams. My mother lived in the attic. It was a well furnished attic but still it was an attic. I shall have my own manor. My children will bear titles.

SIR RALF. And what, young lady, if I report your cynical words to my master?

CLOTILDA. Oh Sir Ralf . . .

SIR RALF. Oh Sir Ralf isn't going to help you.

CLOTILDA. Yes he is. Lord Dumfrey knows that you want to separate me from him. When he sees my tears and hears from me how much I love him, how helpless I am against well-meant slander, he'll know that you can't be telling the truth. But if he does believe you —

SIR RALF. You'll threaten to make a public scene, you'll set the world on fire.

CLOTILDA. I didn't say it, Sir Ralf. But he stands to lose more than I. An orphan has to protect herself. Everybody hates me.

SIR RALF. An orphan! If your father had known! Poor Bennyworth!

CLOTILDA. His grandchildren will be great in the world.

SIR RALF. And poor Lady Margaret! I have heard too much today. Peter! What now?

(Enter Peter, holding a gored sheep in his hand)

PETER. The last sheep of the earl's last flock, Sir Ralf.

SIR RALF. I am no longer surprised.

SCENE TWO

(The hothouse: Lady Margaret's Garden of Exotics. Lady Margaret is guiding Lord Theefton)

LADY MARGARET (snipping a leaf off a flowering plant). It has the softest fur. There. (She rubs it against the baron's cheek)

BARON (ravished but nervous). Amazing. Yes. Again . . .

LADY MARGARET. Isn't it?

BARON. Yes. One hardly — it's altogether . . . What is the plant?

LADY MARGARET. The *Kalosperma gloriosum.*

BARON *(wiping his brow)*. Kalosperma . . . How do you do. *(He titters)*

LADY MARGARET. Observe its flower. These long supple filaments, reaching anxiously over the corolla.

BARON. What are they, Lady Margaret? I am full of scientific wonder.

LADY MARGARET. They are simply the stamens.

BARON. Oh yes.

LADY MARGARET. The male organs. The flower is a sexual animal, why deny it? Even we women learn to speak with erudite detachment, we name the parts, we observe the actions — well, perhaps we do feel a tiny shiver trespassing on our composure — but we no longer blush — that is the beauty of science.

BARON. Admirable . . . Science doesn't blush . . . *(He feels the stamens with his palm)*

LADY MARGARET. They tickle. *(He giggles)* Look close. *(She bends close to him over the flower)* Each filament bears its bud, swollen, distended with the male particles, the pollen, and waiting for a touch to break open, and to pour itself out.

BARON. Without blushing . . .

LADY MARGARET *(moving to another flower)*. And yet this one is even more fascinating. Really shameless. Look at this elongated pistil, erect in the calyx. For a flower!

BARON. Yes, for a flower — exactly — it's —

LADY MARGARET. We call it the *Priapisca vehemens.* But I'll surprise you, my lord. This is a female flower.

BARON. This? This . . . thing? Female?

LADY MARGARET. Nature is a brawl, a tumult, Lord Theefton. Expect anything. The pistil contains the flower's womb. Feel it. Do, my lord.

BARON. Almost —

LADY MARGARET. Like flesh. *(The baron wipes his brow)* When the plant is ready, when the time of longing comes upon it, the time of union, why not say the time of love —

BARON. Exactly — the scientific term.

LADY MARGARET. The pistil grows, it lifts itself stiffly and yearningly, it seeks and we might even say it calls for the pollen, namely through the perfume it secretes. There is no modesty, no hypocritical reticence here. Come to me, the flower cries. I want you to stroke the tip with your finger, Lord Theefton.

BARON. Oh!

LADY MARGARET *(laughing warmly)*. What you feel is the pistil's secretion over its thousand fine hairs — the damp warm cushion which retains and sucks in the pollen. As for the pollen itself — but you're uncomfortable, my dear friend, your face is flushed — perhaps —

BARON. No — not at all! — Margaret — Lady Margaret — go on!

LADY MARGARET. I don't know — should we?

BARON. Yes yes! You were saying . . .

LADY MARGARET. Something about the male granule which lies here. Suddenly it wakes into activity, it sends a long slender finger deep into this pulp until it meets the ovule in its sack. And there the impregnation occurs. The wonderful mysterious entrance.

BARON. Nature! (*He leans over another flower*)

LADY MARGARET. Not so close, my lord!

BARON (*jumping*). Oh!

LADY MARGARET. You're inhaling the *Iasonus sceleratus*. Some call it the most fragrant flower of the tropics.

BARON. Heavenly gods, it is!

LADY MARGARET. The Persians chew its petals for — for unmentionable purposes. It seems to me that merely breathing it — (*She breathes it*)

BARON (*weakly*). Merely breathing it — like this —

LADY MARGARET (*weakly*). The people call it St. Anthony's bane.

BARON (*weakly*). St. Anthony's bane?

LADY MARGARET (*weakly*). They say that St. Anthony himself couldn't have resisted the fragrance. Even I . . .

BARON. Even you? . . .

LADY MARGARET. Perhaps I shouldn't have breathed it. If only . . . But we must be detached, we must.

BARON. Must we? Margaret . . .

LADY MARGARET. And yet, if one could be like this exotic twiner — the *Lekkerkuss gloriosus*. Watch the curling tendrils, see how they reach out towards a stem as if in adoration — and when they find it —

BARON. And when they find it? What then?

LADY MARGARET. They grasp it quickly, violently — because they are fearless — because they know no law or prohibition — because they need — need — need — and what they need —

BARON. They take!

(*He flings himself on Lady Margaret and kisses her passionately*)

LADY MARGARET. My lord!

BARON. Margaret! My Margaret! I am your tendril! I need you and I take you!

LADY MARGARET. Robert!

BARON. Yes, call me Robert, and you — my love, let me kiss you again, my flower, my nectar, my sorceress —

LADY MARGARET. Robert, if I had known . . . What is happening? Robert! since when?

BARON. Since always! Can you ask? I could bear it no longer at Theefton. Surely you know why I came here. The unicorn was a pretext for me. Too many years had gone by — oh Margaret, Margaret, Fate came between us.

LADY MARGARET. Not so loud, my dear, hush, there are people nearby.

BARON. My goddess, confess it now that you love me — oh these blessed flowers — you answered my kisses — you didn't thrust me away — you wanted me to grasp you in my arms —

LADY MARGARET (*weakly*). No, Robert . . .

BARON. Didn't we play together as children, years before Umfrey saw you, and hadn't we celebrated a solemn mock wedding in the rose garden, you were eight, I was nine . . .

LADY MARGARET. How was I to know this meant anything to you? Or that you'd remember these childish promises?

BARON. Oh Margaret, that was the culmination of my life — at nine — I have remembered nothing else. You were my wife from that holy afternoon forth. You the heiress of Wyngham, Brigsley, Tuckbetter and Glaswin Epton, I the future Baron Theefton — our lands lying flank to flank. But then — miserable times — you were orphaned; King Stephen gave you to Umfrey — to my friend! He an earl, I his vassal. I bowed, I wept, I withdrew, I decayed. But now — look down, ye gods, Margaret is in my arms again.

LADY MARGARET. A married woman, Robert.

BARON. Bitterness! And I must think of you lying in his bed — at night — or day! — oh God —

LADY MARGARET. You mustn't torment yourself, my dear; and you needn't. But we were looking at my specimens. My lovely flowers, my only consolations . . .

BARON. Wait, Margaret. You said "you needn't." Why "you needn't"?

LADY MARGARET. It must have escaped me. Don't probe, Robert, for the sake of our happy childhood. Leave an aging woman to tend her griefs alone.

BARON. Griefs? You *will* tell me! I'm on fire, I could smash walls with my bare fists, I am Hercules, confide in me, here, rest your marvelous head on my shoulder.

LADY MARGARET. Oh Robert, if only I had a trusted friend.

BARON. Look at me. I would leap into a gulf full of basiliscs to save a hairpin that belonged to you! Tell me now what it is that weighs on your soul, beautiful Margaret.

LADY MARGARET. Hide my face . . . Robert . . .

BARON. Speak to me.

LADY MARGARET. I am not my husband's wife.

BARON (*astounded*). What are you? Who is your husband's wife? Tell me!

(*Softly*) Tell me, do. Who is his wife?

LADY MARGARET. Clotilda.

BARON. Clotilda Bennyworth — the girl? —

LADY MARGARET. Yes.

BARON. Is his mistress?

LADY MARGARET. His wife.

BARON. I'm lost. Are they secretly married?

LADY MARGARET. No, they are not married, and yet she is his wife, and his only wife.

BARON. His only wife! And you?

LADY MARGARET. I am the maiden Countess of Dumfrey.

BARON. Maiden!

LADY MARGARET. Maiden.

BARON. And I am Robert newborn, newborn this instant! I am forming my first thoughts on this earth! I will liberate you! Before God, you are not married, and never were. You revert to me! Exact an annulment at once.

LADY MARGARET. Umfrey will fight it. He has my lands, Robert, he is in love with my lands.

BARON. Villain!

LADY MARGARET. I could prove his — but that's too loathsome — a medical inquiry — reports to the Pope —

BARON. God forbid! But something must be done! I am driving my ideas about — I'll need more time to think.

LADY MARGARET. I have had years to think.

BARON. You, with your unearthly intelligence — Margaret! Your eyes tell me you have found the way.

LADY MARGARET. Perhaps. The way — a difficult way — I would need all your courage, your —

BARON. — love! My love! My invincible love! In my arms! (*He kisses her*) Use me, I am nothing except the extension of your thought and the execution of your will.

LADY MARGARET. Dear, dear Robert. Could it be that we are meant to be happy yet?

BARON. Here is my oath. By all the saints, Robert shall be twined about Margaret like the — name it for me, my soul.

LADY MARGARET. The *Lekkerkuss gloriosus.*

BARON. Amen. Now; what must I do?

LADY MARGARET. You do nothing at first. The first action is mine, and I have the courage for it at last. Oh I was so miserably alone!

BARON. Angel!

LADY MARGARET. But now all is changed. I will go into the forest with a mirror in my hand —

BARON. And hunt the unicorn! Divine virgin, the unicorn will be yours. How did I fail to think of it! You will capture the unicorn, you of all maidens will not fail! And the world will know that you are no man's wife. Your false husband will be unmasked. The false marriage will be dissolved. Margaret and her true Robert will be joined, stamen to pistil. The archbishop will bless their union. And happiness perfumed with justice will dwell on earth forever. My wife! (*They embrace*)

LADY MARGARET. Be careful! Somebody is approaching. It's Sir Ralf. There's another little door here. Do nothing, say nothing; leave everything to me.

BARON. I will, I will. Once more? (*He offers to embrace her. She smiles, shakes her head, and leaves*)

BARON (*alone*). Heavenly Margaret is mine! Wyngham's grazing lands are mine! The mills of Brigsley are mine! Tuckbetter's corn is mine! The waters of Glaswin Epton are mine! Glaswin Epton, where Ecgfrith defeated Wulfhere in the year 671, and where Theefton overthrows Dumfrey today. Baron cuts down earl, oh savory hierarchical revenge, and even better, I best my best friend. I can't stand the joy of it, I want to write epics, I could drink the North Sea, I'll sneeze a mountain away. Whom can I tell? Halloo, here comes the dear honest fellow — Sir Ralf, here I am, were you looking for me? (*He sings*) "This way, fair maiden, to your lover's arms."

(*Enter Sir Ralf, very glum*)

SIR RALF. I was looking for Lady Margaret.

BARON. The divine Margaret has just left, after giving me a lesson in rare plants I shall never forget. (*Singing*)

      This way, fair maiden, to your lover's arms;
      Your lover with impatience sighs.

SIR RALF. You seem very happy, my lord.

BARON. I seem because I am and I am because I love.

SIR RALF (*more glum than ever*). You too. The place is being smothered with love. (*Sarcastically*) I suppose you'll tell me that you're in love with Lady Margaret, who has adored you since childhood.

BARON. How in the devil's — (*putting his hand over his mouth*)

SIR RALF. What??! I was joking! . . . Oh no!

BARON (*hilariously*). Ha ha ha, you drew it out of me without even trying! Oh no? Oh yes! Ha ha ha! It's the power of honesty, Sir Ralf, it gives you prophetic gifts in spite of yourself. Extend your hand to the happiest man in Britain!

SIR RALF (*pulling his hand away*). Is this *your* joke?

BARON. Joke? Let the world hear it is no joke. I mean to proclaim my love from this *Priapisca vehemens* to the farthest star, not forgetting the

Earl of Dumfrey on the way.

SIR RALF. I'll be insane before the day is out. However, love as much as you like, my lord; congratulations; but I trust my poor Lady Margaret has sense enough to see with her own eyes the difference — I say no more.

BARON (*stung*). Don't, my friend, because you happen to be right again, I return the congratulations; she does see the difference with her own eyes — and with her own lips — and with her own arms — here in the greenhouse she saw it, five minutes ago.

SIR RALF. Lady Margaret?

BARON. Lady Margaret.

SIR RALF. I don't believe it. But I admire your telling these stories to me, who have served Lord Dumfrey from the time he was a child.

BARON. Why shouldn't I? I know enough to freeze you all in your shoes. I have plucked the secrets of this house. I was not in the diplomatic service for nothing. I served in Norway.

SIR RALF. Bluff. You know no secrets — there are no secrets to know.

BARON. My dear Sir Ralf, your loyalty amuses me. But I know as well as I hope you do what connection exists between Lord Dumfrey and the sham virgin Clotilda.

SIR RALF (*astonished*). Who told you?

BARON (*laughing*). An angel — Lady Margaret.

SIR RALF. She knows? She knew? And she told you?

BARON. She knows, she knew, and she told me. (*Singing*)

> Your lover with impatience sighs.
> Fair maiden, swiftly yield your charms . . .

Hmm, that heavenly fragrance. Marvelous flowers — the Arabs chew them for — unmentionable purposes. I must have them at my wedding. Yes, Sir Ralf, I have culled the secrets of this house. Your loyalty is useless. Remember, I am an old hand in the diplomatic service. I know who is the true virgin in this house, and I know who is the false virgin.

SIR RALF. I don't follow you.

BARON. Useless discretion. At the hour of my choosing, the public will be invited to inspect Umfrey's bedchamber. And I shall address them as follows: "Your master, good citizens and reverent judges, has failed to perform even once his conjugal duty in the five vacant years of his spurious marriage. Here, however, is Mistress Bennyworth." And all the rest. Oh, you and I could chat like old friends, Sir Ralf, old friends drinking a tankard of ale over an old oaken table. Don't stitch up your lips on *my* account. (*Singing*)

> Fair maiden, swiftly yield your charms,
> Else your woeful lover dies.

SIR RALF. Excuse me . . . Failed to perform? . . . Lord Dumfrey?

BARON (*suddenly solemn*). A crime, Sir Ralf; his soul and body are sold out to that witch Clotilda. Because of his greed for land and more land he tears Margaret from the bosom of her doting parents. Then he violates the sacrament for five unholy years — refuses to consummate — allows her to wither. Thank God the poor orphan preserved her purity, which now devolves on me.

SIR RALF (*weakly*). How, on you? What do you intend to do?

BARON. That is my secret. But as sure as the Pope and King Stephen are alive, Margaret will be mine, along with Wyngham, Brigsley, Tuckbetter, and Glaswin Epton.

SIR RALF (*flaring up*). This is plunder! Wyngham, Brigsley — Vulgar plunder!

BARON. Vulgar?

SIR RALF. Why didn't I see it before? The unhapppy woman looking for comfort, staggering in the darkness, and stretching out her innocent hand to a smiling claw! However, there's still Ralf Basset. I'll make your designs public, Baron Theefton.

BARON. Piffle. Say one word, and I fling your master to the mob. But you misunderstand me, Sir Ralf. My designs are pure. I love Lady Margaret. We played together as children — this is sacred — I knew her long before Umfrey set eyes on her — we had exchanged oaths in a bower, she was seven and I was eight, the spirits of the woods were undoubtedly listening, we were Aeneas and Dido, only younger; the nymphs and the goblins declared that we should ultimately be united; for, Sir Ralf, these lands, I ask you to note, these lands border upon mine, they are my natural extension. I am amputated without them.

SIR RALF. They also border upon this earldom.

BARON. But they bordered on me before Umfrey knew Margaret. No, Sir Ralf, this is the beginning of my ascent. The Theeftons are destined to eclipse the Dumfreys. Three weeks and two days after I was born, a bolt struck down the church steeple in Dumfrey Bottoms. The heavens don't speak in vain, my friend.

> Dame Fortune can whirl
> Baron to Earl,
> And one more fluke
> Turns Earl into Duke.

Shall I make cottage laws, Sir Ralf, do cornfield justice, educate muddy-shanked milkmaids and build windmills when I could be multiplying my estate and branding my name into the chronicles?

SIR RALF. My lord, I ask you to excuse me. You want no company just now to keep yourself entertained.

BARON. Wait. Let's be friends, Sir Ralf; I'm in a temper to have no enemies; may the sun shine on all men alike. Perhaps you should do something underhanded too, like the rest of us sinners. I think you'd feel more at home among us if you did.

SIR RALF. In plain words, are you suggesting an alliance between yourself and me?

BARON. Why not? I need good men. The Theeftons are obviously in the ascendant. And your master is beyond help. Oh you can warn him about me — much good may it do him! I'm galloping into the future, Sir Ralf, saddle your horse and ride with me before I'm out of sight.

SIR RALF (going). Excuse me.

BARON. Right you are; time to join our good friends again. I promised Umfrey I'd go trotting with him about the countryside. We might catch a glimpse of the unicorn. (He laughs and puts his hand on Sir Ralf's shoulder) Coming, Sir Ralf?

SIR RALF (disengaging himself). I was about to forget — I promised Lady Margaret to label a few of her plants. Go without me, my lord.

BARON. I will. Think of the Theeftons, Sir Ralf. (He leaves singing)

SIR RALF (watching him through the window). Ruffian! Dancing down the path. What now? He's stopped by the roses. Plucks a rose and puts it in his sleeve. Sting him? Not Theefton it wouldn't! Theefton is in the ascendant! Ha! He's leaping over the hedge with his arms out like a pair of wings! Enough, enough. (He turns away and sits on a stool) I've lived too long, I've heard too much . . . Poor Lady Margaret . . .

SCENE THREE

(Same as Scene One. Next evening. The room is even warmer and more lovely in the evening than it was during the day. The Earl, the Baron, and Clotilda are playing cards)

EARL. Don't we need more lights?

BARON (ogling Clotilda). No — why? — this half darkness is enchanting. It sets a man dreaming. Perhaps a lady too?

CLOTILDA (flirtatious). Ladies have to be careful about dreaming, Lord Theefton. I open with six.

BARON. Charming!

EARL (annoyed). Well, I think it's getting too dark. Peter! More lights.

BARON. Three of spades.

CLOTILDA. I take two. My lord?

EARL. Snip with a jack.

BARON. Not bad. Another card for me.

(Enter Peter with lights)

EARL. Here. Is Lady Margaret about the house, Peter?

PETER. I believe she has retired, my lord, but I'm not sure. Shall I inquire?

EARL. No, never mind.

PETER. Thank you, sir. (He leaves)

CLOTILDA. Double-hook and beat seven. Your turn, my lord.

EARL. Oh yes; I flip a queen of hearts.

BARON. I pass.

CLOTILDA. My lord?

EARL. Oh, one whisket with the king.

BARON. I place five in a dash.

CLOTILDA (triumphant). Snip-snap!

EARL and BARON. Again!

EARL. The pot is yours, my dear.

(Clotilda rakes it in and carefully puts the money in her purse)

CLOTILDA. You're allowing your minds to drift tonight, gentlemen.

EARL. Oh I don't know.

BARON (ogling Clotilda). I plead guilty. My mind is drifting, guess where? Mistress Clotilda, your bracelet is a marvel. May I? (He leans over her forearm)

CLOTILDA (charmingly). Do you really like it? It's perhaps too much for an orphan. A friend gave it to me. A former friend.

BARON. A friend who would resign himself to being your former friend, Clotilda, must be an unfeeling clod.

EARL (extremely annoyed). The game's over for tonight and thank God it's almost time for bed. Margaret must be waiting up for me.

BARON (sarcastic). Very likely.

(Enter Sir Ralf, carrying papers)

BARON. Sir Ralf, will you take Lord Dumfrey's place at the card table?

SIR RALF. No thank you. I am working on the Dumfrey tercentenary celebrations.

EARL (gloomily). Celebrations.

BARON. They'll cheer you up, Umfrey. Your house is almost as ancient as ours of Theefton. That's something to be proud of.

SIR RALF. I've asked some of the musicians to come, my lord. They want to introduce a song or two.

EARL. Let them. A little music before bedtime can't do any harm. Or maybe it can. (Sound of the unicorn) Oh my God, listen!

BARON. Fairly close, I'd say.

EARL. Merciful heaven, take this plague away and forgive us our sins.

SIR RALF (muttering). Deserve it first.

EARL. Sir Ralf?

SIR RALF. Nothing, my lord. Let me sit in a corner.

EARL. It's too dark for you there.

SIR RALF. The darker the better. *(From the corner)* Leofa is in the kitchen, grumbling among the cooks and the maids.

BARON. Why don't you hang the rascal, Umfrey?

CLOTILDA. That's what *I'd* like to know.

BARON. I don't tolerate grumblers on my lands.

EARL. Fine. But I'll thank you not to hang my taxpayers for me. *(The unicorn's trump again, now very close indeed. Everyone is startled)* Listen! The beast is in my park! Practically under the window! Robert, go see — Sir Ralf —

(The baron and Sir Ralf go to the balcony)

EARL. This is for my sins. Sorceress! And flirting under my nose. But I'm sending you away.

CLOTILDA *(flaunting her double triangle)*. You'll never send me away!

EARL *(covering his eyes)*. I will, I will!

(Exclamations from the balcony)

BARON. There! There! By the hedge! Beyond the basin!

EARL. What? What do you see? Sir Ralf — *(Enter Sir Ralf)* Sir Ralf! Your face is white. What did you see? Don't tell me —

(Clotilda runs to the balcony)

SIR RALF. My lord — the unicorn —

(Scream from Clotilda)

EARL. Oh.

SIR RALF. Go look —

EARL. I don't want to.

(The baron enters, followed by Clotilda)

BARON. The unicorn is caught!

EARL. Who —?

SIR RALF. Your wife.

BARON. Caught by Lady Margaret! Caught by a virgin! Tremble, Lord Dumfrey! *(The earl is dumb)*

CLOTILDA. This is a dirty scheme to ruin me, Umfrey. Your wife is leading in the unicorn and holding up a mirror as though she had caught him.

EARL *(choking)*. Where is she going?

CLOTILDA. Into the house. This is a plot devised against me.

BARON *(with a laugh)*. On the contrary, my dear Clotilda; we're going to help you.

SIR RALF. He knows everything, my lord. So does your wife.

EARL. How? . . .

BARON. Brace yourself, Umfrey. Your unmarried wife has confessed herself to me. Leofa is in the house. Capitulate, or in a few minutes your People's Delegate will trumpet the news that Lady Margaret is a virgin.

EARL. Capitulate?

CLOTILDA. Hypocrite — viper! Umfrey, do something!

EARL. The world is coming to an end. What is Robert's part in this? How did Margaret —? Explain, somebody, the villain is standing here —

SIR RALF. My lord, I too know more than what you chose to tell me. You kept the worst from me. Your neglect of Lady Margaret. The unhappy woman wants to save herself from all of you — villains — yes — I open my mouth and say villains. You Lord Dumfrey — a shameful alliance — you Clotilda —

CLOTILDA. Nobody wants your sermons. Do something, Umfrey. She's in the house now with the unicorn.

BARON. There's nothing to do for anyone.

SIR RALF. You — manipulating Lord Dumfrey to serve your ambition. And you, Lord Theefton —

BARON. I'm a guest.

SIR RALF. Playing with Lady Margaret's affections to swallow her estate —

EARL. My land! He wants my land! Never!

BARON. Too late, Umfrey, Margaret is mine!

EARL (drawing his dagger and going for the baron). Not for long.

(Clotilda screams and Sir Ralf interposes)

SIR RALF (loud). Who are you to punish a man, sinner? (The earl's arm falls) There is only one innocent being here — your wife — fumbling to save herself from the wolves!

CLOTILDA. Ha!

EARL (sinking into a chair). Where is she? Go look, somebody . . . Oh God, what happened? Robert, what have I done to you?

BARON. You have done that you stole Margaret from me.

EARL. Deep corroded villain!

BARON. I love her, she loves me, we were pledged to each other years before you knew her — I was twelve, she eleven — children, pure and prophetic. All is fulfilled. Umfrey, the time has come to yield up your so-called wife, declare the so-called marriage null, and restitute the land you took from her. If you refuse, out with it all, the whole revolting story, your sordid affair with Clotilda —

CLOTILDA. Protect me!

BARON. All of it conveyed to King Stephen. You'll roll from your chair of state straight to the Tower.

CLOTILDA. I'll be with you to the end, Umfrey. Only you and me.

(The door opens. Enter Lady Margaret)

EARL (with his last breath). Where is the unicorn?

LADY MARGARET. In the wardrobe. (She shows a key)

EARL. Who saw you?

LADY MARGARET. Nobody.

EARL. Who saw the unicorn?

LADY MARGARET. Nobody.

EARL. Leofa? The porter? The butler? The maids?

LADY MARGARET. Don't be a bore, Umfrey. I said nobody.

BARON. Margaret. Heroine!

LADY MARGARET. Not yet.

BARON (*low*). But why at night? Why in secret? I don't understand.

LADY MARGARET. You will.

SIR RALF. My dear lady, are you quite safe? Did the beast try to harm you?

LADY MARGARET. Thank you for asking, Sir Ralf. He tried, but I held the mirror, he became meek; gently, gently he followed me. I have not even a stain on my dress, nor a spot on my hands.

BARON. Miraculous woman.

EARL. Margaret, speak to me . . . I *am* concerned for you . . .

LADY MARGARET. And I for you, my husband. I set you free to marry Clotilda.

EARL (*groaning*). You knew.

LADY MARGARET. Of course. (*Clotilda faints*) The little toad has fainted; Umfrey, help your mistress. (*Sir Ralf attends to Clotilda*)

EARL. Margaret, I don't want to be set free. I was bewitched. *You* belong to me.

LADY MARGARET. You mean Wyngham, Brigsley, Tuckbetter and Glaswin Epton belong to you.

BARON. Precisely.

EARL. This is unjust. We've lived together for five years — peacefully — you accepted my deep respect — you can't wish a scandal to break over my head, surely.

BARON. What scandal? We'll do it quietly.

EARL (*furiously*). Stay out of this, mongrel —

BARON. By thunder, I'll call Leofa! Here I fret over your reputation —

CLOTILDA (*who has come to again*). Umfrey, my dearest love, listen to him, do as they say, we're powerless against them . . .

BARON. That's a sensible girl. She's all yours, Umfrey. You can afford to marry whomever you wish, you're not a lowly baron afraid of a misalliance — a man like you is immune to whispers. Take Clotilda — the poor girl loves you and you're mad about her. Nobody will be told that Margaret caught the unicorn, it could be anyone else — why! the unicorn could have drifted into the wardrobe by himself. Leave it to me, I've had experience in diplomatic life. All that's required of you is a friendly settlement with Margaret, a donation to the church, and a gift to the Pope — I have it! you'll send him the unicorn's tusk in a velvet case — and the story ends with toasts and violins.

EARL. I'm dizzy.

CLOTILDA. Here, my dear; let me take care of you. (*She gives him some wine*) You see, the evil wind has blown some good to us after all.

EARL (*weakly*). Go away . . .

LADY MARGARET (*regally giving her hand to the baron*). My lord . . .

BARON (*devoutly*). My own!

SIR RALF (*throwing himself at Lady Margaret's feet*). Dearest lady, listen to me, listen I beg you, don't take refuge with Theefton of all men! If you knew his real purpose!

BARON. Introduction to slanders!

SIR RALF. Your husband has done you an immense wrong — I know it — but he repents — look at his face! — while Theefton comes here lusting only after your land — he told me so himself —

BARON (*laughing*). Told him so myself! Very likely! Congratulations on your mouthpiece, Umfrey — he deserves his wages — but here thank God there's no one to believe him.

LADY MARGARET. Yes there is. Rise, Sir Ralf, rise, I believe you.

EARL and BARON (*contrasting pitch*). Margaret!

SIR RALF. Lovely lady, I've opened your eyes, I've saved you.

EARL. At least you've seen through this puppet. So far I'm happy.

BARON. Margaret!

LADY MARGARET. I see through all of you.

BARON. This is a dream. Margaret! I adore you. You fell into my arms this afternoon —

EARL. I don't believe it.

LADY MARGARET. Thank you, Umfrey.

BARON. Why did you hunt the unicorn?

LADY MARGARET. In order to crush you all. Sir Ralf, you didn't open my eyes. Poor man. I like you, but at bottom you're a fool, you're an infant. I knew Theefton's greed from the beginning. He stole my favorite puppy when I was ten.

BARON. He ran away! Finders keepers!

LADY MARGARET. And I knew my husband's deceit, and I knew Clotilda's ambition. But I waited for my day. Which came. Now I shall make you all cringe. Umfrey, choose; either you drive your mistress out, come to my bed, and give me my rights as Countess of Dumfrey, or else I leave you demolished in your ruins and marry myself and my lands, eyes wide open, to your enemy Theefton.

SIR RALF. She loves her husband, you see!

LADY MARGARET. Sir Ralf, you'll die the same baby you were born. But phrase it as you like, I'll love my husband, so be it, from the moment he does my will, my justice, my good. And do or don't, by all the saints in paradise who have witnessed my patience —

EARL. What, my dear?

LADY MARGARET (*fiercely*). I'll be avenged!

SIR RALF (*collapsing in a chair*). God destroy me!

CLOTILDA. Protect me, my lord. Show her what you are. Protect the defenseless.

LADY MARGARET. Peter!

(*Enter Peter*)

PETER. Madam.

LADY MARGARET. Warn Leofa to be here in exactly ten minutes; not nine and not eleven; ten minutes from this. (*She snaps her fingers*)

PETER. Yes, madam. (*He leaves*)

LADY MARGARET. All right, Umfrey.

EARL. Clotilda will leave.

CLOTILDA. Oh!

BARON. Wait! You're not rid of me yet. Umfrey, I order you to keep Clotilda. Like it or not, Margaret will be Baroness Theefton.

LADY MARGARET. I will be Countess of Dumfrey, like it or not. Countess!

BARON. Baroness! Umfrey, once more I order you to keep Clotilda. Or else Leofa, the people and the king will be told how you and Clotilda have broken the sacrament, poisoned the land, and inflicted the unicorn on it. I will ruin you. You will end your days on a pallet in King Stephen's clammiest dungeon. Robert Theefton has played his trump.

LADY MARGARET. And what if I refuse to become your mate? What will you have gained?

BARON. Vengeance. Like yourself.

LADY MARGARET. What if, instead of vengeance, I were to offer you land?

BARON. Land? Where and when?

LADY MARGARET. Tuckbetter and its corn; at once.

BARON. Hm.

LADY MARGARET. Besides, remember where you are.

BARON. Where I am?

LADY MARGARET. Namely, in Lord Dumfrey's stronghold, with few retainers at your side.

EARL (*delighted*). That's true. I'll try him on the spot for treason against the earldom, and have his head before he can open his mouth.

CLOTILDA. But I'll cry his story from the rooftops.

LADY MARGARET. Shut your mouth, my child; we'll come to you in a minute. Well, Robert? Think of the scaffold. And think of Tuckbetter's cornfields.

BARON. I'd prefer the mills of Brigsley.

EARL. They're yours.

SIR RALF. Oh God destroy me!

LADY MARGARET. Allow me, Baron Theefton. (*She pours him some wine*)

BARON. Thank you. Political questions can always be settled, provided there's a little good will all around, a little sincerity. Here's my hand, Umfrey.

EARL. What about the falling into your arms this afternoon?

BARON. An obvious lie.

EARL. Here's mine. Brigsley is yours. We'll draw up the papers tomorrow morning. And Margaret — Margaret — come here — my wife — (*Kissing her hand*) a great stone has been lifted from my chest. The earldom is saved, my soul perhaps too.

CLOTILDA (*throwing some pewter on the floor*). Brutes! Brutes! Plotting together to tear me to pieces. But I'll get even with you! Liars! Schemers! (*To Umfrey*) You, I was your slave, I forgot all thoughts of marriage for your sake, I allowed you to wallow in my bed night after night, and how you loved it, how you slavered after me, let the Countess hear it, others can bite too, she's not the only viper, because I'll expose you all, myself too, I don't care, I'll make you repent, Leofa is coming, I'll make you grovel —

BARON. A little reason, Clotilda!

EARL. What'll we do with her? Margaret! I do, I do owe her something. (*He covers his face*)

LADY MARGARET. I agree. The woman who caught the unicorn should be rewarded.

ALL. What?

LADY MARGARET. Why do you look surprised? Clotilda went into the forest early this evening —

(*The door opens*)

PETER. Leofa, the People's Delegate.

LADY MARGARET. Leofa, how good of you to come; come in, come in.

(*Enter Leofa; he kneels before Lady Margaret and kisses her hand*)

LADY MARGARET. Stand, excellent friend, and attend to my words. Clotilda left the castle this evening, longing to succeed where she had failed before, and anxious to restore her reputation in the eyes of the people she loves. She found the foul unicorn — yes! she caught him; she led him back —

LEOFA. The unicorn is caught! Where is he?

LADY MARGARET. In the wardrobe. And here is the key.

LEOFA (*taking the key*). Heaven be thanked!

LADY MARGARET. Heaven be thanked, of course; but heaven's instrument as well.

LEOFA *(kneeling before Clotilda and kissing her hand)*. Mistress Clotilda, the sweet saints in heaven rain their goodness on your pretty head. Our children will be told the inspirational story of your lily life. You have justified the people's confidence.

CLOTILDA. I've always loved the people, Leofa.

LEOFA. No husband will be too great for you. Kings will ask for your hand from Asia to Constantinople.

LADY MARGARET. That will do, Leofa. Go tell the people the happy tidings.

LEOFA. At once. Long live the house of Dumfrey!

BARON. Amen. *(Exit Leofa)* He's right, Clotilda, you will find a splendid husband as soon as the news has spread.

CLOTILDA. Well, I hope nobody here expects me to be grateful. I'm lying for your sakes.

EARL *(low to Sir Ralf)*. Do take the girl away, Sir Ralf.

SIR RALF. No, I am sick at heart. The little hussy. And you, Lady Margaret, cold from your brains to your womanhood. You, Lord Theefton, false friend and plunderer. You my lord, liar and adulterer. And myself, fool of fools.

EARL. I'm afraid we're a fearful lot. But now we're reconciled, Sir Ralf, and are we any worse than the usual?

BARON. Rather better, if anything.

LADY MARGARET. Look at other places.

CLOTILDA. Paris, for example, where Sir Ralf has promised to send me.

BARON. Are there not clouds in the sky?

CLOTILDA. Does it not rain in June?

LADY MARGARET. Don't swans for all their beauty honk?

EARL. And didn't Christ himself lose his temper?

(Enter Peter)

PETER. The musicians are in the antechamber!

EARL. Let them play, let them sing!

PETER. Play musicians, and singers sing!

*(Music is heard, and then a song)**

> When God said
>   Let us make the earth
> What did he do
>   He took a heap of dirt
>
> He took a heap of dirt
>   And made a muddy ball
> and that is why oh why
>   we're muddy one and all!

*The musicians can of course be brought on stage at this point.

EARL. All together!

(All except Sir Ralf sing the song and dance in a circle to the music)

EARL. More wine! *(Peter pours)*

BARON. We're reconciled!

CLOTILDA. We're reconciled!

LADY MARGARET. We're reconciled!

EARL *(toward Sir Ralf)*. We're reconciled!

SIR RALF *(in loud agony)*. I am not reconciled! *(The music stops and he rushes to the balcony)* I've had enough! My revels are over!

EARL. Sir Ralf!

LADY MARGARET. Stop!

BARON. Peter, stop him!

(Peter catches hold of Sir Ralf already standing on the balustrade and ready to jump off)

PETER. Sir Ralf! Don't jump! Don't disobey Lord Dumfrey!

SIR RALF. Let me go! I've had enough. Lie and cheat without me!

EARL. Sir Ralf, Ralf my good friend, come down for God's sake. I need you. You're my counselor.

CLOTILDA. We all love you, Sir Ralf.

BARON. Why don't you be like the rest of us?

EARL. The king will give you a barony! He owes me twenty favors!

BARON *(shocked)*. You're going too far.

EARL. Basset, I'll build you a manor, come back, Ralf my friend.

SIR RALF. Let me die.

LADY MARGARET. Stand aside, all of you. Peter, you too, let him go.

EARL. Margaret will do it.

LADY MARGARET. Sir Ralf, turn again and look down. Look down, and what do you see? Darkness, you see darkness. Look down, Sir Ralf. What is the weather of the darkness? I will answer for you. A cold wind mutters over a colder stone. Now look up, Sir Ralf, look at the sky. What do you see in the sky? I will answer for you. You see discarded, dispirited, homeless bodies. Now look at yourself. What of yourself? I know. The wish that you could wish to live. Now turn again, Sir Ralf, and look at me.

SIR RALF. I am looking at you.

LADY MARGARET. What do you see now? A wicked beautiful woman. Around my neck and arms? Jewels happy to be there. And on my body? Soft silk softly resting against the flesh. And what do you see in the room? Warm candles, silver shimmering, our good homely oak of tables and chairs, foolish deceitful familiar people, and the wine more purple than the grape it came from. And what do you hear? What do you hear, Sir Ralf?

SIR RALF. Human words swimming in a water of music. *(He reenters the room)*

EARL. Not water. Wine. Drink, Sir Ralf, the moment has come.

SIR RALF. I don't know, my lord. *(He drinks)*

EARL *(embracing him)*. Forgive me, Ralf.

SIR RALF. I'll try. Pay no attention to me.

CLOTILDA *(aside to Lady Margaret)*. I have always admired you so much. May I . . . ?

LADY MARGARET *(friendly and regal)*. Of course. *(She offers her hand for Clotilda to kiss)*

CLOTILDA. Thank you!

(Leofa rushes in, holding a gored chicken and rabbit in his hand)

LEOFA. My lords, treason, a new unicorn in the woods!

ALL. Oh!

LEOFA. Look! Gored, gored again, everything is starting all over again. When will it end? Lord Dumfrey, say something!

EARL. I'm calling a meeting of the privy council tomorrow! *(General hilarity)* I'll name a commission . . . I'll launch an inquiry . . . Sir Ralf — Lord Basset — suggest something.

SIR RALF *(bitterly)*. Keep dancing.

ALL. Bravo!

EARL. Provided you join us.

SIR RALF. No.

EARL. In the ballad of Sir Blot!

LADY MARGARET. Music! Clotilda, you begin, and Sir Ralf, you obey.

(Music and dance)

CLOTILDA.   Sir Ralf, say after me,
              "My liege, I bend my knee."

SIR RALF. Must I?

ALL. Yes!

SIR RALF *(reluctantly)*.   I bend my knee
                      In dismal flattery.

EARL.   Sir Ralf, declare aloud
                      "I am a baron, rich and proud."

SIR RALF.   I am a baron proud and rich,
                      Ten slaves relieve me which I itch.

LADY MARGARET.   Sir Ralf, obey me and entreat,
                      "I want twelve bankers at my feet."

SIR RALF.   My slimy avarice demands
                      Twelve bankers licking my two hands.

BARON.   Sir Ralf, repeat with me and say
                      "I slew a brace of unicorns today."

SIR RALF.   Truth and modesty my devil scorns:
                      Yes I slew a hundred unicorns.

No, children, stop, I don't want to play, I can't, let me crumble in peace, let me mourn for the world; I'll become a monk.

EARL. We want you to stay with us. With us, Sir Ralf!

SIR RALF. No.

ALL. Yes!

SIR RALF (*strongly*). No!

ALL. Yes!

SIR RALF (*plaintively*). No.

ALL. Yes!

(*All this in the figure of a dance, and dancing to their Yes and his No they pull him along with them and leave. Peter and Leofa remain on stage. Peter stretches his body to listen. Then the music vanishes*)

PETER. What was the last word, yes or no?

LEOFA (*puttering about, still clutching the chicken and rabbit*). How should I know? (*Looking at the animals*) I don't think we'll ever be done with unicorns. Well, their lordships seem to have left most of their wine in the cups. That's nobility for you.

PETER. Yes no yes no yes no. Now I'll worry and worry.

LEOFA. What do you think you'll do with all that wasted wine?

PETER. What's that?

LEOFA. What are you going to do with all that wasted wine?

PETER. I don't know. (*Drinking*) Here's what.

LEOFA (*falling to*). That's my boy. Here's what.

PETER. Don't touch the decanter.

LEOFA. What do you take me for? Don't I respeck private property?

PETER. And what are you going to do with those?

LEOFA. Those what?

PETER. Those chicken and rabbit.

LEOFA. Give 'em to the wife for cooking, what did you think? I've got five children to feed.

PETER. And the holes?

LEOFA. I've got holes in my shoes, holes in my pocket, holes in my windows, there's a hole waiting for me by the church, I've got a hole in my roof, and there's a steady dumb hole in my stomach. Why should I mind a hole in my boiled chicken? Drink up.

(*A unicorn is heard in the distance*)

PETER. Might as well.

LEOFA. Cheers.

PETER. I wouldn't quite put it that way.

(*They clink and drink up*)

THE END

ISLAND

CHARACTERS

HERACLES

ODYSSEUS

PHILOCTETES

DEMODOCUS

MEDON

CHORUS OF TEN SOLDIERS

SCENE

Before Philoctetes' cave on the island of Lemnos

NOTE: Although the rule calls for a stress on the third syllable in the name of Philoctetes, the ear is better pleased — in English — with a second-syllable stress, which I therefore recommend. The same is true for Demodocus, where, luckily, the second-syllable stress is the accepted one.

PROLOGUE *with drum*

HERACLES. I am Heracles, once a man, a hero, invincible. I ransacked Troy
before Agamemnon was inspired to try again; but I singlehanded,
he with ten thousand soldiers. I died and, as was my due, became
a God; and my word as God is my word when I was man: War!

And this is the island of Lemnos: long uninhabited, always
rugged, a bed for inhuman nature, sunned and winded in silence,
except for the stumble of the Aegean against its flanks.

But now two aliens live here: Philoctetes and his companion
Medon. Ten years this cave has been their house. Philoctetes: the
same who stood twenty years ago at my side on Mount Oeta, where
I died, and who kindled the flame of my pyre, and ever since like a
smoke I have concealed him from death, the bitterness to mortals.

And ten years are gone since Agamemnon, tall, hard king of
Argos, gathered the nations of Greece and sailed for Troy. But Troy
stands. Achilles is slain. Half the army has buried the other half.
The living half crumbles. Sand erodes the names on the epitaphs.
And Troy stands. Its wall frowns into the plain. Yet long it shall
not stand.

Ten years ago Philoctetes, the most skillful of the Greeks, sailed
with seven ships from Malis, his home, in alliance with Agamemnon.
His father, the king of Malis, gave the order. Philoctetes, a prince
of resources; explorer of the Danubian and the Scythian wilderness;
mathematician; builder of aqueducts and baths, harbors and war
machines. Ten years ago he led his soldiers and seamen and found
Agamemnon at Aulis. Those were the days of trumpets! But at the
island of Chryse they stopped, landed, midway to Troy, to sacrifice
at the altar of the island's nymph; and there — was it Hera, my old
enemy, who wanted to spite my friend? — there a viper bit Philoctetes
through the ankle. The wound stank in the air. No man could endure
the stench.

And now the oracle spoke through Calchas: "Let Philoctetes
be divided divided divided from the Greeks." Philoctetes fell to the
ground like a dead man. The sacrifice to Chryse was stopped: pol-
luted by the presence of this divided, excluded, malodorous man.
Odysseus, the other Greeks consenting, lifted Philoctetes into his
ship, stopping his nostrils with spices, rowed him here to Lemnos,
and left him with Medon and gear enough to survive, perhaps.
Poor man. He opened his eyes, he wept. The years passed.

This cave houses him. He dug wells and made pulleys; he
kept a calendar; he culled fruit from the trees; he curved a bridge

across a stream; he cut weapons for the hunt; and, in long hours of delicate thought, he devised in his mind a bow so strong, so far-shooting that its possessor will drive his enemy, the Greeks will drive Troy, into the hated grave. Such is the will of the Gods.

I call up War! Philoctetes, arise, unite with your brothers. On the plains of Ilium the son of Achilles, beautiful and brutal Pyrrhus, waits for you. His the hand that cracks the city open, his the fire that guts old Priam and the Trojan stock; but yours the weapon in his hand. Give him your secret intelligence. The war is resumed. Reach out your intelligence to Greece. Come, Philoctetes! Come from the hunting of birds. Hunt Troy! Already the grey soldier Odysseus and the poet Demodocus have landed on Lemnos, brought here by the voice of an oracle to take you back. Do you hear them? And in sight: trampling the beach, resolute. Do you guess them while the string of your bow thuds and the wild bird dies in the sky? Do you hear the human word? War!

What is a man? Carnivorous, predatory, angry, imperious, cruel, embattled: he bleeds, and he bleeds. To live is to do. To do is to fight. I who fought perfectly rose among the perfect Gods.

If only Zeus nodded and I could strike down the arrogant wall of Troy with this club! But I obey the master of Olympus. *(Exit)*

Scene One

FIRST SOLDIER. No one is here, Odysseus. Follow me.

ODYSSEUS. The old horrible stench. I remember it. All but unbearable. Come, my friends. I recognize the area. Soldiers, spread out and look for our man, each in a different direction.

(The eighth, ninth and tenth soldiers leave)

DEMODOCUS. Are we really on the spot, Odysseus?

ODYSSEUS. On the spot or near it. The darkness of Lemnos under the heavy trees. The stairways of rocks and caves. The inhuman silence. Here, Demodocus, I myself brought the unhappy man ten years ago at the command of Agamemnon.

FIFTH SOLDIER. Men! Here's a cave, and the remains of a fire!

DEMODOCUS. A recent fire, I should say. Would this be his shelter?

ODYSSEUS. Go in, my friend. Take your sword in hand. Caution!

DEMODOCUS *(within)*. It *is* the cave, men! Furnished. Almost a house. A villa!

ODYSSEUS. What do you see?

DEMODOCUS. Strange. Two couches covered with skins — Medon is still alive. Wooden utensils — table, benches, a few knives — bronze basins and pots —

ODYSSEUS. More than we left him!

DEMODOCUS (*emerging*). Stone tools. A hearth. Sunlight penetrates from a high opening in the rock. But why do you hang back, Odysseus, with your hand on your sword? Go in yourself.

ODYSSEUS. Soldiers, keep looking about. Too many trees for comfort here. A man might be concealed anywhere with a bow in his hands.

DEMODOCUS. Do you think he will be hostile to us, Odysseus? After ten years?

ODYSSEUS. Ten years may have made him forget, or they may have deepened his hatred. We must be prepared for the worst.

DEMODOCUS. Capturing the bow may be easy; but taking him back with us —

ODYSSEUS. And voluntarily! Freely offering us his skill!

DEMODOCUS. I see great difficulties in that, Odysseus. Volunteer to join the atrocious miseries of the war?

FIRST SOLDIER. Don't dwell on difficulties and miseries, Demodocus; it's the wrong approach for a soldier. After all, if he won't come back of his own free will, I suppose we'll tie him up and argue with him later.

DEMODOCUS. Force him back with us, like an enemy; but I'm afraid he'll never reveal his secrets to us if we do.

ODYSSEUS. And yet force him back we must if he refuses to come. Have you considered, my friends, that the Trojans are sailing towards Lemnos too?

FIRST SOLDIER (*deeply alarmed*). The Trojans? How would *they* know about this weapon?

ODYSSEUS. Why, have the Trojans no oracles of their own? Are not the same Gods in their sky as in ours? The danger is greater than you think. Perhaps they have landed already; perhaps they have made friends with Philoctetes, and learned from him the secret of how the bow is made.

SECOND SOLDIER. Odysseus, what are you saying?

ODYSSEUS. Calm yourselves. While we are here, the rest of our forces are patroling quietly around the island, with instructions of their own. But I trust that we have landed first. And we too have our instructions. We must persuade Philoctetes to return with us. But what if he refuses? Shall we allow him to be approached by a Trojan delegation? In his bitterness against us he might yield to them, traitor, without so much as a bribe.

SEVENTH SOLDIER. What must we do, Odysseus?

ODYSSEUS. Persuade him if we can, compel him if he resists, kill him if we must.

THIRD SOLDIER. Kill him?

ODYSSEUS. The man has a murderous weapon. Who made him contrive it? He himself compels us either to attach him to us, or to destroy him.

DEMODOCUS. This was kept from us till now.

ODYSSEUS. Are you ready, each one of you, to carry out Agamemnon's orders?

SECOND SOLDIER. If we must, Odysseus, if we must.

FIFTH SOLDIER. Who can blame us for keeping this weapon out of the enemy's hands?

THIRD SOLDIER. God knows we are loyal. Yet God forbid we should pour out the blood of a fellow-Greek.

FOURTH SOLDIER. God forbid. Yet you know best what fighters we have been, always at your side; and how else is this endless, sorrowful war to end?

(Enter the eighth soldier)

EIGHTH SOLDIER. Odysseus, I found footprints!

ODYSSEUS. How far from here?

EIGHTH SOLDIER. About two hundred yards away; on a sandy spot; but leading down from the cave, not returning to it.

ODYSSEUS. One or two men?

EIGHTH SOLDIER. Two.

ODYSSEUS. Good. Medon is with him. Old or fresh?

EIGHTH SOLDIER. Fresh, Odysseus, fresh!

ODYSSEUS. Splendid! Go back, soldier, and look sharp. Give us a warning the moment you see him. (Exit the soldier) Men, are we ready to disappear at the snap of a finger?

FIRST SOLDIER. We are, sir.

ODYSSEUS. Now, Demodocus, the rest is yours. Here he will find you, a poor lonely shipwrecked Greek.

DEMODOCUS. I know my part, Odysseus.

ODYSSEUS. You were not chosen for this mission without good reason. Me and the other chiefs Philoctetes hates, as though we and not the serpent had bitten his ankle. But you are a lieutenant: noble in your own right, a man I have always placed near myself at my table, among my dearest companions, young as you are; though not yet in the highest authority. You are a stranger to Philoctetes. He can hate you only as a Greek, but you will easily persuade him to like you as a man. Furthermore, you are skilled with your speech. To whom else do we turn, after the fighting or during a feast, for a love-ditty, or a hymn to battle, or a ballad of old heroes? Though even as a spearsman you are by no means a man whom the enemy would ignore. Your role it will be, therefore, to enchant the heart of Philoctetes with sinuous, inveigling words and strong appeals. Invoke the glory that shall come to him when Troy falls. Paint for him the suffering of the Greeks: and here you will stir in his heart the emotion of kinship, the longing for one's own which makes even their crimes bearable. Speak to him of prizes and rewards, and particularly the gift of young women. Praise the balm of human companionship: what man can desire this terrible solitude? Who does not long now and then to hear the cozy squabble of a marketplace, the hubbub of a tavern, the cries of children at play, the soft, unique word of a woman in love, the advice of a cautious friend? Bring these to his mind, Demodocus, make him weep.

DEMODOCUS. But what if he suddenly reproaches us for abandoning him on Lemnos?

ODYSSEUS. Swear to our innocence and our good will. Did we plot the serpent's bite? Did we bribe the oracle? He was one of ours, we loved the man! No; counter with a solemn note: duty, Demodocus, duty to our nation and to our cause: the call to arms. What man shall disobey? Troy, sitting like a harpy across the Hellespont, cramming down our ships, our goods, our sailors, Troy must be, shall be cut down!

SIXTH SOLDIER. Grant it, oh Gods!

ODYSSEUS. This is war! Not a children's game. Impress him with this, Demodocus: that you are serious; that there is no room in these matters for selfish resentments and private quarrels. You yourself are here on a mission, under orders — not on a holiday in the islands: a Greek, not a rootless outlaw or a savage. We are not animals; we are citizens, citizens of Greek states; and he too, on Lemnos or in India, is a citizen. Let him indulge his tastes and his antagonisms and his appetites; but only, I say, only after having done his duty to Greece.

FIRST SOLDIER. This is soundly spoken, Odysseus. What a pity Philoctetes is not here now. You would have persuaded him already.

DEMODOCUS. Yes, your words carry a great deal of weight, as always, Odysseus. You are a king. It is only human to have misgivings, of course, but I will do my best to follow your instructions. Shall I let Philoctetes know that his father is dead, and that his son, like your own Telemachus, eagerly sends for news of him?

ODYSSEUS. What do you think?

DEMODOCUS. I should like to. How moved he will be! And then thankful to us, which is important.

ODYSSEUS. Nevertheless, I have to overrule you. No doubt he will ask you for news; but you will pretend to know nothing of his affairs. This will whet his appetite for a return among those of us who know. Perhaps you can say that you have heard rumors, but are they about him or about somebody else? You don't know. *You* would give him security, even the security of misery; *I* will play on his anxiety.

DEMODOCUS. It will be hard for me.

(Enter the ninth soldier)

NINTH SOLDIER. Odysseus, away from here!

ODYSSEUS. Is he coming?

NINTH SOLDIER. Yes! I saw two men from my hill — still in the distance, but coming this way; one limping, carrying a bow; the other, two steps behind, birds in his hands. Philoctetes and Medon, who else?

ODYSSEUS. Good work. Recall the other men. Run. Demodocus — let me see — not in the cave — here perhaps — *(he shows Demodocus a hiding place)* Excellent. You know what to do. When he grows soft, suddenly I appear. I disclose the oracle's revelation. You and I, astonished to meet. Have we left traces here?

FIRST SOLDIER. I think not.

ODYSSEUS. Where — ah!

(The ninth and tenth soldiers return)

TENTH SOLDIER. We've signaled the other man, Odysseus; he'll be here in a minute.

ODYSSEUS. Good. Remember: not a word about Calchas and the prophecy. Nor about the Trojans. That's for me. Where is the fellow? He'll ruin — there! *(The last man arrives)* Hurry up, fool. All here? No one missing?

FIRST SOLDIER. All present, Odysseus.

ODYSSEUS. You will all withdraw to a safe distance but without leaving Demodocus exposed. *(To the tenth soldier)* You follow me to the ship. *(To the first soldier)* You deploy your men according to plan and send runners to report to me. Demodocus, good luck.

DEMODOCUS. Depend on me. *(Odysseus and the tenth soldier leave)* Friends, I think I will stand a little farther off, not here. I'll observe their coming from a safe point and make my appearance at the best moment.

(He leaves)

THE CHORUS SPEAKS *with flute and drum*

SECOND SOLDIER. Does your heart beat like mine, comrades?

FIRST SOLDIER. Zeus! Be with us. Zeus! Now this man comes, and already the stench of him sickens us. Zeus! Make him pliant, bend him to us, let him shift his ways like the stream when it parts and yields before the commanding rock. Zeus! Sharpen the words of Demodocus, let each syllable be a hook to catch the soul of this man. Zeus! We are your people. Will you forsake us? Are we to die in the futile plain where bones of our brothers lie, men once ordinary, men once reasonably content, lying now where the oak, the tamarisk and the myrtle grew, become a barren country, yellow with war, pocked with spears and rusted swords and shreds of armor, while the vultures scrape in the skulls for meat. Zeus! Give us this man and his weapon, and the end of this abomination!

SEVERAL. So be it!

THIRD SOLDIER. Men, do you know how old I was when I enlisted for the war? Twenty years old, having barely tasted the pleasure of being a man, of attracting a woman's sly glances, of taking my place in the Assembly, uttering my first words there, surprised almost that I was taken seriously, no longer a boy, beginning the best years of a man; and these years, oh my friends, these lovely years in which I should have found a kind wife, in which I might have established a house and grown in wealth and reputation, I have spent them like a beast among beasts in the sand; yes, my mouth filled with sand when we crawled on the beach and drove back the Trojans in the first onslaught, like a beast sweating and growling, muck-covered, swearing over dice, scratching the blood off the rings I stole from the dead — me, the son of a good man, Schedios of Pronnoi, before whom even now I would blush to say a foul word.

FOURTH SOLDIER. This is my story too.

FIFTH SOLDIER. Fifteen years we are children, fifteen years we are old men; and the little space between, must we spend it howling in the attack, luckless if we die, luckless if we live, life either killed or wasted? And why? Why? What is it to us, I ask, though timidly?

SIXTH SOLDIER. Why are we driven and driven?

SEVENTH SOLDIER. Because.

EIGHTH SOLDIER. Because.

NINTH SOLDIER. Because.

(Three drum-beats)

FOURTH SOLDIER. Zeus, give us quick victory!

SEVENTH SOLDIER. Give Philoctetes and the mysterious bow to us who are dumb, we confess it, to us who fight as our fathers fought, who cannot devise and invent, whose minds are daily and weekly; nice people, effective enough, reliable, and loyal even when we grumble, but with minds not adequate to the extraordinary, needing help when troubles grow outrageous.

EIGHTH SOLDIER. What can that weapon be?

NINTH SOLDIER. Oh the beaches of Troy, though we move away, will hold our shadows as if engraved on the sand.

SIXTH SOLDIER. Even the living have epitaphs.

(*Demodocus appears*)

DEMODOCUS. He's coming! Scatter! Back to the ships!

FIRST SOLDIER. We'll move a little way off, Demodocus, in case you need sudden help.

(*All leave*)

SCENE TWO

PHILOCTETES. Let me stop awhile, Medon. The cycle of pain begins again. We could sit down awhile. (*Medon offers to help him*) No no; sit farther off. Why should you suffer my suffering? This stench oozes into my very sleep and pollutes my dreams; and you so patient, with a divine pretense of not noticing. Let me rest. The breeze cools my wound and sings like an old nurse. Clean Lemnos. I feel better. Medon, I'll help you pluck our catch for the day. No masters and servants here. Philoctetes works with his hands. Look. Thick. Hard. Efficient. I am now, good sir, become worthy of being a slave, having learned to work. Did you see how I shot the wild geese? I hardly aimed. As though my arrows had an intelligence of their own. Retrievers. I would have been Troy's horror — all Troy a great shadowing kingfisher, and my uncanny arrow — now! — dying it falls, moaning, and then my knife in its belly. Ugly thought, Medon. How cool it is. If only I could smell the fragrance that must be here. Yes, I know, the birds must be plucked. I am so tired. Why should I lie to you? The pain is mounting again. God, what have I done to deserve this? Go into the cave by yourself, Medon. Leave me. I must be alone.

(*Medon enters the cave. Philoctetes sits moaning, his bow across his knees, and loses consciousness. Demodocus appears. He stands motionless at a distance from Philoctetes. Gradually Philoctetes regains consciousness. He opens his eyes and sees Demodocus. He leaps up and aims an arrow at Demodocus*)

PHILOCTETES. Medon! Your sword! Men on the island!

(*Medon rushes out of the cave, armed*)

PHILOCTETES. Stand back!

DEMODOCUS. Peace, my friends. I am a man who can do no harm. A castaway.

PHILOCTETES. A liar, maybe. Stay where you are. Who is here with you?

DEMODOCUS. No one. I am alone. No one else survived.

PHILOCTETES. You were shipwrecked?

DEMODOCUS. Yes.

PHILOCTETES. Your clothes are dry. You don't look exhausted.

DEMODOCUS. I had a calm journey of it on my raft for a whole day. And I slept a full night in a tree by the beach.

PHILOCTETES. Search him, Medon.

(*Medon does so and seizes a knife, which he gives to Philoctetes*)

DEMODOCUS. You are welcome to it, my friends, whoever you are.

PHILOCTETES. What's your name?

DEMODOCUS. Demodocus, son of Terpius.

PHILOCTETES. A Greek!

DEMODOCUS. A citizen of Ithaca. Your voice fills me with fear. Will you treat me as a guest or will you injure me? I have neither money nor goods.

PHILOCTETES. Money! The Greek says money! You'll come to no harm unless you look for it. How did your ship go down? An enemy? A storm?

DEMODOCUS. A storm. Will you not tell me where I am? Did I land on an island? Tenedos, perhaps?

PHILOCTETES. This is Lemnos.

DEMODOCUS. Lemnos! Then you — is it possible? You are Philoctetes! Alive!

PHILOCTETES (*lowering the bow*). You know my name.

DEMODOCUS. Who doesn't? Philoctetes! Unbelievable! How many times your story has been retold around the campfire, and you have been pitied, and we have wondered, is the brave Philoctetes still alive, and is his companion with him?

PHILOCTETES. What campfire? Not before Troy, surely?

DEMODOCUS. Troy too surely. Lucky man, not even to know. Yes, before Troy. Still before Troy.

PHILOCTETES. Amazing. And you are one of the Greeks? An officer?

DEMODOCUS. I am.

PHILOCTETES. I don't remember you.

DEMODOCUS. I was never among the first, and then ten years ago, Philoctetes, I was a mere boy. You couldn't know me then. And even now I am better known among the Greeks for my singing than for my fighting, though even as a fighter I am not helpless.

PHILOCTETES. And was it for singing a false note, my friend, that the honest Greeks set you on a ship and sent you off?

DEMODOCUS. No, I am not an exile. I was sent to levy a thousand men in Arcadia — laggards! — but the storm wrecked our ship, and I, perhaps, am the only survivor.

PHILOCTETES. The war is hungry.

DEMODOCUS. Unendurably hungry. Last year —

PHILOCTETES. Tell me no stories. I think I would vomit. No, my friend, take advantage of your accident; explain it as intended by the Gods. Come. sit down; stretch your limbs, and feel what peace is like.

(Medon brings a bowl of water and a dish of fruit)

DEMODOCUS. I feel it already in every bone, kind Philoctetes. The change is so sudden, I keep wondering, is it myself talking here? And to Philoctetes! Who would have thought it! Talking under trees. Trees! If you saw the plain before Troy. Scarred, sacked, cracked, every leaf and every blade of grass blasted. The heather uprooted. Bones and sand and mud. And now I sit here drinking clean water and eating figs.

PHILOCTETES. Tonight you will eat a curd of boar's milk and honey we call "Gods' food." Other dishes too, oddities I promise you'll enjoy. Not a bad place, is it, for a man who was at the point of drowning this morning?

DEMODOCUS. Yesterday, Philoctetes. Oh, this is Elysium.

PHILOCTETES. Later we'll walk halfway up a cliff to watch the night drifting in. Night without ambush. Night without thief. Take it: the island is yours. It lies in the Aegean like a pillow for the weary sailor.

DEMODOCUS. You are infinitely courteous. Ten years of solitude have not coarsened you. But tell me. I suppose that other men have landed here, recently perhaps.

PHILOCTETES. Possibly.

DEMODOCUS. Who. When?

PHILOCTETES. I don't know. We've seen no one.

DEMODOCUS. No one? In all the years?

PHILOCTETES. Why do you ask so suspiciously?

DEMODOCUS. Not suspiciously, my friend, only with surprise. The Trojans, we understand, sail fairly often in this direction.

PHILOCTETES. They are welcome if they land here.

DEMODOCUS. The enemy?

PHILOCTETES. You are my enemy too. Mankind is my enemy.

DEMODOCUS. Why do you say such a thing, Philoctetes?

PHILOCTETES. Why do I say such a thing! Medon, did you hear this? I thank you of course — you made a gesture — oh, I notice! — yet you mastered yourself. But your fellow Greeks did not make the effort; no, they kicked me out of their ranks, like a leper, like a murderer. They're bleeding before Troy, thank God; that's justice of a kind. Kicked me, I said. My rank was nothing, my opinion wasn't asked. In my collapse they carried me here — your master Odysseus, you know it as well as I, carried me here and threw me on the ground like odious garbage and thought I would die. But I didn't die. Here I am to curse them yet.

DEMODOCUS. Forgive me, Philoctetes. My words were rash.

PHILOCTETES. Peace. I flare up too easily. But ten years with no one except Medon to complain to! I make more noise than damage, however. Besides, I have no grievance. This island has been my happiness. Never had I dreamed when I was a boy, wishing I could be another Heracles, that I could find this perfection. Yet I hate the Greeks who brought it to me. Take the paradox.

DEMODOCUS. I understand. It was not perfection they meant for you. And yet — let me ask you — is there not a thrust in your flesh toward your own brothers? Do you ever wonder, do you ever feel a small questioning ache, would you not like me to tell you whether your old companions are still alive, or how they fare — Agamemnon and pitiful Menelaus, the mountainous Ajax, Meriones, audacious Diomedes, old Nestor, Achilles perhaps and his companion the generous Patroclus, or even, even my own master Odysseus?

PHILOCTETES. Your master Odysseus! That ragged, thirsty, patched-up king of Ithaca! Ithaca — excuse me — where people eat stones for supper! Ithaca had a king! Go on, be offended, my lad, but don't I remember him in the early days, when he saw himself sitting in Troy on a red cushion, a leg of mutton in each hand, and ten coffers of gold stowed away in his ship! And Agamemnon — no fool, I'll grant him that — invincible Agamemnon had visions of himself Emperor of Asia, he envied the centipedes because he had only two feet for people to kiss. I was more modest. A little gold, a little reputation, a few slave girls, I didn't ask for much, I was a villain of the tenth rank.

DEMODOCUS. You are a hard man, Philoctetes. Are we all bandits? Wasn't there a shred of justice in our going against Troy?

PHILOCTETES. Of course there was! Plenty of justice, my boy, Troy was a nest of pirates. Tons of justice; and there's the beauty of your human affairs, crime and justice are bosom friends, famous allies; why, nothing's more deadly than a cause stinking with justice; but I, Philoctetes, I shook it all off the way a dog shakes the water off his back after a dip in the sea. A man stops being a bandit only when he's alone.

DEMODOCUS. Terrible, terrible words, Philoctetes. But you've convinced me that I should not tell you anything about these men, these criminals. Not even who died.

PHILOCTETES. Ah? Some of them died? Some of the great ones, I hope.

DEMODOCUS. Can you expect otherwise, after ten years?

PHILOCTETES. I will ask you one question. I had a father at home, a wife, a son — a son eight years old — and two younger brothers . . .

DEMODOCUS. I don't know anything, Philoctetes. If only I did. Bad news is better than none. If you were among us again, you would find out, but here —

PHILOCTETES. I can live without news. My question was only a form. I've become another man. I will show you my world by-and-by; what I and Medon have accomplished; the tools we use; the comforts we knocked out of nature; the machines we made. *You* will ask the questions, believe me. *My* question was only a form. I've captured the sun's rays; a river moves wheels for me; I made this bow, and could make — God knows what; I have an orchard; the hedgehog and the mole give me their hides; I have hemp for my nets; reeds for my arrows; the porcupine supplies me with needles. The wild olive grows here, and wild barley too. I gather saffron on the hillsides for spice. We baked our first bread from crushed acorns, will you believe it? Sometimes we kill a boar. From the sea we catch mullet, bass, bream, and tunny; from the air and ground pheasants, quail, geese, rock-doves. And more, and more: wonders! But greatest wonder of them all, here where men left me to rot, in this silence I can think at last; my mind bounds unimpeded to the constellations and the tentative realms of all the ultimates. You, poor fools, your claptrap thoughts, as soon as they are outdoors, they stumble over "Why is my income lower than his?" or "Will the neighbors laugh at me?" or "My wife is getting fat!" Pah! Give me no news, I beg you. My question was pure form. News! A child of ten has all the news the world will ever provide — that a man will be honest only if he is scared. How is *your* honesty, my friend?

DEMODOCUS. Don't ask me, Philoctetes. I'm so troubled, so uneasy. Your freedom makes me dizzy. When I stand before Agamemnon, I dare not even *think* an unpleasantness against him. Agamemnon is still alive, you see.

PHILOCTETES. Ah?

DEMODOCUS. And Menelaus too.

PHILOCTETES. Achilles defending them, of course, with a great bluster.

DEMODOCUS. No more, Philoctetes.

PHILOCTETES. Impossible. Achilles could die? Who killed Achilles?

DEMODOCUS. Hardly believable, but Paris did, with an arrow. A fluke, a mere fluke.

PHILOCTETES. Well, what's all that to me? But you're still hungry, I'm sure. Medon! Will you bring our young soldier and me a loaf of bread and some plums? I talk like a lord! No wine, alas; but we do have bread of a kind. (*Medon brings the dishes and reenters the cave*) Barley, you see, unleavened, not fit for a young nobleman, of course.

DEMODOCUS. Excellent. Excellent. I marvel at you. The longer I am here

— no, I daren't say it.

PHILOCTETES. Dare! Dare! I am perfectly meek.

DEMODOCUS. Then I will dare and tell you that I have a great wish, in spite
of your anger, to lure you to Ilium with me — even on a raft. We need
your hundred skills, your godly genius. At every council you, Philoctetes, are openly missed. And think of it — Achilles dead, Patroclus
dead, Idomeneus dead, Leucus dead, Orsilocus dead, Creton dead,
Menestheus dead —

PHILOCTETES. Yes yes yes yes, slaughter, dead dead dead. Enough, you are
trying to make me weep; and I do, I do. Scoundrels! Yet there they lie
in the sand, their brains smashed or their stomachs splattered on the
ground. But your Odysseus, is he still alive? No, tell me no more;
what is it to me?

DEMODOCUS. He is still alive, God be thanked, and Diomedes too; but the
glory is gone, and we remain on the plain of Ilium by a kind of
habit, hardly remembering why and what for.

PHILOCTETES. How should anyone remember the lies he told himself ten
years ago? Come, Demodocus, forget Troy. We have been two in this
colony these many years, and now we'll be three.

DEMODOCUS. How is this possible? I was sent on a mission.

PHILOCTETES. I spit on your mission. Digging a grave for a thousand men.
Look about you, my friend, and thank God he has delivered you out
of the criminals' hands. I need another man here. To work with,
but also to talk to. Perfect solitude is unbearable.

DEMODOCUS. And Medon?

PHILOCTETES. I wouldn't have survived without him. But three is better
than two; you would refresh us.

DEMODOCUS. Strange as this may sound, Philoctetes, I think I could bear
perfect solitude. So much I have learned in these ten years. I am sick
of the noise and smell of other men, the hearty and disgusting
comradeship, the bellowing in unison. Not even a privy to oneself.
Beds — on the ground, of course — with fifty other beds. A large
table where a hundred eat together. No thought without a chorus.
Then, out of despair, you begin to confide over a cup of wine to a
dozen bearded, swilling solitudes — out go your dearest secrets —
you hate it afterwards; you are emptied into a gutter. Am I a man,
you cry, God, am I a man or am I the cell of a polyp?

PHILOCTETES (in pain). The cell of a polyp. My friend — don't stop, I heard
all you said — I'm glad — welcome now —

DEMODOCUS. You're ill! What can I do?

PHILOCTETES. The pain is returning to my foot. The hideous cycle. Don't
call Medon. He has troubles enough with me.

DEMODOCUS. But tell me what I can do.

PHILOCTETES. Nothing. I'm going to lose consciousness. Hold me. No. Stay away. (*Demodocus is averting and covering his face*) My friend — pity me — the Gods have cursed me. I don't know why. Yes I do. I didn't love their war enough! Pity me.

DEMODOCUS. I do. Forgive me and let me help you.

PHILOCTETES. No, I'll lie down. I'll sleep an hour. It's a kind of sleep. Stay here. Wait for me. I can bear it.

DEMODOCUS. Let me hold the bow for you. I'll wait here.

(*Philoctetes gives him the bow*)

PHILOCTETES. You are kind. Medon! Medon!

(*He stumbles into the cave*)

DEMODOCUS (*looking at the bow*). Kind? Oh Philoctetes, if you could see the black liar's heart in me!

THE CHORUS SPEAKS *with drum*

SIXTH SOLDIER. Demodocus!

DEMODOCUS. Yes.

SECOND SOLDIER. Not so loud.

FIRST SOLDIER. We heard everything. Masterfully done!

SECOND SOLDIER. Masterfully!

FIRST SOLDIER. At first we worried. "Why isn't he following instructions?" we asked each other. And then you call out to him — "Give me the bow" — and he gives it to you like a child.

SECOND SOLDIER. You have to remember he doesn't know how important it is.

(*Enter the third soldier*)

THIRD SOLDIER (*to the first soldier*). We've sent the man, sir.

DEMODOCUS. Where have you sent what man?

FIRST SOLDIER. One of our men to contact Odysseus. He should know.

DEMODOCUS. Know what, busybody? Is it your duty to spy on me?

FIRST SOLDIER. No sir, I assure you. I thought I was simply obeying Odysseus' orders. But why wait for Odysseus to come? We've got the bow.

THIRD SOLDIER. Now's the time to bolt.

FOURTH SOLDIER. But is this the bow we want?

FIFTH SOLDIER. Of course! Oh, I could dance and shout!

FIRST SOLDIER (*to Demodocus*). May I — ?

DEMODOCUS. Hands off! What I do with the bow concerns me.

FIRST SOLDIER. Do with the bow? What *can* you do with the bow? We have it! Have it!

SEVENTH SOLDIER. Why stand and wait here, Demodocus? Let's go and meet Odysseus halfway.

EIGHTH SOLDIER. I know why he hesitates.

SECOND SOLDIER. Why?

SIXTH SOLDIER. He has made friends with Philoctetes.

EIGHTH SOLDIER. No I didn't mean that. Don't you remember that we really want Philoctetes himself? Who knows whether we can copy this bow? Whether we can handle it? What's it made of? Why does it have that curious knob in the middle? What kind of arrows does it take? I wouldn't dare use it. With this bow, the oracle said, we are doomed to win the war. But it's come into our hands too easily, that's all.

FOURTH SOLDIER. Are we sure this is really the bow itself?

FIRST SOLDIER. Always a doubter in the crowd. Always a questioner. Demodocus, no more of this — let's take the bow to the ship and reason with Philoctetes afterward.

SECOND SOLDIER. From a position of strength.

THIRD SOLDIER. A bird in hand.

DEMODOCUS. A man who trusted me in the middle of my lies gave me the bow to safekeep for him.

FIRST SOLDIER. You asked and took it.

DEMODOCUS. He gave it to me! What if I walked into the cave while you stare at me and placed it in his companion's hand, scoundrel that I am?

FIRST SOLDIER. And the war?

FIFTH SOLDIER. We've got orders, Demodocus.

SIXTH SOLDIER. The whole army!

THIRD SOLDIER. Let's rush for it.

FIRST SOLDIER. Insubordination.

SECOND SOLDIER. Demodocus has made friends with Philoctetes.

SIXTH SOLDIER. That's what I said before.

SEVENTH SOLDIER. Why not? Philoctetes is a Greek.

EIGHTH SOLDIER. A Greek! Did you hear him talk about the Greeks? He would eat us all boiled and salted if he could. And Demodocus was supposed to win him over. Instead it was Philoctetes who won *him* over.

FIFTH SOLDIER. The Trojans will get the bow! I see it!

SEVERAL. Quiet! God forbid! What next?

THIRD SOLDIER. Yes, the Trojans! Why not? They'll send Pandarus or another one of their professionals, somebody who won't mind a few lies and a length of dagger in the back if that's the way to purchase the bow.

FIRST SOLDIER. Demodocus, come with us.

THIRD SOLDIER. Don't hesitate.

FIFTH SOLDIER. In another few minutes it will be too late.

SIXTH SOLDIER. Odysseus is your master.

SEVENTH SOLDIER. Woe to you if he hears.

EIGHTH SOLDIER. And if you anger him.

SECOND SOLDIER. Stop! I hear steps.

(Enter, running, the ninth soldier)

NINTH SOLDIER. Here is Odysseus! Stand ready!

SCENE THREE

(Enter Odysseus, accompanied by the tenth soldier)

FIRST SOLDIER. Odysseus, we've got the bow!

ODYSSEUS. Childishness. Where is Philoctetes?

DEMODOCUS. He became sick. He's in the cave, unconscious.

ODYSSEUS. Medon is with him?

DEMODOCUS. Yes.

ODYSSEUS. What did you tell him?

DEMODOCUS. I served him the lie about the raft; I shrewdly aroused his longing for home and companionship; I successfully concealed your presence; I secured his sympathy by envying his manner of life; and I skillfully extracted the bow from his fingers. No, I did so well he almost foisted it on me.

ODYSSEUS. What have we here?

FIRST SOLDIER. See for yourself, Odysseus.

ODYSSEUS. An attack of sarcasm! What's the meaning of this? Hand me the bow.

DEMODOCUS. Why?

ODYSSEUS. Am I to give reasons? Hand me the bow!

DEMODOCUS. Odysseus, I wish to wait here until Philoctetes comes to again. With your permission I will reveal the truth to him and ask his pardon for my lies. I will even return the weapon to him. Then man to man, openly and clearly, you can request him to accompany us to Troy. This will be the real glory for us: to win over the man by honest persuasion.

FIRST SOLDIER. Don't stand for this, Odysseus. If you'd heard Philoctetes as we did, you'd know nothing will make him fight on our side. He says "Greek" the way a tiger growls.

ODYSSEUS. Is this true?

DEMODOCUS. Let me speak with him again. Give me more time. If I can prove our honesty —

ODYSSEUS. No. The man is obstinate. I know him well. The oracle's message must be conveyed to him without more preambles. I am glad you have the bow, however. I like him better disarmed. Take it back to the ship, my son. I'll wait here, talk to him as quietly as I am talking to you, and persuade him to return with us.

DEMODOCUS. And if he refuses? Now that he is helpless?

ODYSSEUS. Go back to the ship.

DEMODOCUS. What if, in his anger, he prefers the Trojans?

ODYSSEUS. Go back to the ship.

DEMODOCUS. I wish to stay here.

FIRST SOLDIER. This is open rebellion, Odysseus.

SECOND SOLDIER. I'm not surprised. Always two steps behind everybody, and arguing, arguing, arguing.

THIRD SOLDIER. Argue Troy down if you can!

FOURTH SOLDIER. One man leaps up a battlement, sword in hand; another argues whether swords are fair weapons.

FIFTH SOLDIER. He acts as though he were the only man tired of war.

SIXTH SOLDIER. Ten years of bloody filth and now we're to lie down and die because we're too delicate!

SEVENTH SOLDIER. An idealist, that's what he is.

EIGHTH SOLDIER. Give us the bow!

ODYSSEUS. Patience, my friends. All will be done gently. I myself, as it happens, do not question the loyalty of Demodocus. I understand his scruples. And yet, I don't know, I am no weakling; and we are many against one. We might have a scrap, shed some blood, but we could subdue him.

DEMODOCUS. What are you saying? Would I fight you? Never! No, I ask you simply as a man —

ODYSSEUS (*changing his tone*). Ask me nothing. Men, draw your swords. Demodocus, I order you to take the bow to the ship. If you refuse, I advance on you myself. As I do, let the rest of you rush against him; if I die, take the bow, kill him, and kill Philoctetes.

DEMODOCUS. You're not serious!

ODYSSEUS. We'll see. You take me for a coward or a clown. (*He draws his sword. Demodocus half raises the bow. Odysseus throws his sword to the ground and slowly advances on the puzzled Demodocus. Demodocus retreats as far as he can*)

DEMODOCUS. Stop! Stop! (*He leaps away and disappears in the direction of the beach. Odysseus picks up his sword and sheathes it. The others do likewise*)

ODYSSEUS. Follow him. (*The ninth soldier leaves*)

SEVENTH SOLDIER. Well done.

FIRST SOLDIER. He is still a traitor, Odysseus. Will you arraign him before the Assembly?

ODYSSEUS. Nonsense. Most men are traitors to their country, but they keep it secret. We must teach the boy to hide his feelings, and that will give us another patriot.

THIRD SOLDIER. Anyway, we've got the bow.

FIRST SOLDIER. Now for Philoctetes!

ODYSSEUS. Now for Philoctetes. Stand aside, men. I shall sit here.

FIFTH SOLDIER. In the open?

ODYSSEUS. Man to man.

(*The chorus withdraws, except for the tenth soldier*)

ODYSSEUS. Stay.

TENTH SOLDIER. Yes, sir.

ODYSSEUS. I learned from Demodocus what I sent him for: how bitter the man is against us. I expected the worst; the worst is what I found.

TENTH SOLDIER. Yes.

ODYSSEUS. I will try again.

TENTH SOLDIER. God grant you success.

ODYSSEUS. I may fail. (*The soldier looks down*) Are you and the others ready?

TENTH SOLDIER. My lord —

ODYSSEUS. Are you and the others ready?

TENTH SOLDIER. Yes.

ODYSSEUS. Look out for my signal. If Zeus is merciful, I will not give it. If I give it, be prompt. The blood is on my head, not yours; but yours will answer if you disobey.

TENTH SOLDIER. You are the master, Odysseus. I am ready.

THE CHORUS SPEAKS *with harp and flute*

FIRST SOLDIER. Let us speak in praise of our master Odysseus. To speak his praise is a lovely task, because whatever the brain shapes privately concerning this man, the mouth is glad to utter, and not only in the house, to father or wife or children, but in the market place, in the Assembly, to all men. It makes a man happy when he means his praise, when he bows because of the veneration he truly feels, when he presses a hand because he loves. Now, as is fitting, I will be the man to begin.

SECOND SOLDIER. What will you praise in Odysseus?

FIRST SOLDIER. I will praise his rank among the Greeks. Though he rules a harsh land, Ithaca, which has not grain enough to feed itself, and where few trees grow among the many-colored rocks, he is the man most honored by Agamemnon. Achilles was the stronger man; but he was proud, fierce, and factious. Menelaus is Agamemnon's brother, but he is a weak soldier, one who always leans against another. Diomedes is supreme in the battlefield; but he fights even in his dreams, even in his tent at supper, even in the Assembly. To every concern brought forward in the Assembly, he answers, "Fight!" Idomeneus was the richer man; he was king of Crete; he could plunge a hand into the treasury of magnificent Egypt; his palaces were thick and strong, with deep foundations; he called us rustics; yet because of all this, half of his mind stayed at home and only with the other half did he attend to our war. And still he died. No. Agamemnon's true brother is Odysseus, though Odysseus came to him with only twelve ships — he had no more. Odysseus is strong, wise, loyal: in the fight a fighter, in council a counselor, and, I will add, at supper a merry man. Agamemnon has said in public, "While Odysseus remains at my side, I will not lift the siege of Troy, I will never be disheartened. But if Odysseus chose to despair and withdrew from us, I too would give up." So much has Agamemnon himself said.

SECOND SOLDIER. Now let me speak of Odysseus the ruler of Ithaca. How did he come to rule? By means of conquest? By sly murder of his betters? By bribing the old men? By promising the riches of the Hesperides to our poor country? Not so. But by unanimous applause and election, promising nothing, threatening no one. And I ask you all, my friends, to tell me his achievements.

THIRD SOLDIER. He taught us to build ships to carry our own goods.

FOURTH SOLDIER. He cleared the roads of bandits by hanging some and giving work to others.

FIFTH SOLDIER. He gave the poor justice without robbing the rich.

SIXTH SOLDIER. He proclaimed the festival of Pallas Athene, at which the young compete in the chariot race and the wrestling and the javelin-throwing while the whole island, assembled, relaxes, takes sides, and is refreshed by idleness.

SEVENTH SOLDIER. He rescued the debtors from prison and proclaimed a full remission of all unpaid taxes.

EIGHTH SOLDIER. He gave us courts of justice and made an end of private revenge and family vendettas.

THIRD SOLDIER. He gave us peace without sloth —

FOURTH SOLDIER. And prosperity without vice.

FIFTH SOLDIER. Let me speak in my turn of Odysseus the master. I was a smith in his household before I became a soldier. And you too, my friend —

SEVENTH SOLDIER. I was a farmer.

FIFTH SOLDIER. You shall witness the truth of what I say. Did he ever speak brutally to any of us? No. Did he work us half to death, so that we lacked the living life on which to spend our earnings? No. Rather he came among us, taught us what he knew, and amazing to us, the poor, he asked to be shown; took the hammer in his own hands, spat like one of us, rolled back his sleeves, and worked.

SEVENTH SOLDIER. Once he took the plow from my hands and walked a furrow behind the ox.

FIFTH SOLDIER. Singing — do you remember? — singing all the while! So that we glowed brighter than the hot iron and worked like Cyclops to please him.

SEVENTH SOLDIER. And he gave us sudden holidays. "Go, my lads," he said, "it's the fifth day of the fourth week after the harvest feast, and isn't that a glorious time for a twelve-hour carouse?" Laughing as he talked, and going about boxing with the boys of the village.

EIGHTH SOLDIER. Now I will speak of Odysseus the husband and father. Noble Telemachus, his son, walks gravely by his side as he visits his people, or sits close by when he delivers judgment. He is less strong, less lively than his father; more sober, perhaps more delicate, more studious. But strong love binds these two men together. Have you seen Odysseus lean toward his son, whisper a question into his ear, receive a reply, and nod in approval? Wise is the father who knows how to flatter his son, who takes, or seems to take, advice from him. And from the day Telemachus was born, Odysseus himself raised him. He did not fear smiles by entering the nursery and seeing that the bottles were washed. He was the boy's tutor, playmate, guide, and father; until it happened that, although Telemachus was only in his seventeenth year when his father left, Odysseus gave him the rule of Ithaca with peace and trust in his soul.

SIXTH SOLDIER. While Penelope his wife, glad and proud, having loved no man before and no man since, waits for the kindest husband who ever lived, in mourning and solitude. And even as she weeps, she is happy in her unhappiness, because the greatness of her present misery measures the greatness of her former joy. Luckless woman, whom the loss of a husband cannot make unhappy! And by this I judge the goodness of Odysseus, that those who knew him best lament his absence most.

THIRD SOLDIER. And in the camp, my friends? Whose tent is empty? That of Odysseus. A man without handy concubines, without purchased whores, without soft-lipped slaves. The others quarrel over a captive and threaten civil war for the sake of a naked woman. They wake at noon from their debauches too destroyed to fight. Only Odysseus keeps faith with his wife. He rises from the banquet gay but clearheaded: even-tempered, his mind firm, his body controlled, his gaze like a prong of light into the dense world.

SECOND SOLDIER. See him now, sitting patiently. His fingers hold the strings of destiny.

FOURTH SOLDIER. Almost a god.

FIRST SOLDIER. Almost a god.

SCENE FOUR

ODYSSEUS. My friends, I hear a stirring in Philoctetes' mansion. Stand ready if you please. Philoctetes!

(Philoctetes appears. He gives a shrill cry. Medon, armed with his sword, stands next to him)

ODYSSEUS. I am Odysseus.

PHILOCTETES. An army of Greeks. I should have known! *(He restrains Medon with his hand)*

ODYSSEUS. I greet you, and I greet Medon, with affection and respect. I thank the Gods who have kept you full of strong life. Give me a hearing, Philoctetes. Do not condemn us before we have spoken. We come as your brothers.

PHILOCTETES. Odysseus, the same old fox. He sends me a young hypocrite to disarm me, he stalks me with a brace of tall ruffians, he stands before me with his sword out, he murders, and as he murders he cries out Brother!

ODYSSEUS. More gently, Philoctetes. We arrived in a strange land. Who could predict what we should find? We are accustomed to war. But I am reassured and I return my sword to its scabbard.

PHILOCTETES. Always the fox. What are you looking for?

ODYSSEUS. You.

PHILOCTETES. You stole my bow. Has the oracle told you that Philoctetes must die?

ODYSSEUS. Far from it. We are here to take you back to our ranks.

PHILOCTETES. That is what your accomplice hinted. How affable to poor Philoctetes! Fancy the Greeks at their Assembly one night, the place stinking with corpses. Agamemnon strokes his beard and says, "How I pity Philoctetes! Never has he had his chance of a nobly torn belly or a gloriously broken skull. My eyes fill with tears thinking of it."

ODYSSEUS. Let me speak.

PHILOCTETES. Then Diomedes takes the staff in his hand and speaks. "Oh my comrades," he brings out between sobs of pity, "let us fetch the poor man back among us to share in our sour wine, our stony

bread, the knocks we get every day, and the evening walks among
the graves." Then they send Odysseus off with a friend, and all for
pity and affection they lie to him, trick him, rob him of his weapon,
and trap him in his cave. Now Odysseus, speak up, good and blunt,
and if it's blood you want, spare me your apologies.

ODYSSEUS. You treat me, Philoctetes, as though I were childish enough to
treat you as a child. I have not come for pity of you. If circumstances
required me to liquidate you, I would of course do so. This we both
know; no fooling between us. As it happens, the oracle pronounces
that your good fortune is ours, and ours is yours. A common interest
binds us. Will you hear what it is? Or will you bite before the hand
is even stretched?

PHILOCTETES. Speak.

ODYSSEUS. The word came from Calchas the soothsayer. "Not by strength
alone shall the Greeks overcome Troy, but by strength allied with
immortal cunning. Let Pyrrhus, the son of Achilles, be our strength.
Let Philoctetes, king of Malis, be our cunning."

PHILOCTETES. King of Malis? King?

ODYSSEUS. Your father is dead and you are king. And in the summer Troy
will be toppled. Calchas saw your bow in a dream: strong, far-
shooting, unerring: its arrows deadlier than those of Crete or Thrace:
your secret. With this bow we shall send into the bowels of Troy a
panic like the trample of a falling mountain. And you, Philoctetes,
you will live; you glorious to the end of time: cherished by Greece,
your disease forgotten, an oracle among men, one of us, Philoctetes,
a Greek again.

CHORUS (low). One of us.

PHILOCTETES. He saw the bow in his dream?

ODYSSEUS. Yes, my friend. Let this persuade you of the truth of all I have
told you. How could I have known that such a bow existed? Who
does know except you, your companion and the Gods?

PHILOCTETES. I can't answer you. You are shrewder than I am. I've become
too simple here, I don't see the mechanism.

FIRST SOLDIER. Noble Philoctetes, he speaks the truth.

PHILOCTETES. Well, the bow is in your hands. Demodocus stole it, if that's
his name.

ODYSSEUS. Be indulgent with us, Philoctetes. The bow fell into our hands;
we should have returned it to you; but we have been soldiers in the
field too long; my men would not relinquish it.

PHILOCTETES. Keep it then, my friends, see if you can handle it, go back
to your ships, let the pinewood oars fly, and good riddance to you all.

ODYSSEUS. And you?

PHILOCTETES. We stay here. I have my world, and like it.

ODYSSEUS. Return with us, Philoctetes. Let the bow be your gift to us. Let us receive it from you, the man himself, and allow us to acknowledge you our friend, benefactor, savior, and master.

PHILOCTETES. I am satisfied here. You took the bow. Go back to Agamemnon.

ODYSSEUS. Ten years of loneliness is enough. Who can bear such loneliness? Medon may die.

PHILOCTETES. God forbid! I am the older man. I will be the first to die.

ODYSSEUS. Perhaps not. And then what will become of you? You will howl on your knees and go mad. A man must live among his kind.

PHILOCTETES. Ruffians! Back to Troy! You are not my kind!

FIRST SOLDIER. Odysseus! I hear somebody running.

SEVENTH SOLDIER. There! There!

ODYSSEUS. Demodocus!

CHORUS. Stop!

(Demodocus rushes up to Philoctetes and thrusts the bow into his hands)

DEMODOCUS. Your bow, Philoctetes! Forgive me!

PHILOCTETES (aiming at Odysseus). Back Odysseus, back! All the arrows, Medon!

ODYSSEUS. Back, men!

CHORUS. Oh God, help us!

PHILOCTETES. Stand back! Medon, look sharp. Now we'll see.

ODYSSEUS (to the Greeks). No violence, my friends. All in good time. I admire Demodocus in a way. I deplore what he did; but I admire him. It was his conscience.

DEMODOCUS. Why do you always jeer, Odysseus?

PHILOCTETES. Hands off your swords, all of you! Eyes open, Medon. Odysseus, don't stand there. Call your gang together and clear the island. The tide will be up soon.

DEMODOCUS. Odysseus, understand me, I beg you. A man has to respect his own soul before everything else.

ODYSSEUS. A speech! It would melt a young girl! Well now, we'll sit here and wait till nightfall.

PHILOCTETES. But if by nightfall you're not sailing in your ship, I will shoot you straight and happy through the heart.

ODYSSEUS. Let that be as it may. Patience. (He sits on a rock and gives a discreet sign with his hand. The tenth soldier whispers into the ears of the eighth and the seventh, and the three quietly leave)

DEMODOCUS (to Philoctetes). I will try to protect you.

PHILOCTETES. What are you doing?

DEMODOCUS. Going back.

PHILOCTETES. Don't be a fool, Demodocus; stay here. Odysseus is waiting to pounce on you. You're a traitor to Greece. Congratulations!

DEMODOCUS. I think not. Odysseus, I beg you to draw Philoctetes to our cause simply and honestly. Let me plead with him, now that I can do so at peace with myself. I think he trusts me now and will give me a hearing.

ODYSSEUS. Suit yourself, my lad.

(*Demodocus advances toward the Greeks*)

PHILOCTETES. Don't be a fool!

ODYSSEUS. Take him! (*The soldiers leap at Demodocus. Medon, ready to rush to his help, is restrained by Philoctetes*)

DEMODOCUS. Scum!

CHORUS. Well done!

ODYSSEUS. Hold the boy. From behind. Lock his arms. Bind his wrists. Now then, that's one.

DEMODOCUS. Fool, fool, fool.

PHILOCTETES (*to Medon*). You're too exposed here. Go inside the cave. (*Medon obeys*) Is that how you'll tempt me to return to Troy? Demodocus, keep heart. The game isn't finished yet. Bandits! Leap at me! Leap! Let me see you take my corpse to Troy. Alive never!

ODYSSEUS. Philoctetes! Once more! Return with us! How easily we could master you!

PHILOCTETES. Stand back!

DEMODOCUS. Philoctetes, they will force you or kill you! They are afraid you'll deal with the Trojans!

(*The soldier forces Demodocus to his knees. Demodocus cries out with pain*)

PHILOCTETES. The Trojans are coming too! Of course! Let Hector have the bow! Why not?

ODYSSEUS. Hector is dead! But you are right, the Trojans are coming. You are more than right: the Trojans have come! (*He claps his hands*)

FIRST SOLDIER. When? When?

ODYSSEUS. Bring in the Trojans! Now my children, watch carefully. Surprise Odysseus? Where is the man? There will be no Trojans to traffic with, Philoctetes; I am going to teach you an unforgettable lesson. (*Enter four soldiers carrying two litters, each with a dead man on it*) Look at your Trojan saviors. They are the last ones you will ever see. You'll rot alone in this place.

FIRST SOLDIER. Odysseus, we are all amazed. What happened?

ODYSSEUS. One of our patrols found a small Trojan craft, and some twenty men ashore. We took them by surprise and killed them all.

FIRST SOLDIER. Did we lose anyone?

ODYSSEUS. Not a man. Come, Philoctetes, come and look.

PHILOCTETES (*without moving*). What is all this to me? Are these my people? Odysseus, I tell you once again, take yourself and your henchmen away. I'm getting impatient.

ODYSSEUS. I understand. And I give up. Let Agamemnon send another embassy. For my part, what matters is that we shall have no competitors. There they lie. You can even keep Demodocus. (*He seizes Demodocus and pushes him toward Philoctetes, who moves farther back*) He's yours. (*He throws Demodocus down with a blow*)

PHILOCTETES. Coward!

(*Philoctetes has left the opening of the cave unguarded. At a signal from Odysseus, the fifth soldier rushes into the cave. Philoctetes utters a cry but hesitates*)

MEDON (*within*). Master!

ODYSSEUS (*shouting*). Kill him!

PHILOCTETES. No!

MEDON (*within*). Master!

PHILOCTETES. Don't kill him!

CHORUS. Kill!

DEMODOCUS. Kill Odysseus! (*Odysseus catches hold of Demodocus and uses him as a shield*)

PHILOCTETES. I can't.

ODYSSEUS. Bring Medon out!

(*The fifth soldier carries Medon's body out. With a mighty effort Philoctetes breaks his bow in two. He flings himself over the body. Odysseus surrenders Demodocus to one of the soldiers*)

SIXTH SOLDIER. He broke the bow!

FOURTH SOLDIER. He broke the bow!

ODYSSEUS. This is not the bow! This is a toy! Does Philoctetes think he can dupe Odysseus? The bow is in his brain and that brain must be ours!

PHILOCTETES. In my brain too, the bow is broken. Force me back if you like. I am naked before you. But I'll never speak. And may the Gods preserve me long enough to see the broken body of every Greek sprawling before Troy's gate, and yours too, Odysseus, but yours, I pray, oh Heracles! let it be left to the dogs, let them devour you and make you their excrement.

ODYSSEUS. Why do you rail at me, Philoctetes? It is you who killed Medon, not I. Your hatred for us has made you insane. We came here, Greek to Greek, brother to brother, offering you and Medon immortal glory, love and reverence. You raved at us as if we, and not the serpent, had bitten your ankle that foul day in the grove of Chryse. Yet still we offer you the haven of our friendship, still we clamor for your help, still we look upon you as our teacher. And such is our awe for a man marked by the Gods that we will not compel you even now. I now abandon you to your hatred and your misery. I shall report

you mysteriously dead amidst a crowd of Trojan corpses, and
exhibit these poor victims in proof. The Trojans will not come again.
Neither will we. Never, never will you see a human being again.
Stubborn to the end, crammed with unnatural spite, you will stink
to your own nostrils. Soldiers! Sack the cave. Destroy everything.

(Several soldiers enter the cave)

HALF CHORUS *(low)*. Alone . . .

OTHER HALF *(low)*. Alone . . .

DEMODOCUS. Philoctetes . . .

PHILOCTETES. What?

DEMODOCUS. I pity you.

PHILOCTETES *(to Odysseus)*. Release the boy, Odysseus. What does it
matter to you now? Let him stay here.

ODYSSEUS. Break everything, men. Break!

CHORUS. Alone . . .

(The soldiers appear)

SECOND SOLDIER. Everything is smashed.

FOURTH SOLDIER. The body, sir?

ODYSSEUS. Take it inside — throw it on the heap. It will be stinking soon,
stronger than Philoctetes himself. *(To the Chorus)* Back to the ship,
my friends.

FIRST SOLDIER. Without Philoctetes?

ODYSSEUS. Without Philoctetes. He will never give us his secret.

SECOND SOLDIER. No pity for us?

THIRD SOLDIER. For us who have to do the fighting?

FOURTH SOLDIER. For us who only obey orders?

FIFTH SOLDIER. We never meant you any harm.

SIXTH SOLDIER. Harm? We wanted to fall at your feet.

THIRD SOLDIER. The common soldier was always your friend.

SIXTH SOLDIER. What have we got to do with oracles, higher strategy, new
weapons, headquarters, military policy?

FIFTH SOLDIER. It is us you punish, not Odysseus, not Agamemnon.

FOURTH SOLDIER. And our wives, our children, who don't even know you.

ODYSSEUS. Away, soldiers. No tears. The bow doesn't matter if no one
has it.

(The Chorus slowly leaves)

PHILOCTETES. Leave me Demodocus! I beg you!

*(Demodocus is carried off. The litters with the dead men are taken away
too. Only Odysseus and Philoctetes are left. Philoctetes is trembling)*

ODYSSEUS. How quiet it is. Only my voice remains. Then I will go. *(He
draws a dagger, rises and advances toward Philoctetes)*

PHILOCTETES. You'll murder me? *(But Odysseus throws the dagger at
Philoctetes' feet)*

ODYSSEUS. When you are sick of the silence.
(He turns and leaves. Philoctetes is alone. He seems bewildered. He enters the cave, and comes out again, a broken man, holding a few scraps. Total silence. A long time passes. Suddenly he flings himself toward the far end of the stage, where the Greeks left, and utters a wild cry)
PHILOCTETES. Take me! Odysseus! Take me! *(The drum beats hard. The fourth soldier appears)* Take me! Take me! Take me! *(He is sobbing)*
FOURTH SOLDIER. Odysseus! Come back! Take him!
A VOICE *(in the distance)*. Take him!
(Philoctetes lies on the ground. His sobs diminish. Heracles appears)
HERACLES. Philoctetes, rise, rise! Heracles calls you. Be reconciled. Rise! The serpent and the eagle shall unite. Troy shall fall. Glory to Greece! Glory to man!
(Reenter Odysseus, Demodocus and the Chorus. All except Demodocus fall prostrate before Heracles)
HERACLES. Rise, Greeks, rise most noble Odysseus. I give you this man, Philoctetes the Greek, to whom glory and imperishable tribute in the hearts of men. Philoctetes and Pyrrhus, spirit and power, shall unite in the common task now and not only now but forever and forever, unbreakable league, wherever man shall live against man, city against city, nation against nation. Take his hand. Honor him. You have mastered him, but now acknowledge him your master. He cowers; he is small and weak; his eyes are filmed with grief and fear; yet he is like a God among you; his thought shall break the citadels. Troy shall fall. And Troy shall be torn out of the earth like a cankered tree.
ODYSSEUS. Humbly, with reverence unutterable, I take back to our thousands, and to Agamemnon the tower above the host, the promise, the certainty, the signature of Zeus.
(The drum rolls. Heracles vanishes)
ODYSSEUS. Soldiers, conduct noble Philoctetes to our ship. The bitter words and the cruel acts are erased. The King of Malis is our commander now. Treat him with fear and veneration.
(The ninth and tenth soldiers escort Philoctetes out)
ODYSSEUS. Friends, our mission is accomplished; not without difficulties, not, alas, without bloodshed, but accomplished, I believe, in a manner which must satisfy the supreme command. Demodocus, you are pardoned. I will leave you to the private obscurity of your shame, your petty emotions, your pampered self-concern and not curb you to the prosecution you deserve. Philoctetes is ours, body and soul. Now let the Trojans land and look for him!
(Demodocus raises his head in surprise)
FIRST SOLDIER. The Trojans? But you killed them!

ODYSSEUS. No, my children. Sooner or later you must know. Harden yourselves against the inevitable. These two men were simple sailors on our craft. They gave their lives, two for ten thousand. We shall never forget our debt to them.

FIRST SOLDIER. Odysseus!

DEMODOCUS. You murdered two of our men?

ODYSSEUS. When you failed us, Demodocus, when your conscience became petulant, you forced me to give the terrible command. With the bow in his fist, Philoctetes was intractable. I made an inhuman desert about him. I destroyed his nest. I broke him.

FIRST SOLDIER. But then, surely, master, you never meant to leave Philoctetes behind, with the Trojans on their way even now! What if he had not cried out for us in the end?

ODYSSEUS. He did cry out for us in the end.

FIRST SOLDIER. I shudder at your cunning, Odysseus. Always in control, even when you are surprised. I will never admit that Philoctetes is an intelligent man, in spite of his inventions.

ODYSSEUS. The intelligent man is not always the clever man. No gloating. Let us be soberly satisfied.

FIRST SOLDIER. Not you, Odysseus. Wherever you go, it seems to us that a shimmer of divinity surrounds you.

ODYSSEUS. Wherever I go, I am knee-high in dung and blood. Come, children, away. Demodocus, are you ready?

DEMODOCUS. Leave me here.

ODYSSEUS. Leave you here?

DEMODOCUS. Yes.

ODYSSEUS. Alone?

DEMODOCUS. Yes.

SECOND SOLDIER. Don't be a fool, Demodocus. Come with us.

THIRD SOLDIER. No one will remind you of anything.

FOURTH SOLDIER. Your place is still your place in camp.

FIFTH SOLDIER. And in Ithaca as well. Do we speak for you, Odysseus?

ODYSSEUS. By all means.

DEMODOCUS. Leave me here. Give me some clothes, a few knives, tools, anything you can or will. Leave me here.

ODYSSEUS. What shall we do, my friends? For myself, I don't care. Let him do as he pleases. Demodocus, we sail when the tide rises and the ship floats free. Come if you wish, stay if you wish. You are too small for my concern. (*He leaves*)

THE CHORUS SPEAKS *with harp*

FIRST SOLDIER. As a man older than you and more experienced by far, I will speak freely with you, Demodocus, and call you a coward. You will tell us that you despise the world, that you abhor mankind, that you condemn life, or perhaps stand — what do I know? — away from it — above it — beside it —

SECOND SOLDIER. All of which are words suitable to a poet.

FIRST SOLDIER. But in reality you fear the world.

SECOND SOLDIER. Your decision is not strength, but spite; not courage, but shame.

THIRD SOLDIER. And the cheering fire in the house? The open door, the embrace? "You've come back to us," they cry. They take off your cloak, they bathe your feet, they offer you wine and honey, they cry and fuss over you.

FOURTH SOLDIER. Human beings.

FIFTH SOLDIER. Others.

SIXTH SOLDIER. Yet yours, your own.

SEVENTH SOLDIER. Invisible strings between you and them.

EIGHTH SOLDIER. Once long ago I quarreled bitterly with my father because he loved my brothers, but me he neglected and even starved; sometimes he beat me; he called me a vagabond. And I left the house; I went to Corinth; I lived alone among strangers. At night I heard the voices next door to mine; I saw the people in the street: families, lovers, friends, or polite acquaintances — I envied them all, even the man who patted a dog; and now and then I saw a man alone, like myself, and that man wore the same expression as mine, a studied air of indifference to conceal his despair. He looks around and seems to say, "Me? I am alone only for the moment! I am expecting a happy crowd of friends. Don't worry about me, I beg you." But inside he cries. He goes home and stares at the wall opposite his chair. He eats an apple. He writes a letter. He mends a stocking. And he sits again and stares. Presently he begins to talk to himself. Then he stops, because he is ashamed. What will he do? He is not tired. What can he do? He paces the floor, lifts a vase from a shelf, places it on a table, he doesn't know why, and sits down again. All he wants now is to see a human being. He knows one at the far end of the city. But this man has a wife and two small children, and it would be a disturbance to knock at his door. What excuse would he have for the visit? He could say, "Excuse me, but I came to borrow the hand-saw you promised me." Perhaps the wife would ask him to come in and share their meal. But if she did, he would reply,

"Thank you, but I must hurry, I have an appointment," lest they ridicule him with pity; and he would go home again, and sit, stare, and suffer. Oh Demodocus, believe me, I returned to my birthplace, I kissed the first friend I met in the street; he thought I was mad.

FOURTH SOLDIER. And the war, for that matter, is that so bad after all?

EIGHTH SOLDIER. No! Better this war all my life, and to lose both my arms, than another month of loneliness.

SIXTH SOLDIER. A comrade keeps you warm too.

FIFTH SOLDIER. In the heat of battle you hear and see your platoon.

THIRD SOLDIER. At night you roar out a song together.

FOURTH SOLDIER. You share a bottle.

FIFTH SOLDIER. A story.

SECOND SOLDIER. A woman.

SIXTH SOLDIER. Show me a good brawler and I'll show you a reliable friend.

SEVENTH SOLDIER. The worst kind is the man who has no enemies. He has no friends either.

THIRD SOLDIER. Cold blood.

SECOND SOLDIER. Sitting in a corner.

SIXTH SOLDIER. He doesn't know it, but if you left him alone on an island, he would clamor for you, though he acted as if he didn't even know your name.

EIGHTH SOLDIER. Yes, it's easy to look self-sufficient when you're in good company.

FIFTH SOLDIER. For whom will you sing? How will you fare without us who are the listeners? When you sang, we sat still and yet we traveled; we were ourselves and yet we became other men; our lives multiplied; wisdoms not our own became ours. Such was your power over us. But without us, where is your power?

FIRST SOLDIER. Come with us, Demodocus. This is too horrible. You will babble at random and finally lose your language. You will crouch on all fours like a beast. Who knows? You will fornicate with an animal, and beget a monster. Demodocus, live among men. Even hate is better than solitude. The universe is morose, the Gods ignore the simple people we are; everywhere you look the stars drive insanely in the dense cavern, and we, we few, we poor few, should huddle here and hold each others' hands and say goodbye to the dying, and kiss their lips with a last warmth. But you will die alone, growling vacantly, your head on a stone, and the wild pigs will eat you.

(Silence)

FOURTH SOLDIER. He won't say a word.

A VOICE (in the distance). Men! The tide is rising, hurry, hurry!

FIRST SOLDIER. Demodocus. If you came running after us, and caught the rope-ladder while the ship moved away, you might cut a shabby or laughable figure. Many a fool will die rather than cut a shabby or laughable figure. Don't be a fool.

(*The Chorus slowly leaves*)

DEMODOCUS. Erased from the records of the city and the temple, I now become free and innocent, not rising, not sinking, dumb as the laurel, still as a comet, clean as a drop of rain, patient as a rock, peaceful as the dust. I will stop singing, being perfect. I will be reticent. I will listen to the sea's liquid speech, not one hypocrite among all its syllable waves. Philoctetes, I see Troy in torment to the end of time, to the end of time I hear the victor's scurrilous mirth, but to me the seagull will report only the fish singing in the sea, innocently devouring, innocently devoured. Now my peace begins. And to begin it, Demodocus must bury a man.

THE END